IMAGES
of America
FAIR OAKS

On the Cover: This c. 1897 photograph shows the magnificent view of the American River from the Fair Oaks Bluff. The location has attracted visitors for over 100 years.

IMAGES
of America

FAIR OAKS

Lee M. A. Simpson and Paul J. P. Sandul

ARCADIA
PUBLISHING

ISBN 978-0-7385-3088-8

Published by Arcadia Publishing
Charleston, South Carolina

Printed in the United States of America

Library of Congress Catalog Card Number: 2005934499

For all general information contact Arcadia Publishing at:
Telephone 843-853-2070
Fax 843-853-0044
E-mail sales@arcadiapublishing.com
For customer service and orders:
Toll-Free 1-888-313-2665

Visit us on the Internet at www.arcadiapublishing.com

CONTENTS

Acknowledgments

We are incredibly grateful and beholden to the tireless work and assistance of many people and organizations that facilitated the completion of this book. Jason Layland, Amber Layland, Natosha Layland, Lola Aguilera, Christopher Marcille, and Larry Bishop provided much needed photographic equipment, expertise, and help. Likewise, the local newspaper, *Fair Oaks Today*, and chief editor David Schold graciously advertised a call for photographs from community members free of charge. Janice Speth, Karl Speth, and Mike Villarreal also helped by not only providing photographs, but also by either providing contact information or contacting prominent community members with remarkable images on our behalf. Community members and friends of Fair Oaks such as Donald Kenmouth, Bobbi Mitchell, Diana Lennon, Hugh Gorman, Jim and Delores Broadley, Linda Morris, Sherry Lynn Wood, and John and Eileen Dewey Thomas cleared time and opened their homes, their family albums, and treasured stories about long ago relatives and Fair Oaks memories. Eileen Dewey Thomas, in particular, provided us with over 200 images (nearly one third of over 600 pictures collected), documents, and hot coffee and could rightfully produce an amazing pictorial book called *The Dewey Family of Fair Oaks*. Local businesses such as the Fair Oaks Coffee and Deli, Oaks Hardware, and the Stockman Club displayed and distributed flyers calling for images. In particular, Dallas Bock, the owner of the Stockman Club, not only distributed flyers, but also provided images and enthusiastic support for the project—he also bought a round or two! Community organizations, such as the Fair Oaks Presbyterian Church, St. Mel's Catholic Church, and The Woman's Thursday Club of Fair Oaks, opened their doors and provided some of the most stunning and important pictures in the entire collection. Likewise, the Fair Oaks Chamber of Commerce, Fair Oaks Water District, Fair Oaks Recreation and Park District, and the Fair Oaks/Orangevale Community Library freed up their busy schedules and allowed us to acquire images from their cherished records. Also, we are grateful to Pat Johnson and the staff at the Sacramento Archives and Museum Collections Center for providing information and images.

Finally the Fair Oaks Historical Society graciously opened up their treasured and prized collection of images. Fair Oaks Historical Society members volunteered their time, aided in the acquisition of images, and provided information and contacts that led to other people and organizations with significant images. In particular, Pres. Russ Monroe and Vice Pres. Sherry Lynn Wood deserve our biggest thanks for the countless hours, correspondence, interaction with historical society members, and their resilience in securing the cooperation of the historical society in sharing Fair Oaks' wonderful and storied history through pictures. All royalties generated from this publication are going to the Fair Oaks Historical Society to aid in their continued efforts to document and preserve Fair Oaks' remarkable and wonderful history. You can learn more about the society from their website at www.fairoakshistory.org. Of course, lest we forget, there are our families and friends who, on a daily basis, encouraged and inspired us so.

INTRODUCTION

The axis of the earth sticks out visibly through the centre of each and every town or city.
—Oliver Wendell Holmes Sr.

Despite the tremendous metropolitan growth in the Sacramento region, approximately 16 miles northeast of Sacramento up the "backbone of America"—Highway 50—sits a small, semi-rural community along the banks of the American River. One quick exit from the busy concrete jungle, the hum of traffic and screams of development are muted and visitors are seemingly transported to a small town from 50 years ago. Watch for roosters on the path and make sure to wave at each received smile or the gossip spread from the wrinkled lips of Alice and Martha in the back of the coffee house will surely follow you around. For you are now in the "Crown of the [Sacramento] Valley," in the "Heart of California," you, my friend, are in Fair Oaks.

Fair Oaks sits on a fraction of land first occupied by the Southern Maidu Indians nearly 10,000 years ago. European occupation of the area occurred in the 19th century when Mexican governor of California Manuel Micheltorena divided the land bordering the lower American River into large private land grants. Joel P. Dedmond acquired the nearly 20,000-acre area known as the San Juan Land Grant. In 1844, it covered all or parts of the present-day communities of Fair Oaks, Orangevale, Carmichael, and Citrus Heights. Here the paper trail becomes a bit murky. According to Grant Vail Wallace's reminiscence printed in the *San Juan Record* in 1948, Charles H. Howard and James W. Wilson of the Howard-Wilson Publishing Company of Chicago secured rights to sell land in the tract in 1895. The publishing company developed a contractual relationship with California senator Frederick Cox and businessman Crawford W. Clarke to market the land although it does not appear that they received title to the land.

Fair Oaks, from 1895 to 1930, experienced typical Western development, particularly for communities owned and operated by absentee land speculators. Like most Western boosters, the Howard-Wilson Company sold what can either be described as a myth (in the negative sense) or a dream (in the positive sense). Fair Oaks contained only potential in 1895, not the services and economy that clearly appeal to home buyers and builders. Thus, the company created demand through a carefully orchestrated marketing plan under the guise of *Farm, Field and Fireside* publications.

By 1897, 300 permanent settlers resided in Fair Oaks and purchased land in five to 20-acre tracts. The successful citrus industry of Southern California provided evidence of an easy and rapid road to wealth through the growing of fruit. Timing, however, worked against Fair Oaks. Few came and investment began to diminish leading the Howard-Wilson Company to withdraw. A group of local and out-of-state businessmen and investors then formed the Chicago–Fair Oaks Association in 1898–1899 to seek support for the "Sunset Colony" by lobbying government and other potential investors and, according to the officially sanctioned history of the Sacramento County Chamber of Commerce, *A Sacramento Saga: Fifty Years of Achievement*, helped in the successful realization of the construction of a bridge at Fair Oaks in 1901. Likewise a group of local businessmen incorporated the Fair Oaks Development Company in 1900 not only to profit from selling the land, but also to build up the infrastructure of the county.

Fair Oaks grew rapidly with the completion of a bridge and railway. The reminiscences of residents in *Fair Oaks and San Juan Area Memories* (1960) indicate that Fair Oaks exploded in a tremendous building and population boom and became a typical small town by the 1910s. For the next two decades, Fair Oaks grew at a steady pace. Also, dredging companies, in search of gold along the American River, dredged up thousands of acres of rich farm land along the southern boundaries of Fair Oaks and made a lasting mark on the landscape.

The freeze of 1932 is one of the single most significant events in the history of Fair Oaks. It hit during the depths of the Great Depression. Two separate freezes effectively wiped out Fair Oaks and other surrounding citrus colonies as major producers of citrus fruit in California. Fair Oaks, however, continued to grow. It became a residential community with its inhabitants primarily working elsewhere.

The rise of the defense company Aerojet General as a major employer influenced the growth rate of Fair Oaks from 1955 to 1965. In 1957, for example, the Sacramento County Planning Department shows that Fair Oaks had over 750 families with one or more members employed by Aerojet General—second only to the Arden-Arcade area. The growth rate slowed noticeably, but growth did still continue because of the increased access to Sacramento by Highway 50 and the construction of the Hazel and Sunrise bridges. This allowed residents of Fair Oaks to find greater employment in the connecting area and for Sacramentans to relocate to Fair Oaks more easily. The former citrus colony transformed into a bedroom community of greater Sacramento and altered residential demography into either white or blue collar workers.

We invite you to meander through the quaint streets of the "Crown of the Valley." Turn down Fair Oaks Boulevard or Main Street and peruse many original buildings, relics of the early 1900s. Travel up Sunset Avenue and Winding Way or take any small road between and discover turn-of-the-century American homes that tell the story of American architecture and vintage suburbia. Take the Old Fair Oaks Bridge that once played a pivotal role in transforming the small community into an agricultural power, down the red bluffs, and toward the rushing waters of the American River. Follow the Parkway Trail northward and notice the evidence of dredging left nearly a century ago. Watch for friendly dogs leaping into the cold water after elusive ducks and cyclists enjoying the cool, river air. The beauty and charm of Fair Oaks is picturesque, timeless, and can evoke memories of an easier time, a simpler past for which we all somehow yearn.

One

COLONIZATION

This modest booklet, then, shall open for you the gate to the Promised Land.
—Fair Oaks Development Company, 1900

The promotion of Fair Oaks as a pastoral paradise began with the Howard-Wilson Publishing Company of Chicago in 1895. One account tells that Gen. Charles H. Howard, a Civil War veteran, christened the colony with the name Fair Oaks after a battle in Fair Oaks, Virginia. The Howard-Wilson Company promoted Fair Oaks as one of their "Sunset Colonies." They advertised Fair Oaks as an innovative and growing citrus colony and promised the construction of a railway and water system. Then, on October 19, 1895, approximately 165 excursionists arrived in Sacramento by train from Chicago. They were taken to Fair Oaks the next day where many of them decided to stay and cast their lots.

When the Chicago publishers withdrew from the colony, a group of local and out-of-state businessmen and investors formed the Chicago–Fair Oaks Association to seek support for the budding colony by lobbying government and other potential investors. The following year Valentine S. McClatchy, editor of the *Sacramento Bee*, helped to form the Fair Oaks Development Company not only to keep the fruit colony from going under, but also to protect his investments in Orangevale and profit from the sale of land in Fair Oaks. The boosters shamelessly promoted Fair Oaks as the "Crown of the Valley" in the "Heart of California."

The development company also advertised Fair Oaks as a growing fruit colony. The company dissolved within a few years, but was successful (in cooperation with the Chicago–Fair Oaks Association) in bringing about the construction of a bridge and railway to Fair Oaks that serviced the local agricultural community and provided for better transportation of fruit for landowners, investors, and farmers.

The *Sacramento Bee* published an article on March 1, 1901, concerning the construction of a railway to Fair Oaks that sums up the desires to promote and develop Fair Oaks:

> This means that Sacramento, which has had no accessible show place, will be able to take Eastern excursionists direct to the orange groves [of Fair Oaks], showing them by the way the rich hoplands and orchards and vineyards of the American River district. . . . It means that the American River district for sixteen miles out of Sacramento City will gradually be utilized for suburban homes, and that the mechanic, for the price of a street car fare, can reach any point along the river within eight or ten miles of the city, and can buy, for less than the cost of a city lot, an acre or two of ground and have his kitchen garden, and orchard, and his cow.

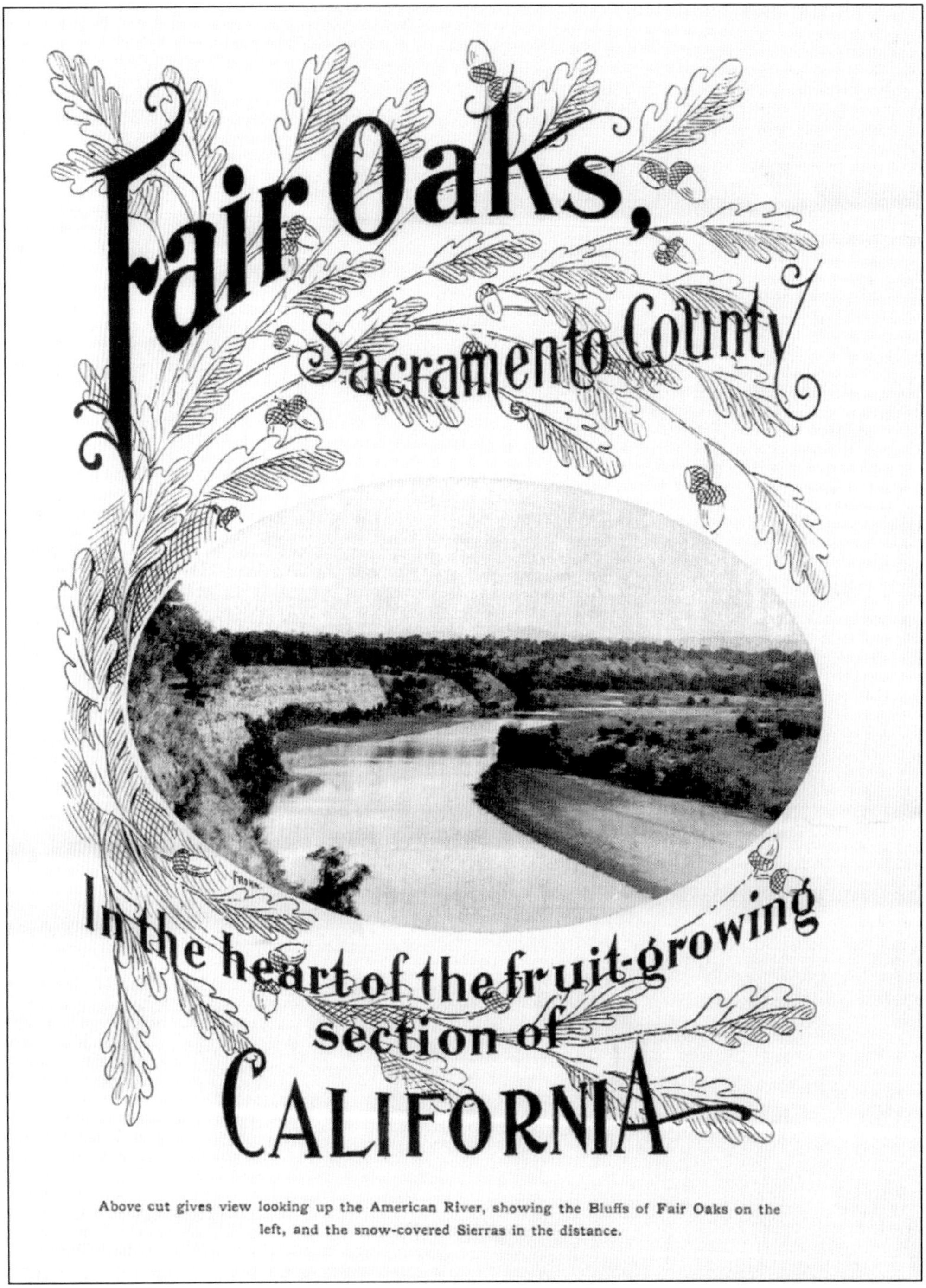

In the early years of Fair Oaks, promotional pamphlets, such as this 1900 brochure, were produced by both the Howard-Wilson Company of Chicago and the Fair Oaks Development Company. The pamphlets were designed to attract Easterners to the "promised land" of Fair Oaks, in the "Heart of California." (Courtesy Fair Oaks/Orangevale Community Library.)

This picturesque scene appeared in the Howard-Wilson Company's 1897 promotional booklet, *The Heart of California*. The caption read, "Among the Scattering Oaks. Landscape View on the American River, in the Heart of California." (Courtesy Fair Oaks Historical Society.)

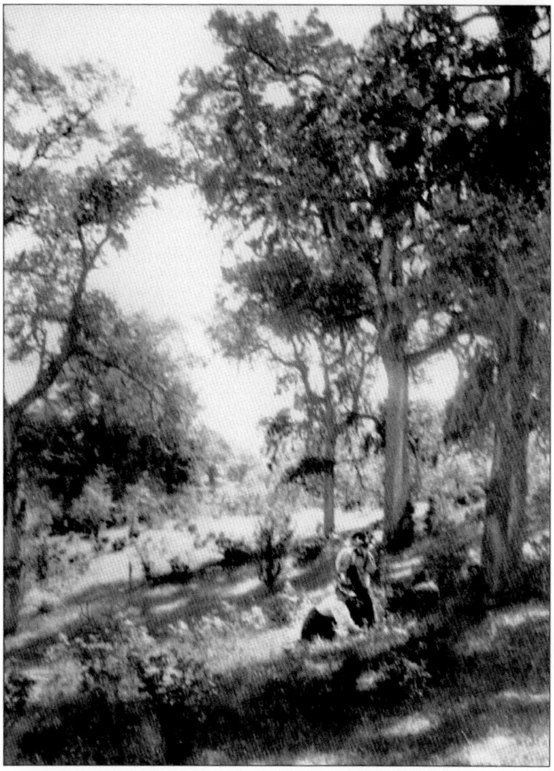

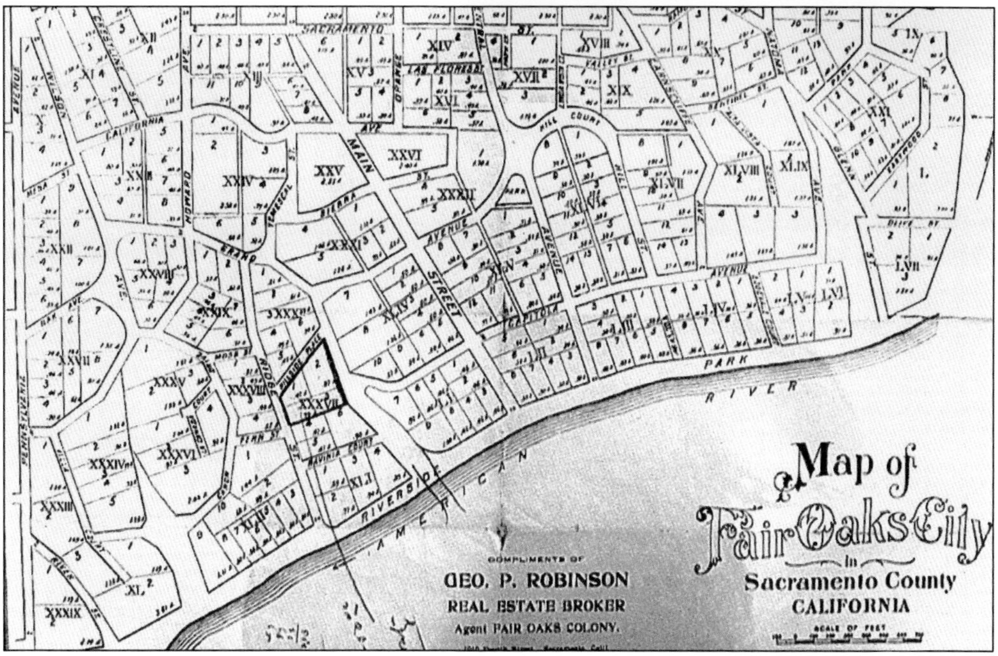

This map of Fair Oaks, produced in 1900, shows not only how the land was originally conceived and developed, but also how the "Crown of the Valley" was advertised as a thriving and growing community with a plethora of streets and roads, as well as vigilantly planned parcels for sale. (Courtesy Fair Oaks Historical Society.)

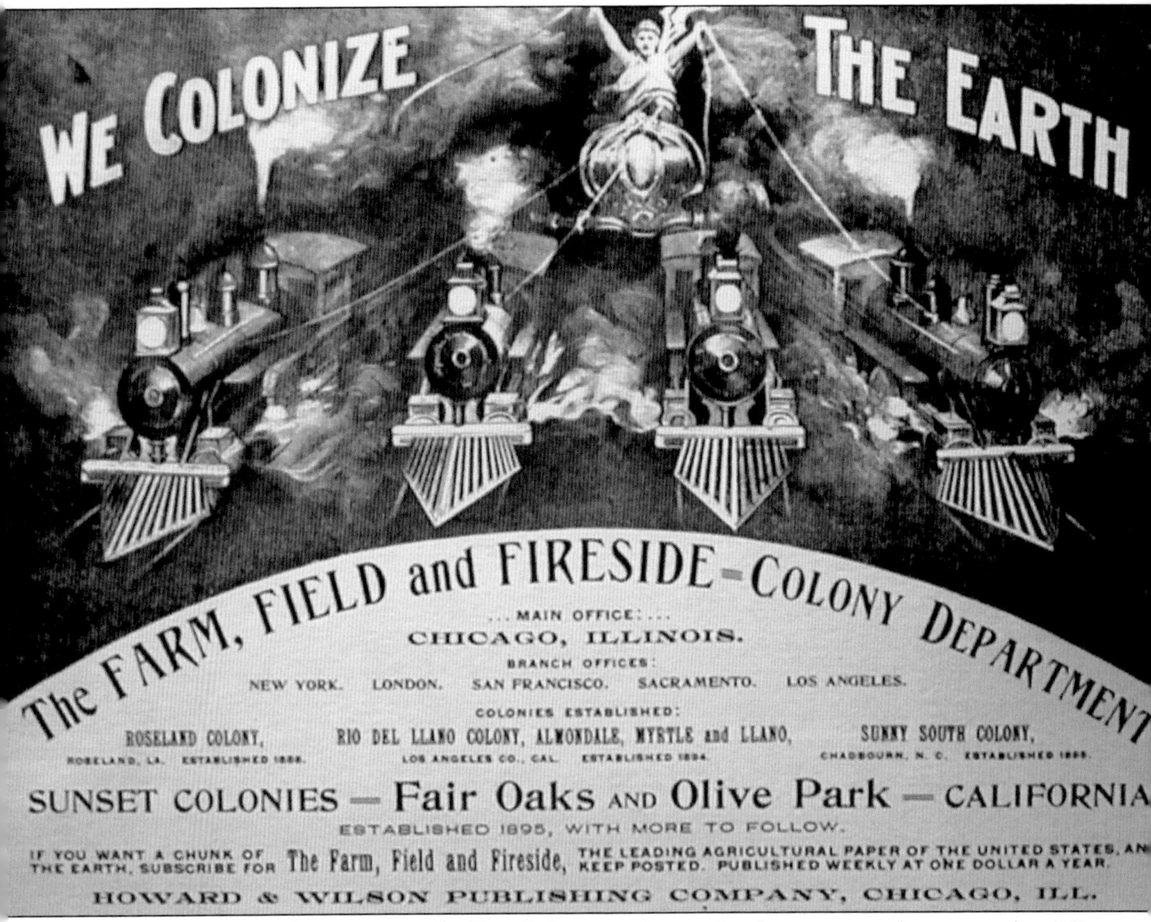

This thunderous booster piece for Fair Oaks, complete with what seems to be an angel or Miss Liberty herself guiding a team of trains in a great and divine mission to go westward, appeared in the Howard-Wilson Company's 1897 publication, *The Heart of California.* (Courtesy Fair Oaks Presbyterian Church.)

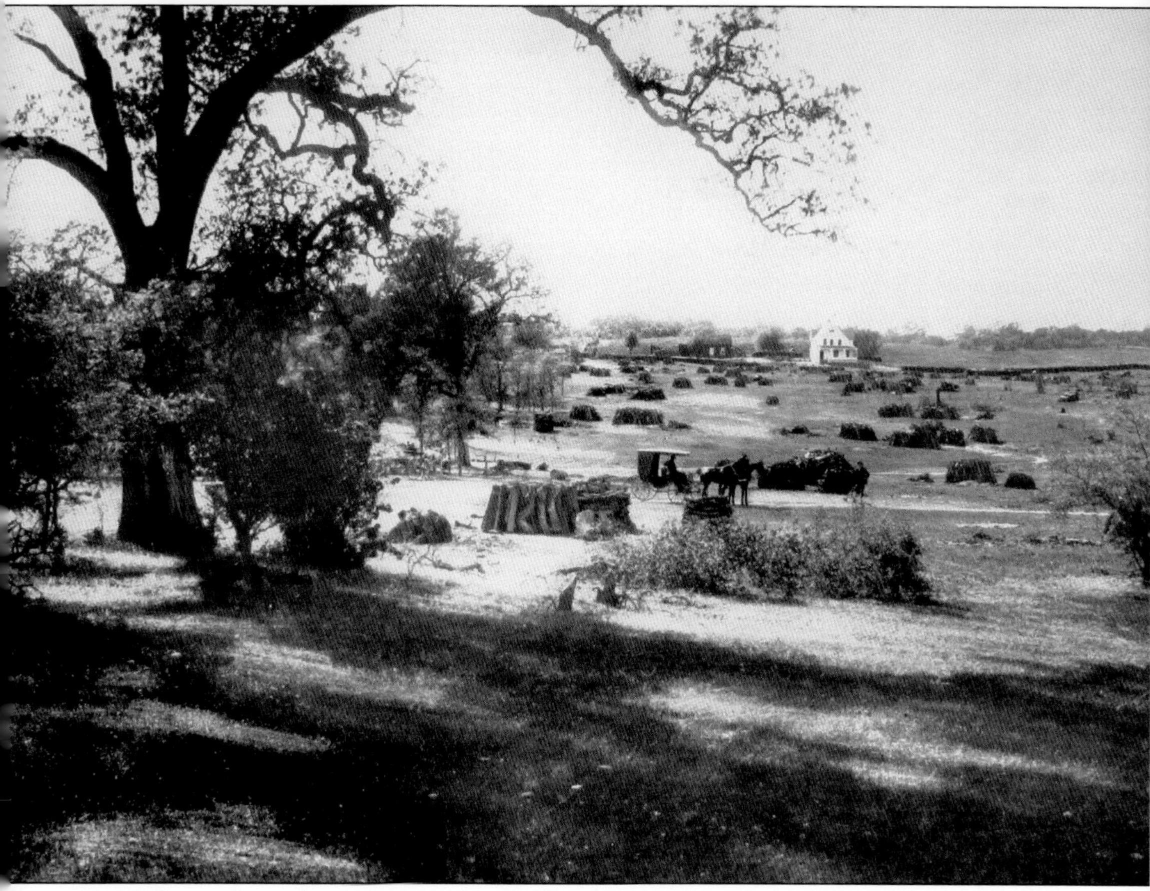

Fair Oaks in the early 1900s was advertised with bucolic imagery. In the photograph above, plentiful haystacks, beautiful trees, and orange fields abound. Open land, ripe for cultivation and complete with a farmstead home, spread as far as the eye can see. (Courtesy Fair Oaks Historical Society.)

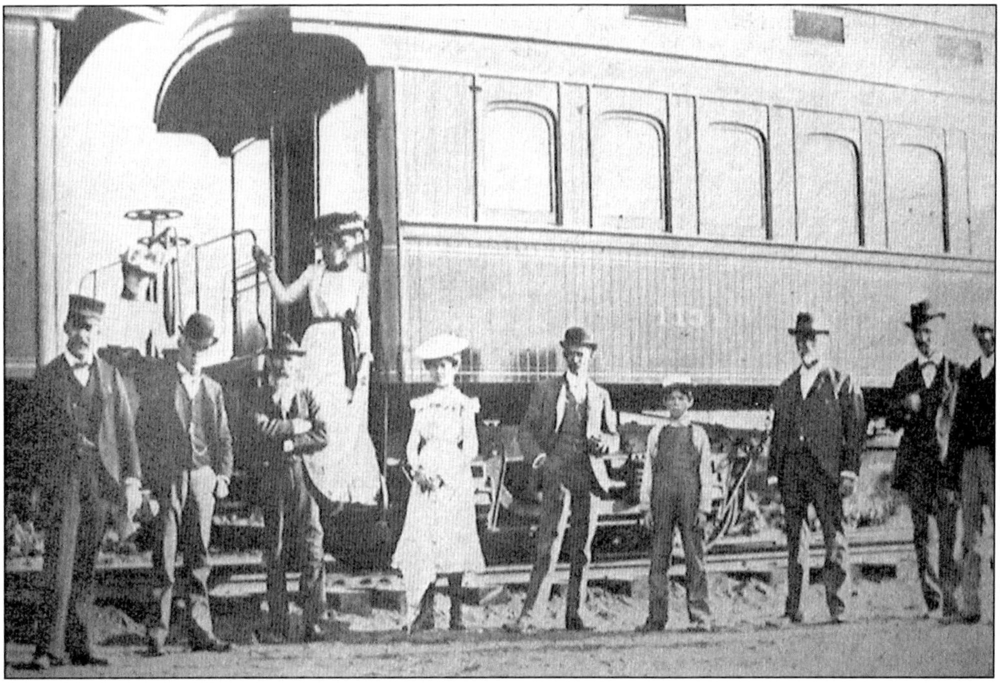

In November 1895, Fair Oaks' original excursionists disembarked after a long trip from Chicago in hopes of finding the "Promised Land" guaranteed by the brash boosters of the Howard-Wilson Publishing Company. (Courtesy Fair Oaks Presbyterian Church.)

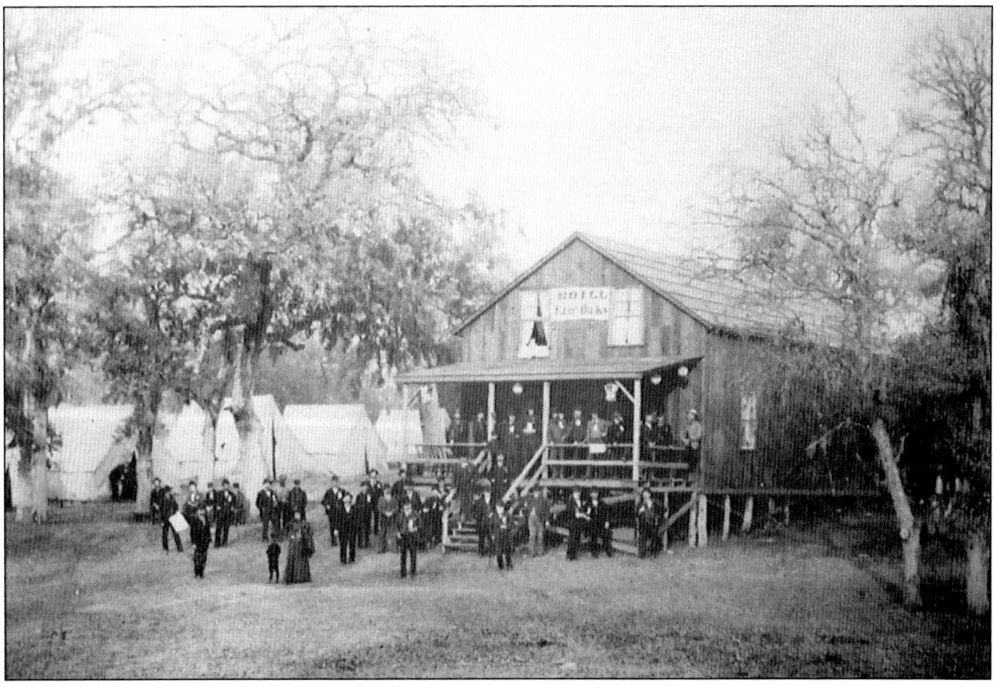

On November 20, 1895, the Fair Oaks excursionists arrived at the Fair Oaks Hotel. The fledgling hotel housed overflow patrons in tents. Excursionists are shown here resting from a long trek to this rural Garden of Eden. (Courtesy Fair Oaks Presbyterian Church.)

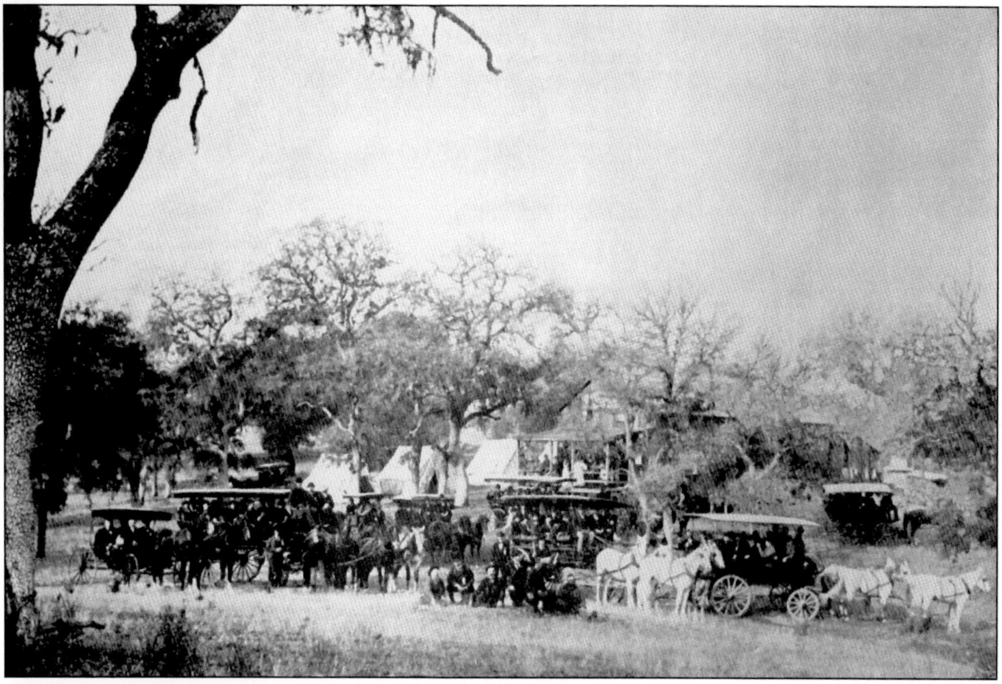

After a brief rest, the pioneering excursionists were given a tour of Fair Oaks and the surrounding areas, including a tour of the prosperous neighboring fruit colony of "Orange Vale." (Courtesy Fair Oaks Presbyterian Church.)

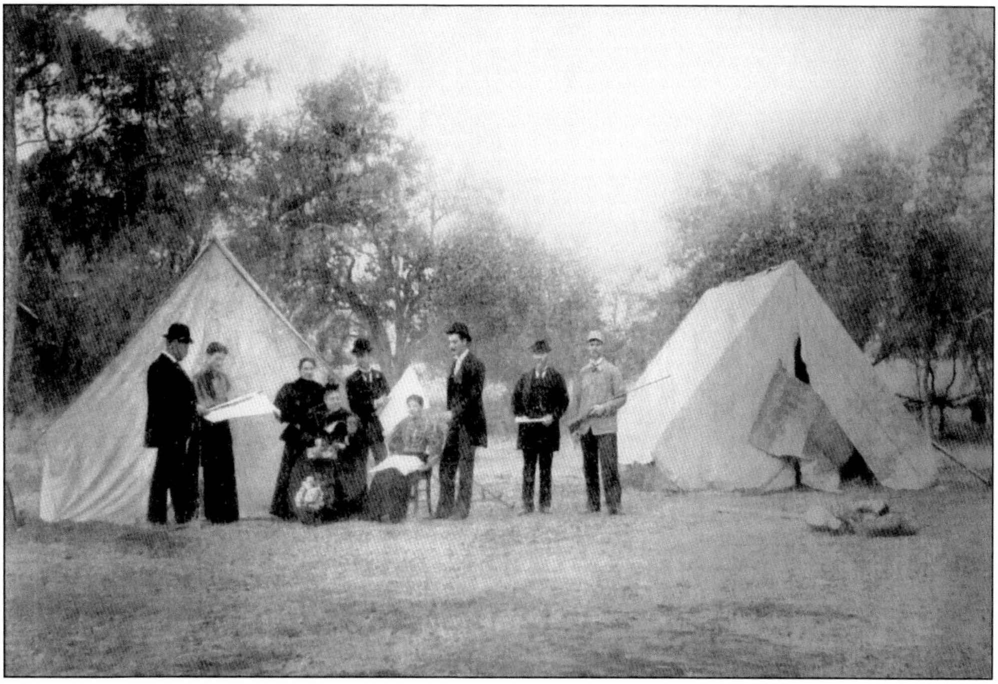

The Fair Oaks excursionists, a reported 165 in all, were so plentiful that they could not all fit into the Fair Oaks Hotel. Many had to set up campsites as they prepared to cast their lots in the "Crown of the Valley." (Courtesy Fair Oaks Historical Society.)

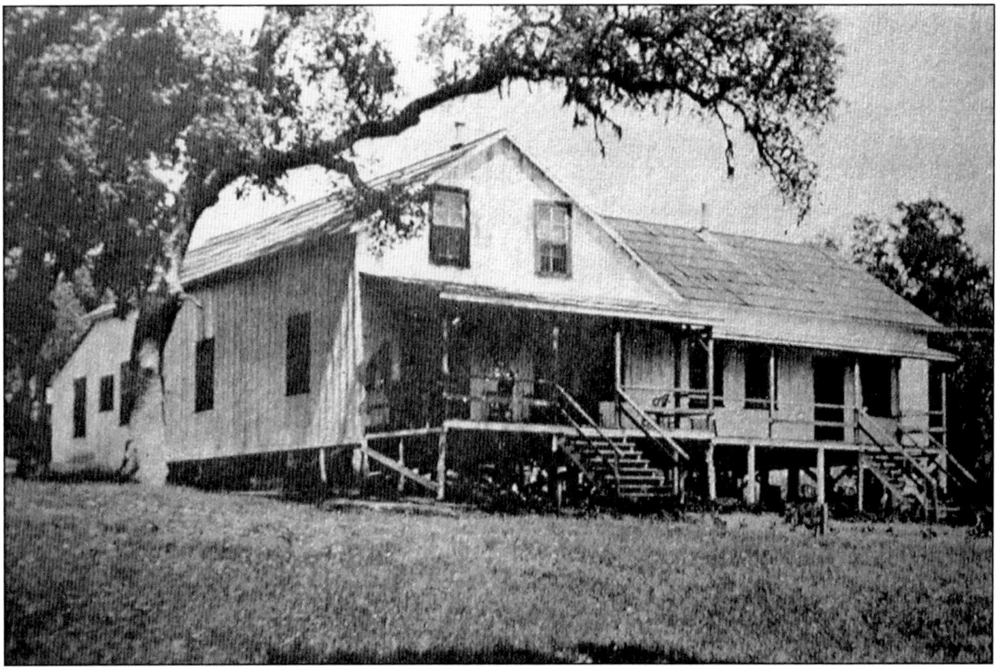

The Fair Oaks Hotel, pictured above *c.* 1900 and bottom, *c.* 1905, sat at the corner of Capitola and Main Street. Originally built around 1890 and used until about 1915, J. Murray Broadley, a pioneering settler from 1897, tore down the hotel in 1923 to use the wood to construct the home his family still lives in today off Main Street. (Above courtesy Fair Oaks Presbyterian Church; below courtesy Fair Oaks Historical Society.)

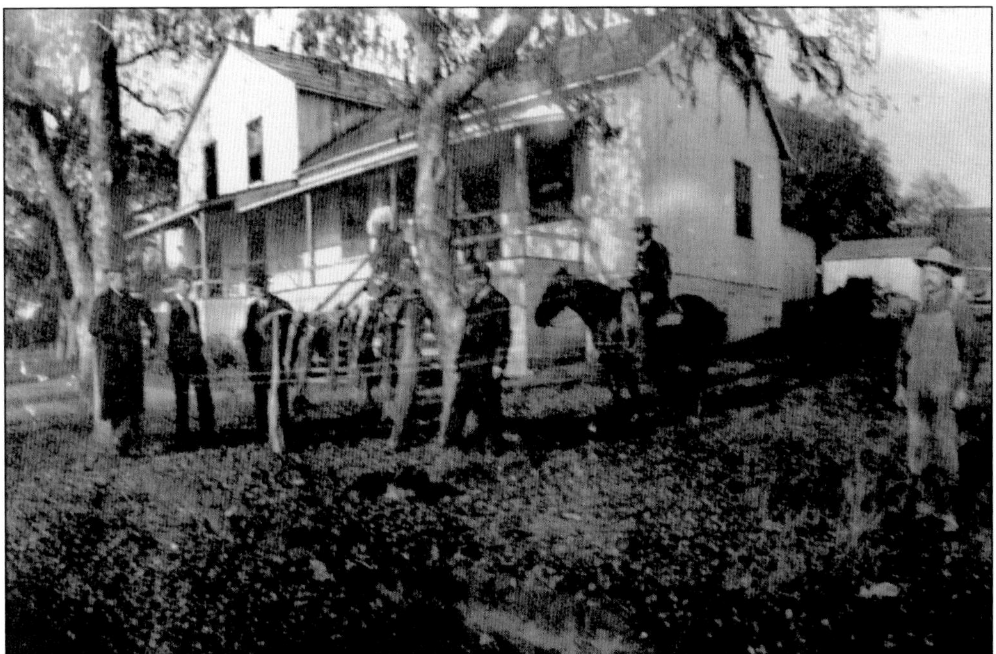

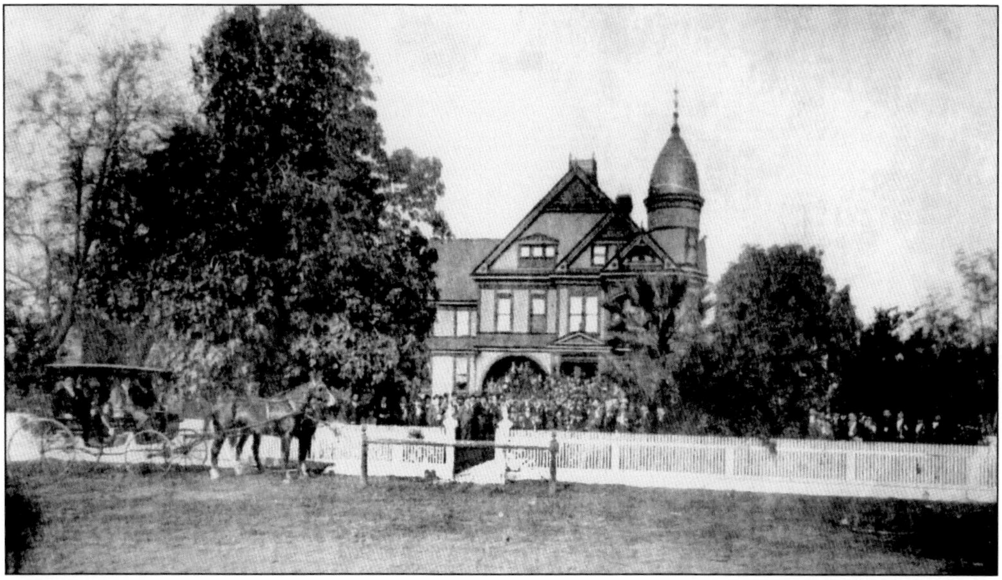

During a tour of surrounding areas, Fair Oaks excursionists were shown beautiful homes, such as the "residence of Hon. R. D. Stephens, on the American River, California." The Howard-Wilson Company used this image of excursionists gathered in the front yard in one of their promotional booklets. (Courtesy Fair Oaks Historical Society.)

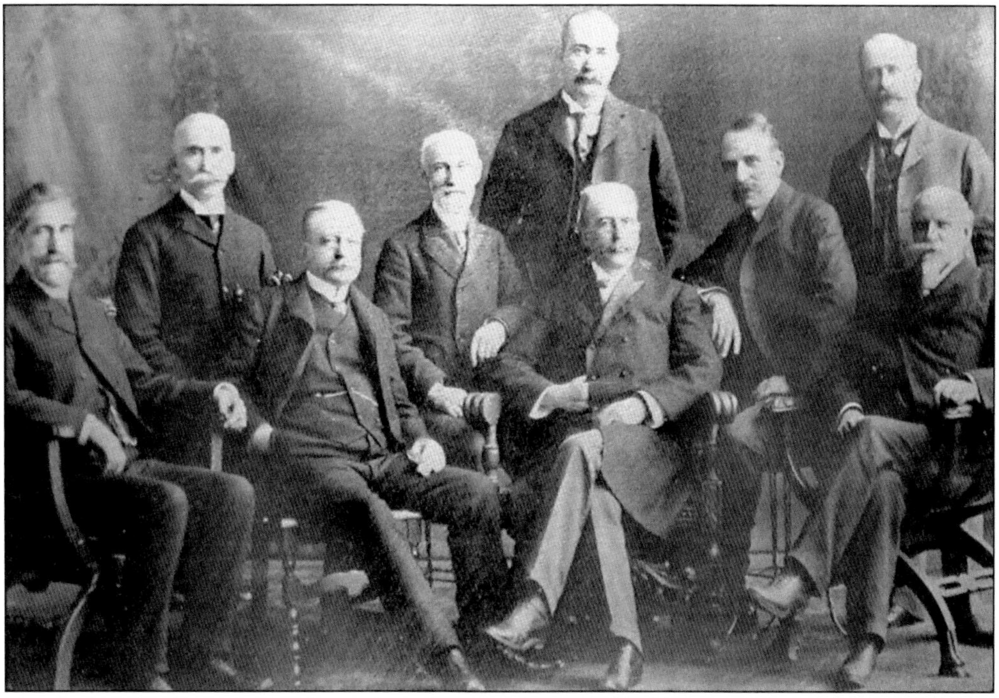

A group of local and out-of-state businessmen formed the Chicago–Fair Oaks Association, pictured here around 1900, to help sustain the budding fruit colony after the Howard-Wilson Company withdrew. The association lobbied the government and other potential investors and succeeded in realizing the construction of a bridge over the American River and a rail station to help the neophyte colony survive and prosper. (Courtesy Fair Oaks Presbyterian Church.)

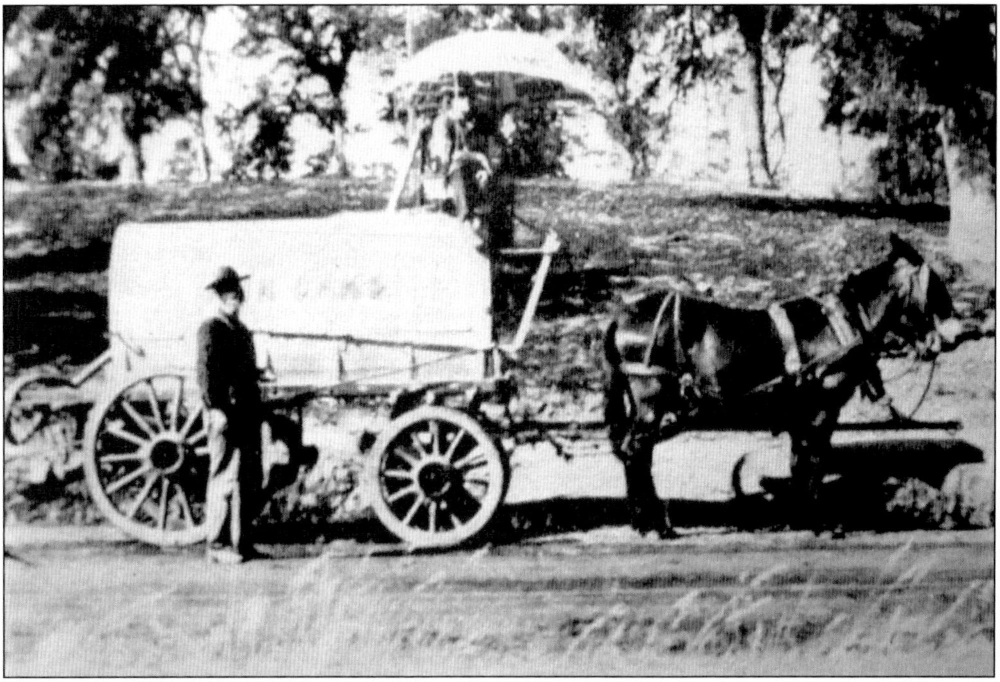

To help sustain the colony, other essential services were provided, such as the delivery of water seen above in an early day water wagon and the construction of roads, as seen below with the still widely used Winding Way. (Courtesy Fair Oaks Presbyterian Church.)

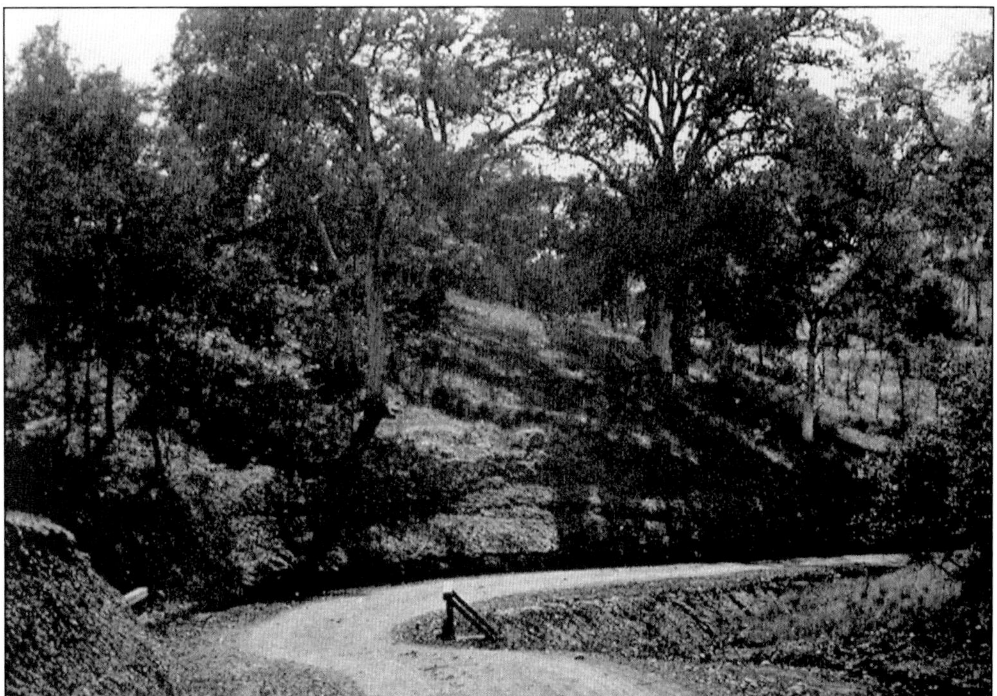

Two

LIVING OFF THE LAND

Cultivators of the earth are the most valuable citizens. They are the most vigorous, the most independent, the most virtuous, and they are tied to their country and wedded to its liberty and interests by the most lasting bands.

—Thomas Jefferson, 1785

Living off the land had been the foundation of life in Fair Oaks for decades before the Howard-Wilson Company first advertised the colony as a rural Eden and the first excursionists arrived to prosper from the growth of "deciduous fruits." The Maidu Indians cultivated the land and prospered for thousands of years, while early pioneers such as the Heintz family had been farming in the area since the 1870s. Advertising Fair Oaks as a rural paradise drew upon this earlier history and reflected the commodification of farming in the second half of the 19th century.

The construction of a bridge over the American River grew out of this economic reality and the need for faster transport of fruit from the newly established colonies at Orangevale and Fair Oaks to markets in the East. It also reflected the growth of the Northern California fruit industry and the maturation of fruit trees planted during the 1880s and 1890s in hopes of competing with Southern California as the citrus center of the world. According to historian Joseph A. McGowan, farmers planted over 250,000 orange trees and 50,000 lemon tress north of Sacramento between 1888 and 1891. The trees bore fruit by 1893 when four carloads of fruit shipped out from northern California. The figure jumped to 81 carloads in 1896, 286 in 1897, and 589 in 1898.

Fair Oaks grew rapidly with the completion of a bridge and railway a few months later. The community experienced steady growth with 2,200 acres of land sold and 1,200 acres planted primarily with lemons, oranges, olives, and almonds.

In 1902, the Fair Oaks Fruit Company incorporated and built a warehouse in Fair Oaks to export its fruit. According to their record book, the young fruit company produced 743 tons of fruit by 1906 and anticipated growth in the future. John E. Holst, an early pioneer of the colony, reported that the fruit company eventually shipped out a yearly average of 150 carloads of oranges and 50 carloads of lemons.

Unfortunately the freeze of 1932 destroyed the fruit crop and took a heavy toll on farmers already burdened by the Great Depression. For several days, the temperature dropped to 18 degrees. Most trees were killed and the few individuals who replanted their orchards were hit two years later with a similar freeze. The freezes effectively wiped out Fair Oaks, and surrounding citrus colonies, as a major producer of citrus fruit in California.

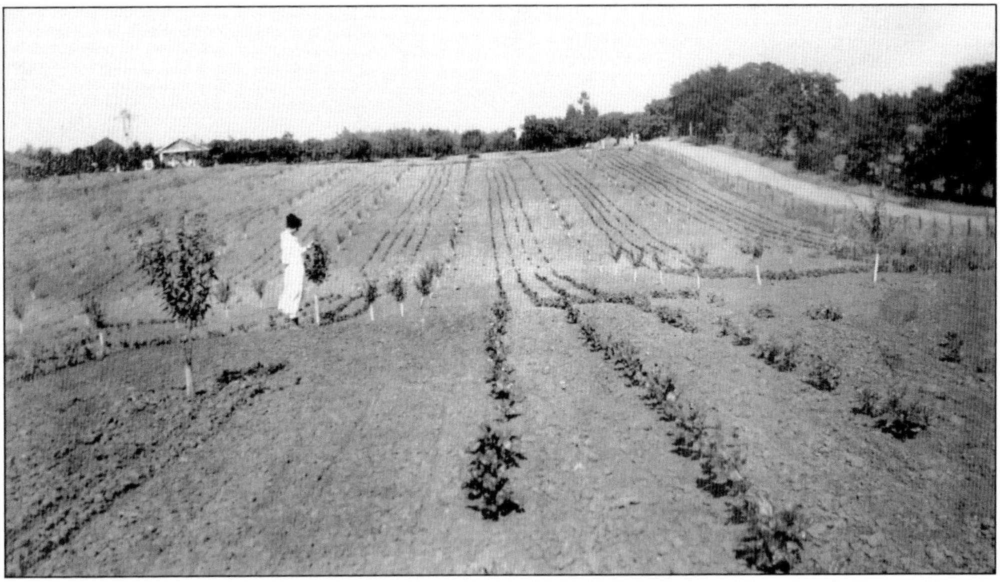

From the 1870s through the 1960s, the Dewey family orchard, pictured here with Emma Dewey inspecting the fields around 1910, grew almonds and cotton (shown here) along with oranges, olives, grapes, cherries, watermelons, and wheat. This orchard was located at the corner of present-day streets Winding Way and Dewey Drive. (Courtesy Eileen Dewey Thomas.)

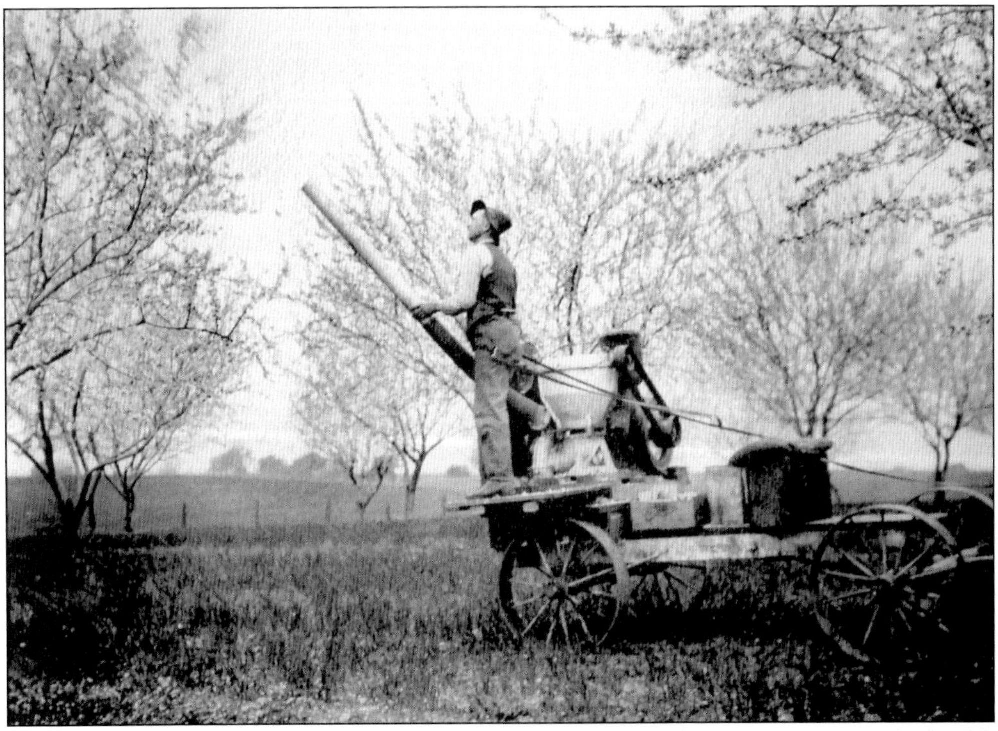

Like many farmers in Fair Oaks, Harold Dewey took the time and concern to insure the health of his family's crop by fumigating his almond trees, *c.* 1915. (Courtesy Eileen Dewey Thomas.)

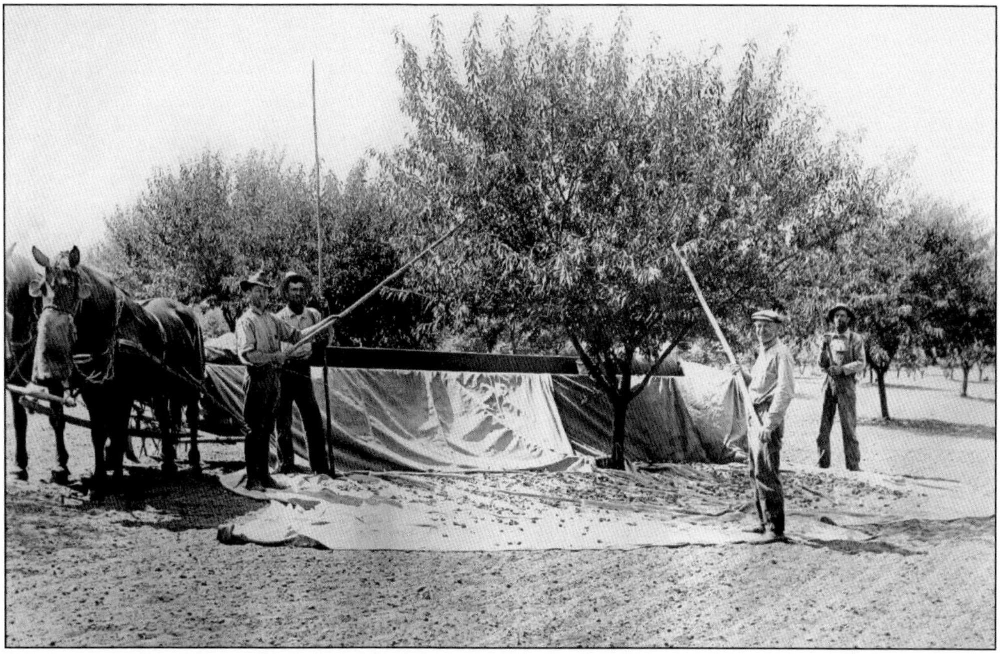

Workers on the Dewey farm, seen here in 1910, helped to harvest almonds and prepare them for sorting, packing, and shipping. The Dewey farm often used local high school boys from San Juan High School, who earned credit through the school's Work Experience Program. The sticks seen here are still owned by the family today. (Courtesy Eileen Dewey Thomas.)

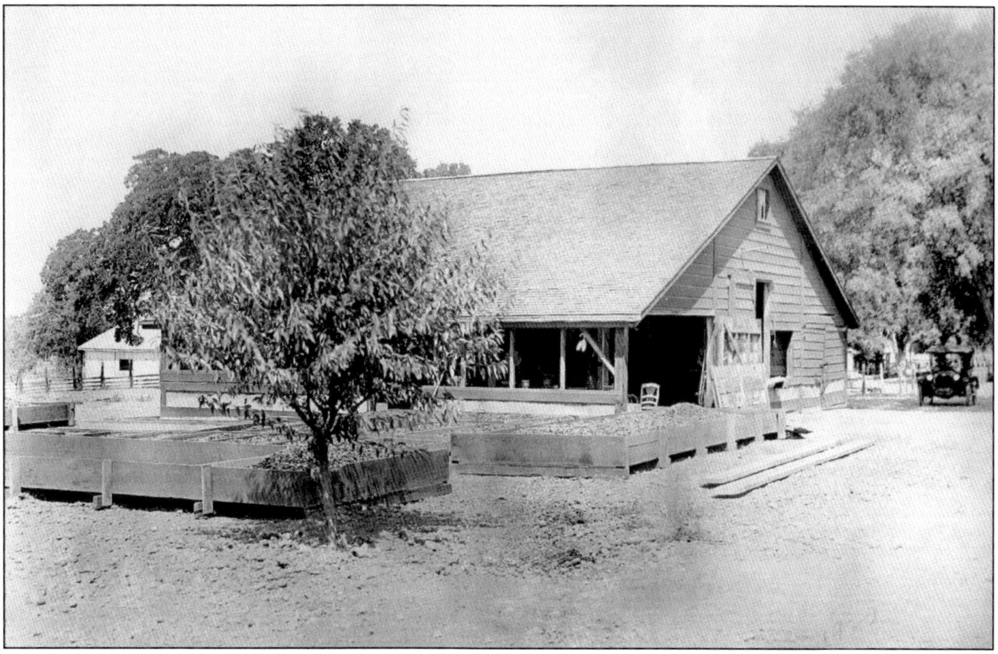

The Dewey barn, shown here in 1920, stored the family's machinery and served as a packinghouse. Built in 1898, the barn had a hard 40 years. One family legend reports a disgruntled worker burned it down (or nearly burned it down). The barn eventually collapsed during strong winds in 1938. (Courtesy Eileen Dewey Thomas.)

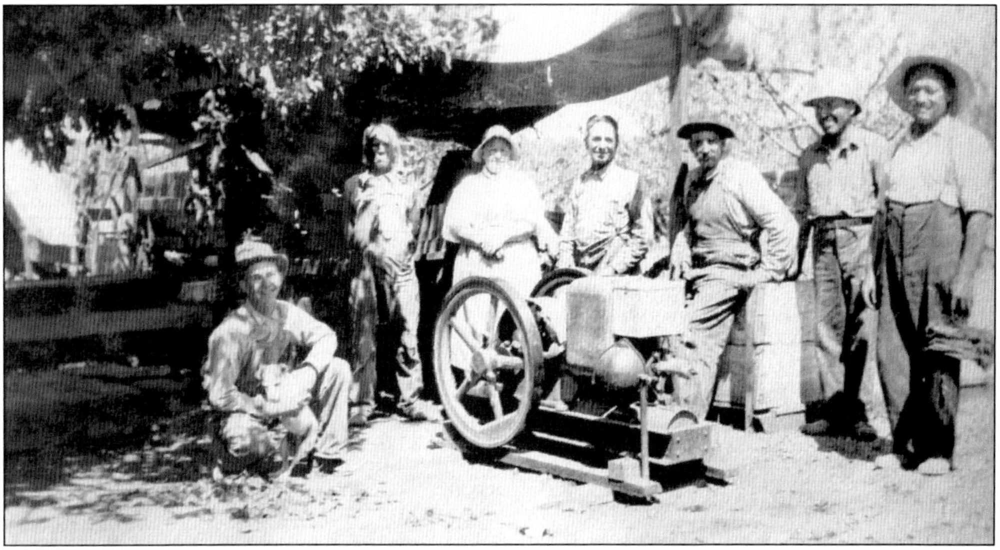

Resting from the hard work of harvesting almonds, Harold Dewey, seen in the middle, poses with workers in 1918. The family often employed Native American workers, as well as Hindi and Mexican immigrants and sojourners. (Courtesy Eileen Dewey Thomas.)

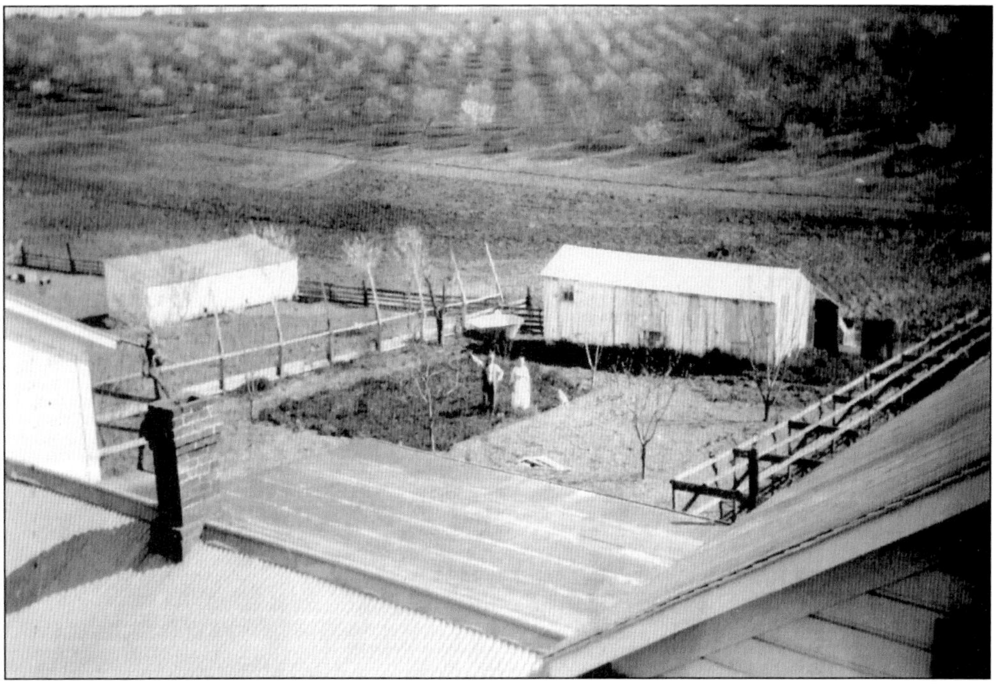

This view of the Dewey farm, taken from the roof of their home around 1915, shows the family's vast acreage, typical of many farms in Fair Oaks, as wells the Dewey's out sheds and even a grape grate in the right corner. Today this area is surrounded by busy streets, houses, and the latest convenience stores. Indeed, a Starbucks and Dairy Queen sit today on what used to be the Dewey orchard. (Courtesy Eileen Dewey Thomas.)

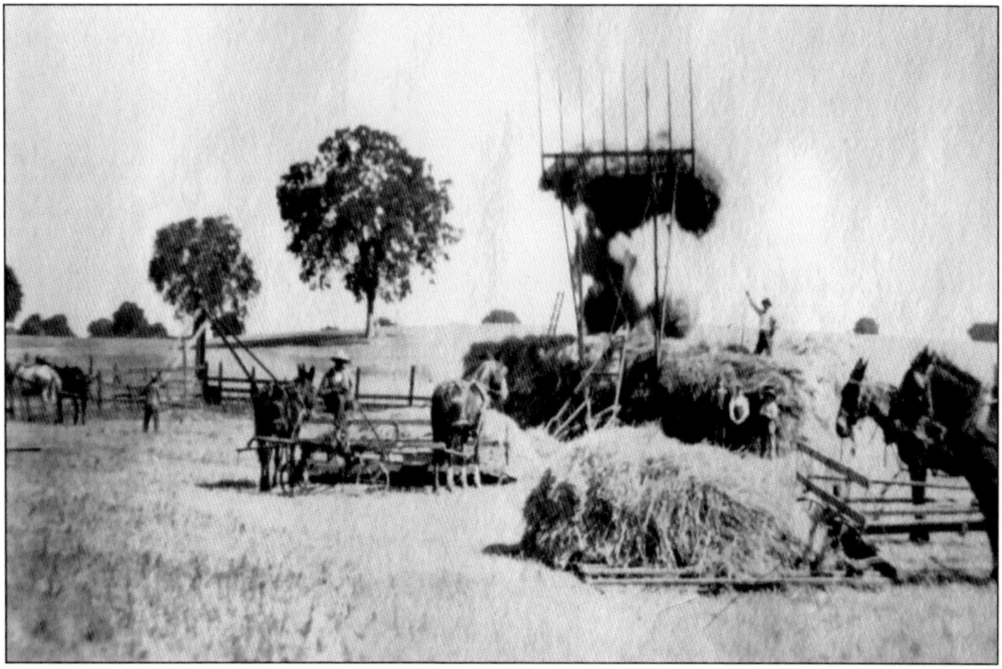

The Deweys and other workers are seen above during the grain harvest around 1915. Typical of many Fair Oaks farmers, the Deweys used a wheat thrasher, which the family still owns. They then had to load the wheat on a wagon, seen below in 1919, to ship produce to local and other markets. (Courtesy Eileen Dewey Thomas.)

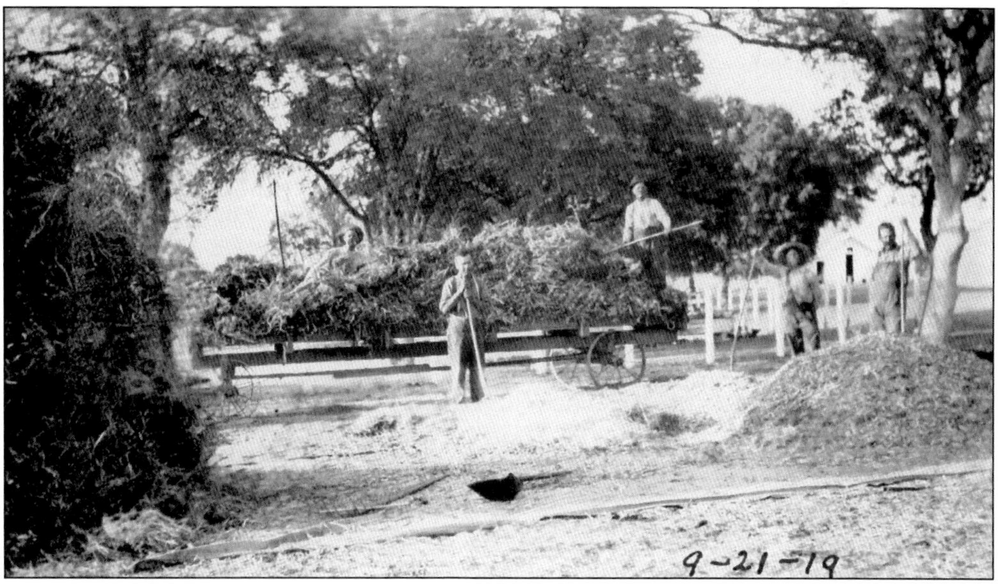

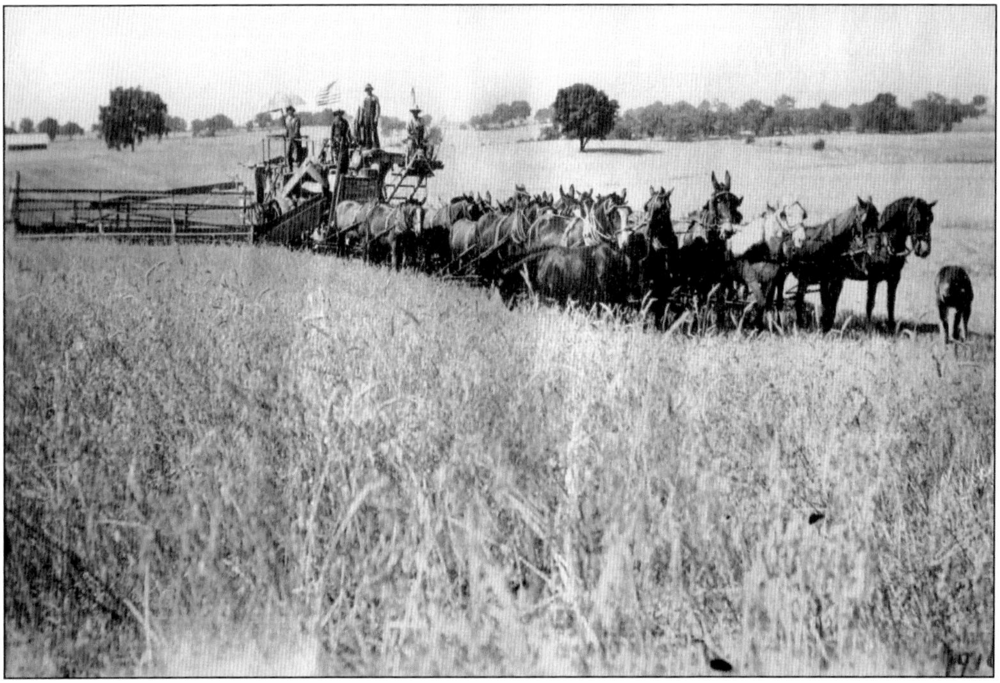

Many Fair Oaks farmers used large combines, like the one seen above in 1916, to harvest wheat. They also used large tractors, like the one below in 1913. Tractors skyrocketed in popularity after technological advances saw the number of sales soar from approximately 600 in use in 1907 to around 3.4 million by 1950. Often families, like a cooperative, would share or rent out equipment, like the Ricketts possibly did for the Deweys. (Courtesy Eileen Dewey Thomas.)

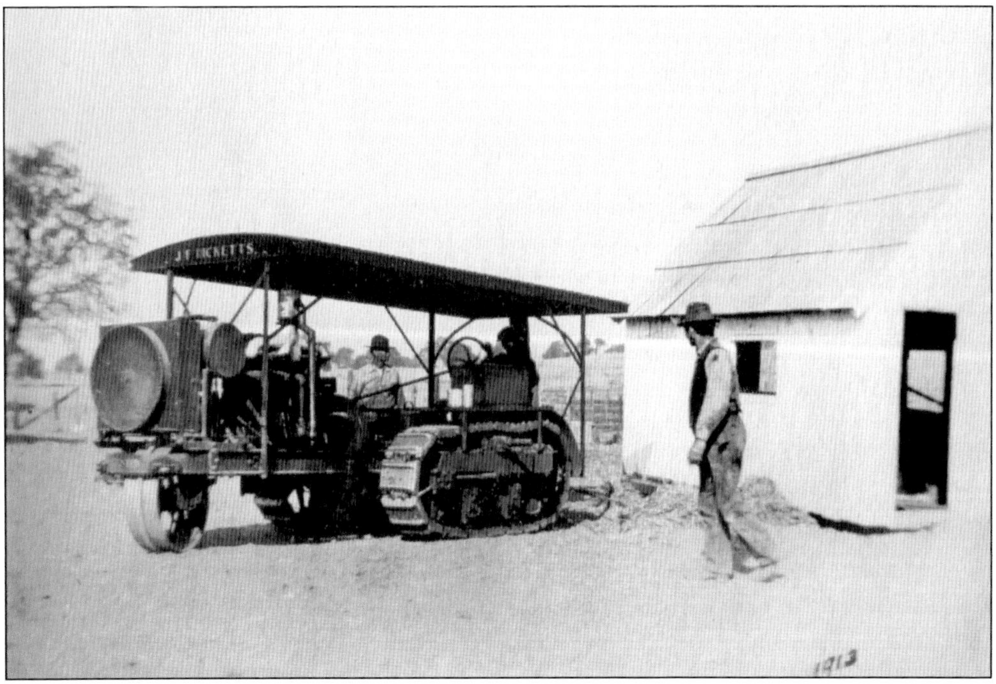

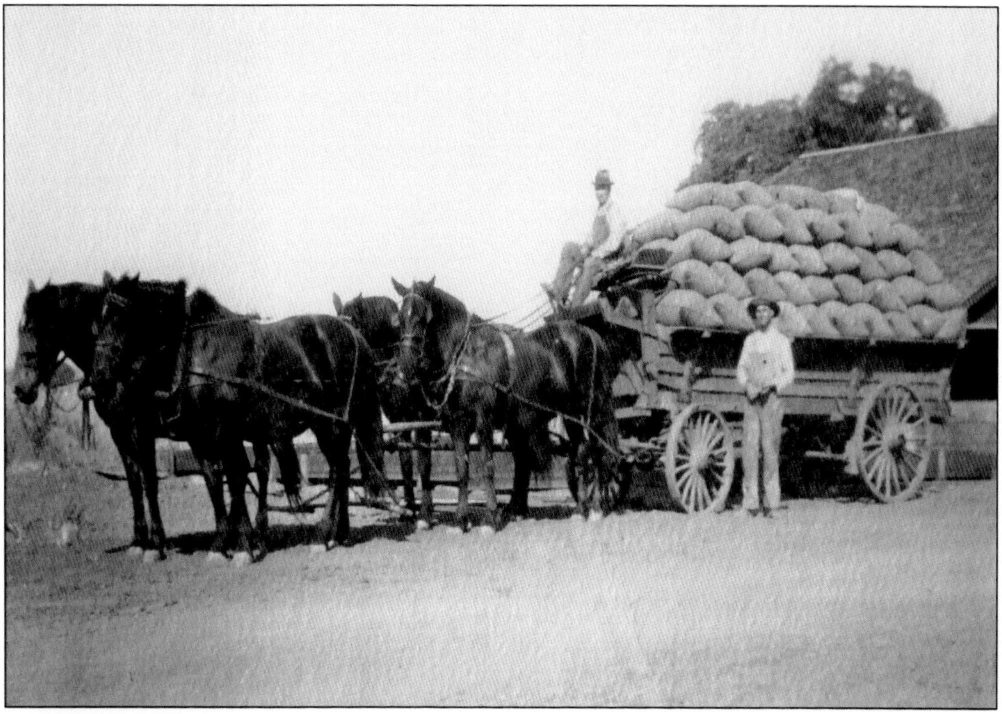

Harold Dewey (driving the wagon) and other workers, seen here *c.* 1915, loaded their wagons with bags of wheat to ship to local and other markets. (Courtesy Eileen Dewey Thomas.)

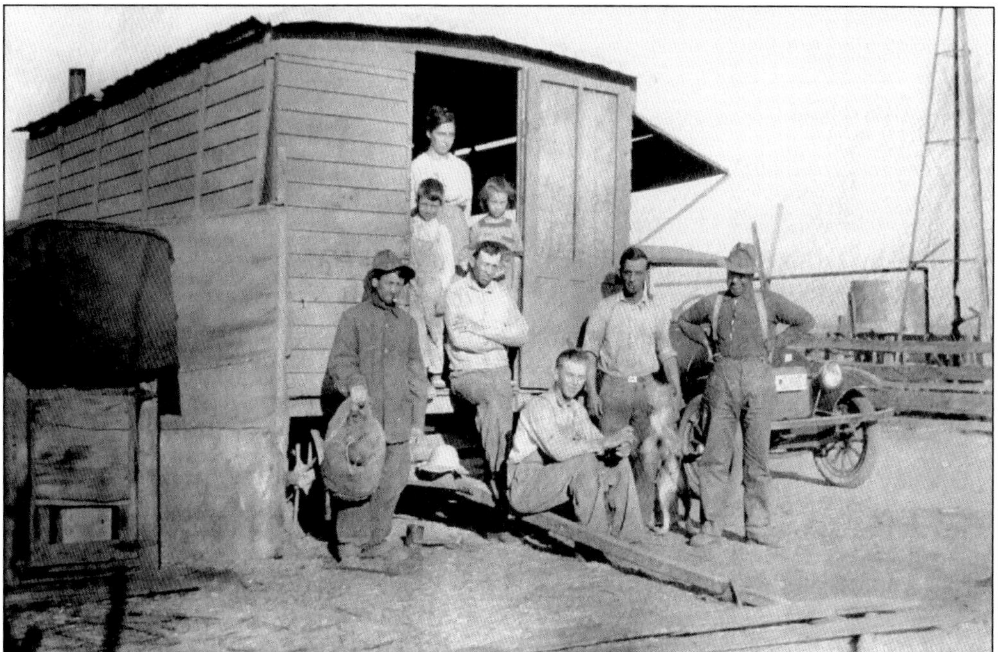

Seen resting on a hulling wagon around 1915 are the Dewey family and other workers. Often workers and families in Fair Oaks, like the Deweys, would hire themselves out to work on other farms during the busy season. (Courtesy Eileen Dewey Thomas.)

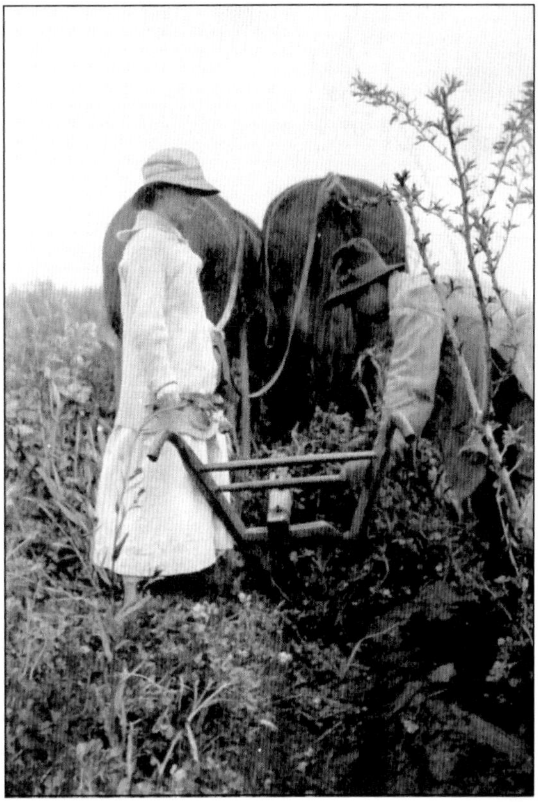

Fair Oaks farmers like Emma and Harold Dewey, seen here around 1915, worked hard with the plow in the large orchards to help sustain crops. (Courtesy Eileen Dewey Thomas.)

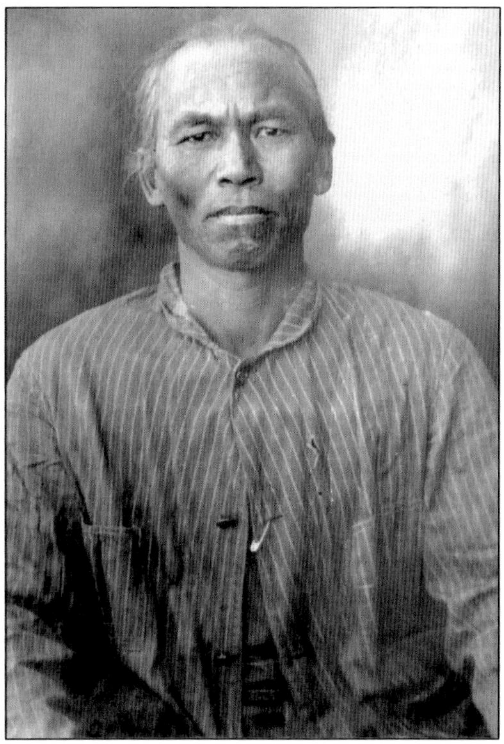

Many ethnic immigrants, including the Chinese, Japanese, Hindis, and Mexicans labored on the farms in Fair Oaks. Pictured here around 1915 is Chinese immigrant Jim Gee. Gee worked and lived with the Dewey family almost his entire adult life. He was buried in the Heintz family plot in the cemetery downtown—the Heintz family originally owned the Dewey farm before Harry Dewey married Bertha Heintz in the late 1800s. (Courtesy Eileen Dewey Thomas.)

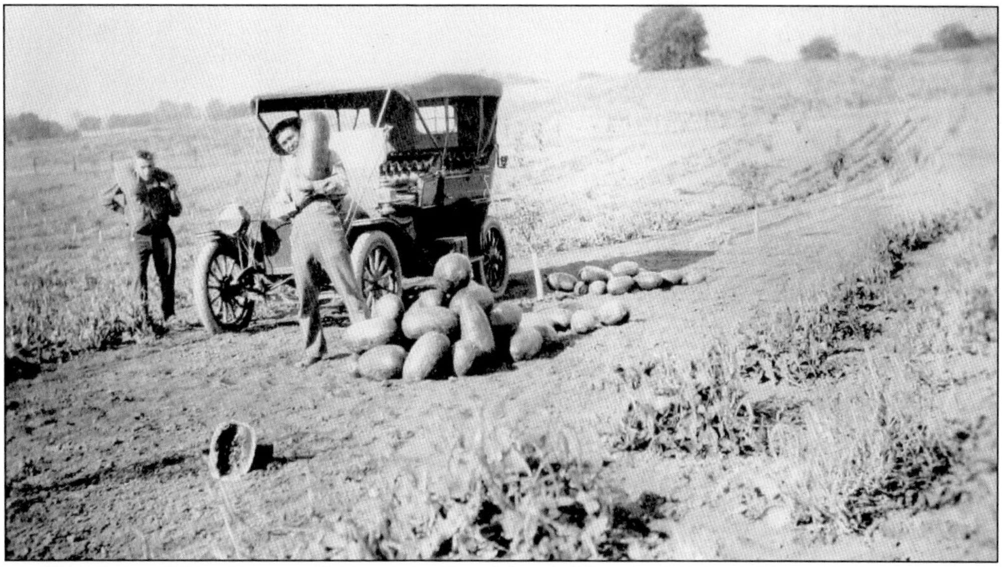

In 1916, Harold Dewey proudly inspected and lauded his large watermelon crop (a marginal crop in Fair Oaks) in front of the family's 1909 EMF 30. Though Fair Oaks mainly produced citrus, particularly oranges and lemons, many farmers grew such produce as olives, watermelons, cherries, and grapes. (Courtesy Eileen Dewey Thomas.)

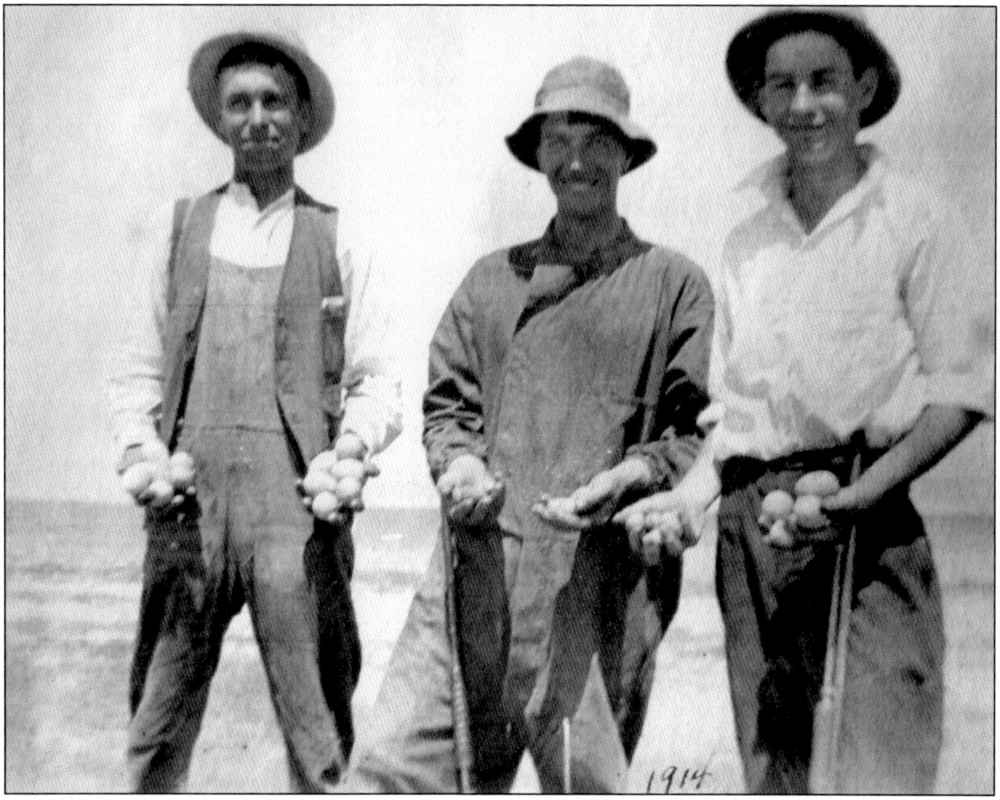

Harold Dewey, pictured here on the left with some friends and family in 1914, gathered eggs to supplement the family diet and income. (Courtesy Eileen Dewey Thomas.)

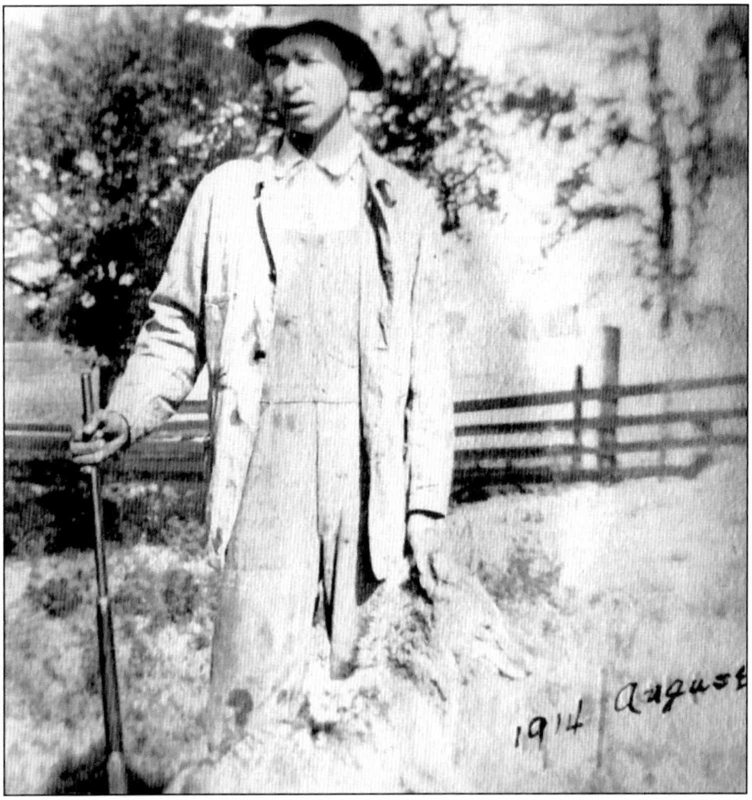

Many Fair Oaks residents, such as Harold Dewey, seen left in 1914, hunted the local wildlife, which included opossums and coyotes, to protect his livestock and chicken farm. Below, Harold Dewey, positioned in the middle, and some of his friends or family display the outcome of their hunt—a coyote. (Courtesy Eileen Dewey Thomas.)

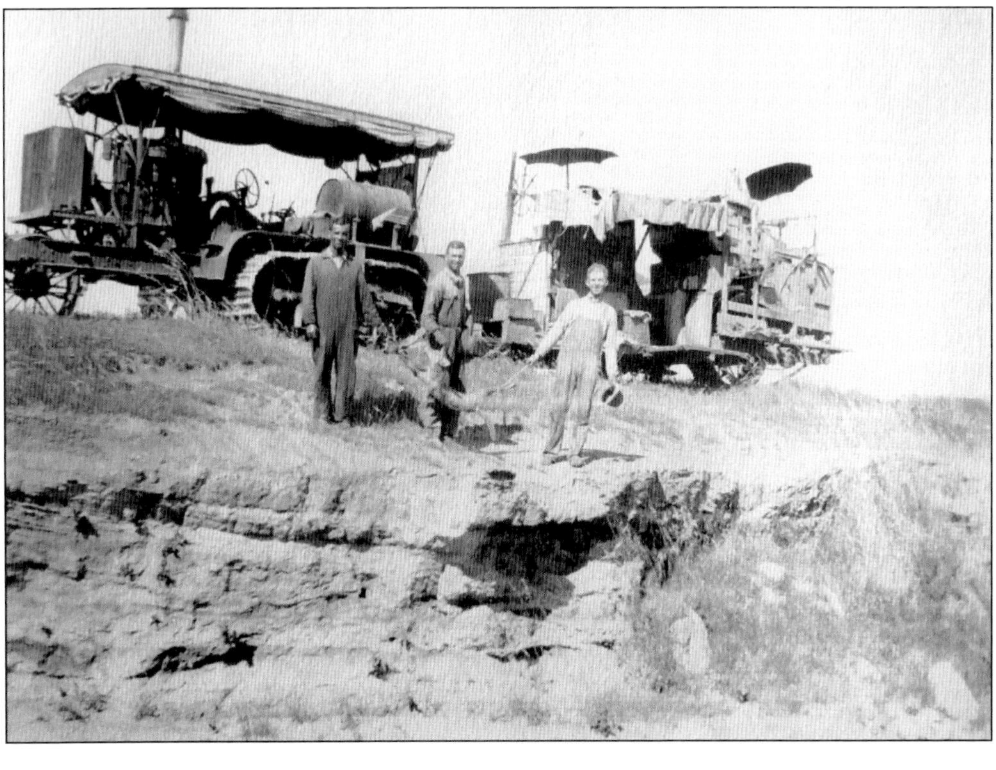

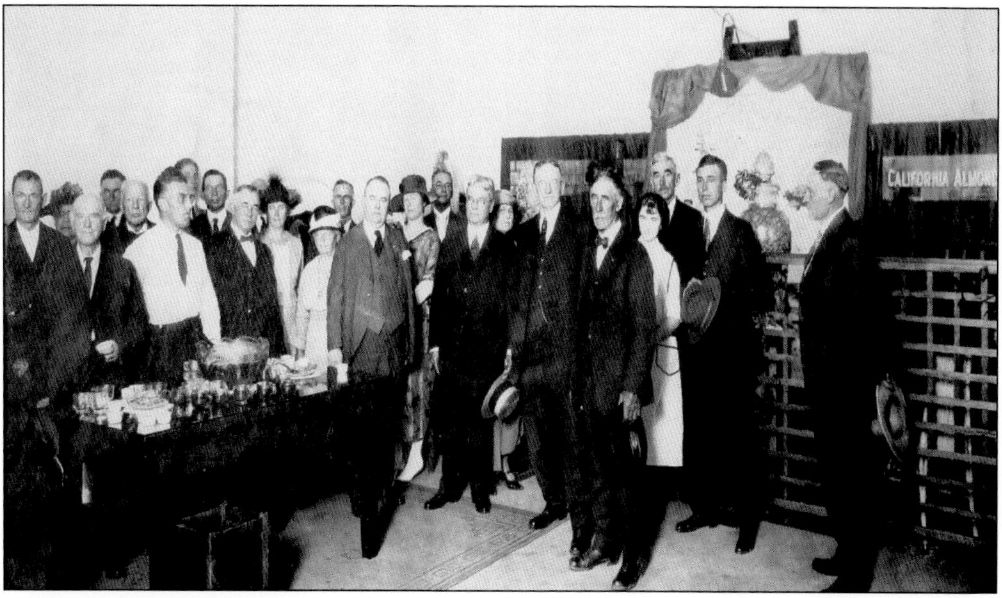

In the mid-1910s, founding members of the California Almond Growers Exchange, Harry Dewey (middle, back row) and Harold Dewey (second to last on the right) met with Gov. Hiram Johnson (middle, holding a hat). Members from nine associations in Antelope, Orangevale, Fair Oaks, Davis, Capay, Sutter County, Live Oak, Oakley, and San Joaquin County formed the cooperative on May 7, 1910. Today the cooperative, known as Blue Diamond, includes 230 of California's almond growers and has 4,000 grower members. (Courtesy Eileen Dewey Thomas.)

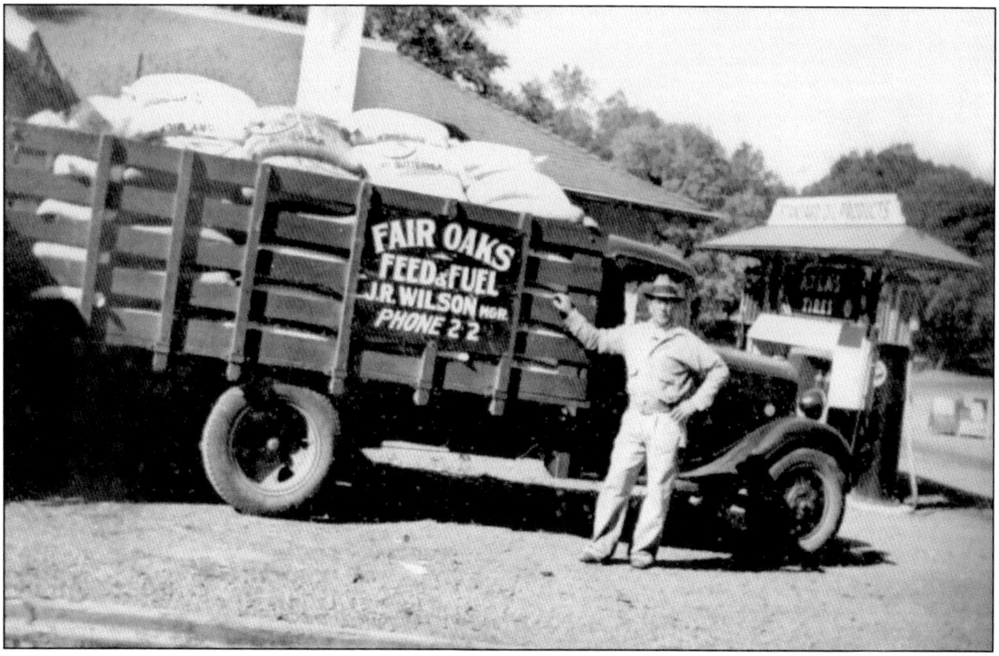

In the early 1930s, Jack "Pop" Wilson posed in front of his Fair Oaks Feed & Fuel truck. Beginning in the late 1920s, he helped to service the local Fair Oaks and surrounding area farmers. He also ran his own service station, gas station, and sporting goods store. (Courtesy Hugh Gorman.)

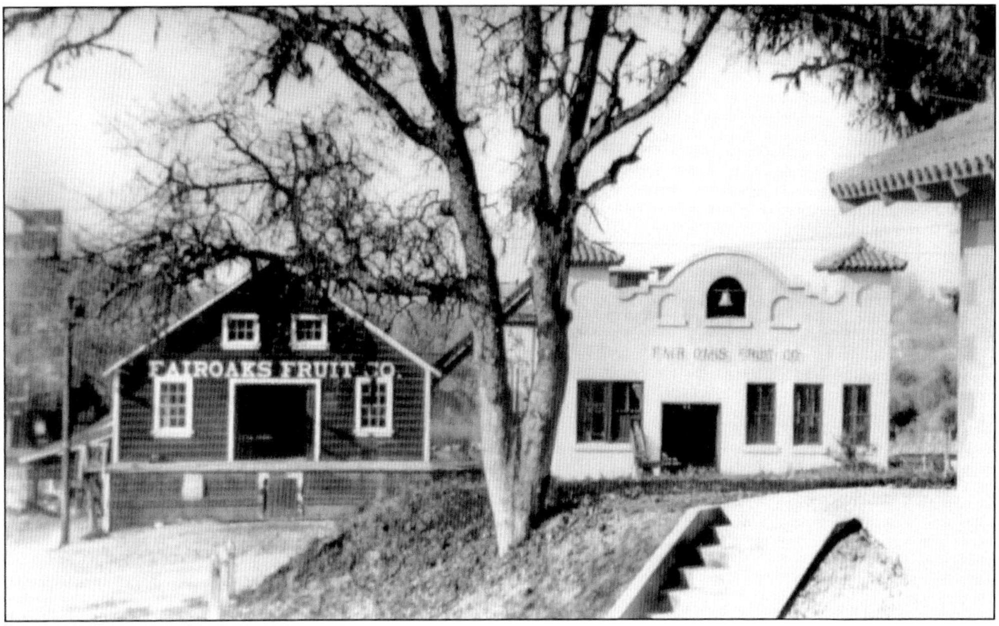

The Fair Oaks Fruit Company, incorporated in November 1902, operated for over 45 years before it dissolved in August 1948. The Fair Oaks Olive Growers Association then took over until the 1960s. Pictured here is the Fair Oaks Fruit Company building, on the left, and the olive mill, on the right, sometime in the early 1900s. (Courtesy Fair Oaks Chamber of Commerce.)

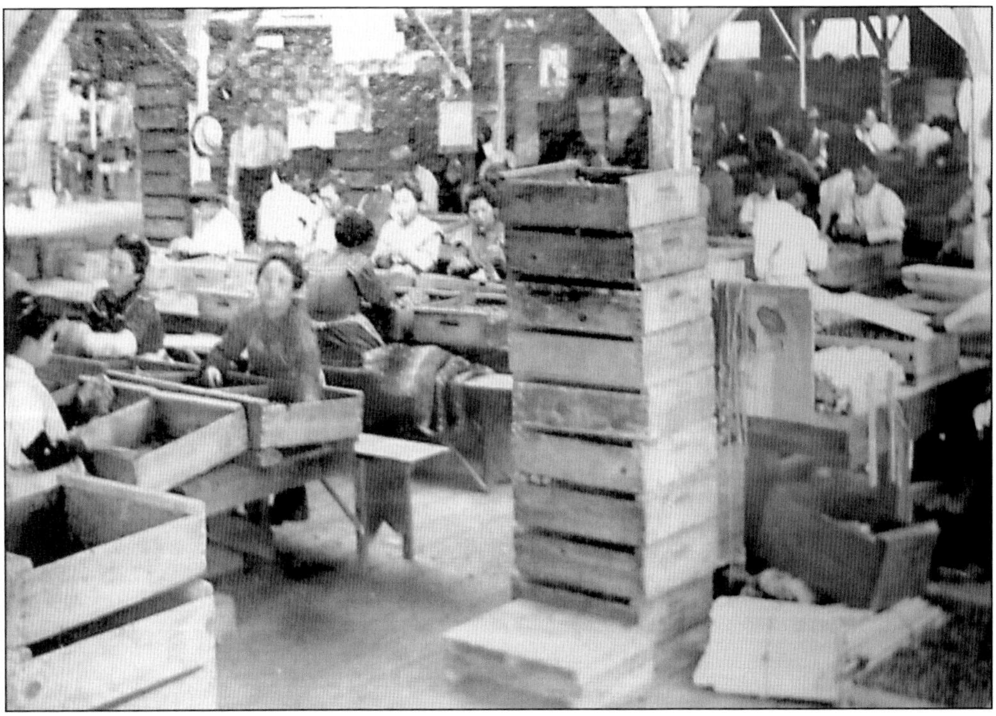

The Fair Oaks Fruit Packing Plant, also known as Pioneer, often employed female Japanese immigrants to help sort, pack, and ship produce. (Courtesy Fair Oaks Historical Society.)

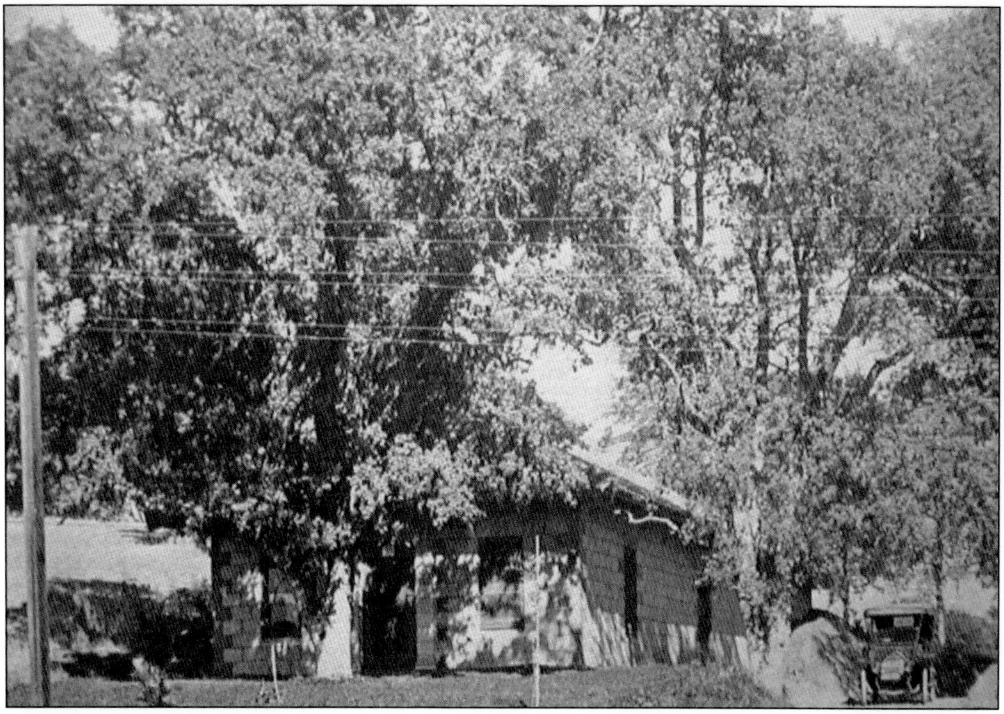

The Fair Oaks Olive Growers Association conducted business from their office on Winding Way and Sunset Avenue, pictured here around 1920. (Courtesy Fair Oaks Presbyterian Church.)

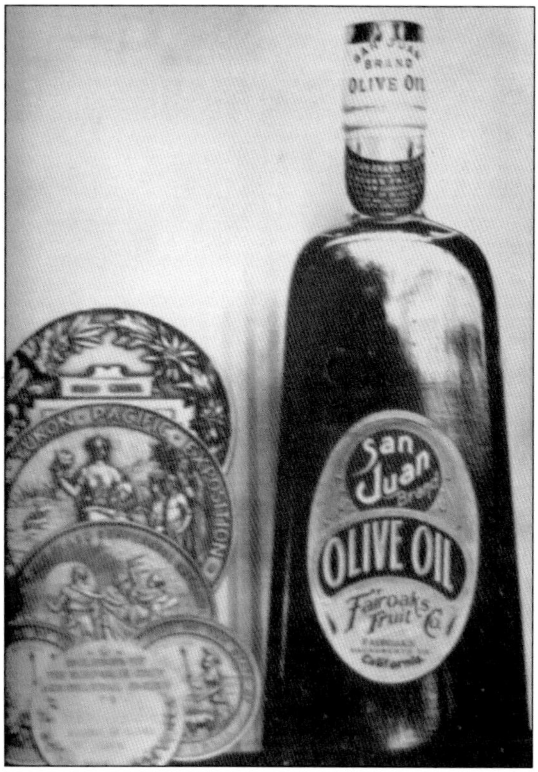

The Fair Oaks Fruit Company manufactured canned olives and olive oil under various labels, such as the San Juan Brand, San Juan Brand Olives, and San Juan Brand Olive Oil. (Courtesy Fair Oaks Historical Society.)

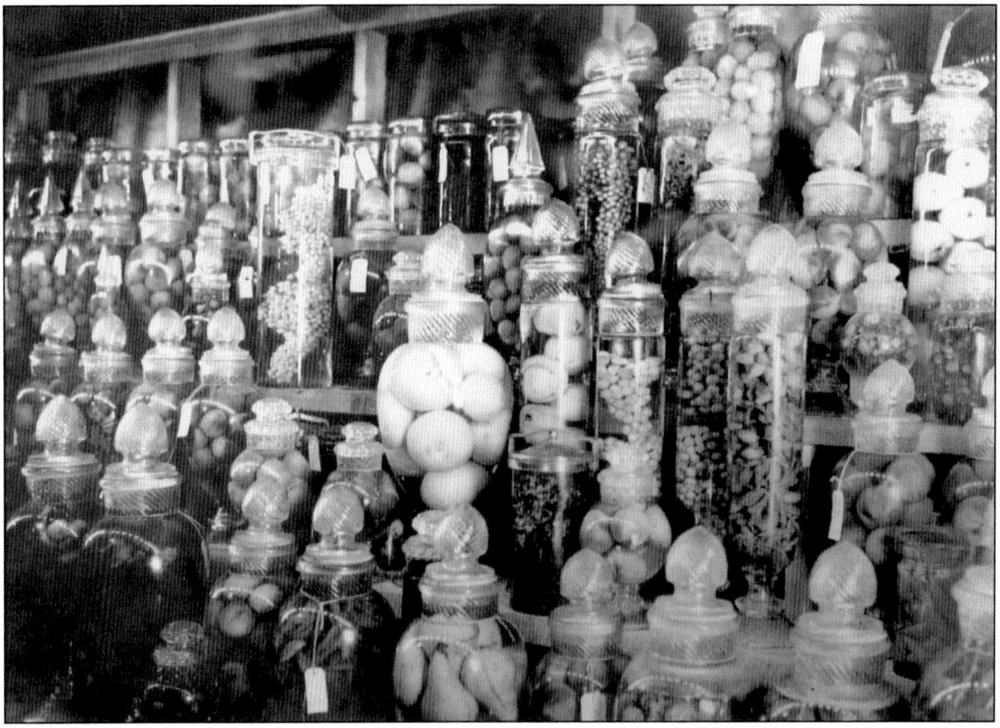

The Fair Oaks Fruit Company displayed its assortment of fruits, olives, and bottles at various forums, including the California State Fair in 1908 (top) and local fruit markets, such as the one pictured below in 1918. (Above courtesy Fair Oaks Historical Society; below courtesy Sacramento Archives and Museum Collection Center, No. 1981/06/1072.)

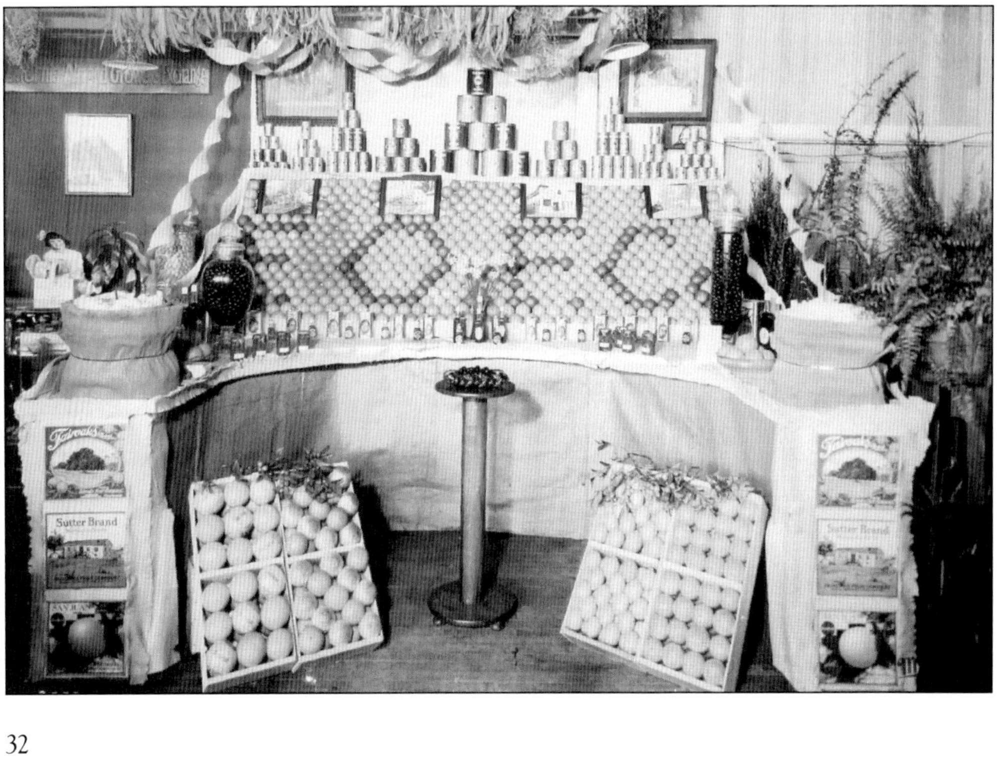

Three

Community Building

If a city wishes to gain in population it must work along esthetic lines. It must improve its schools, it must establish libraries, parks and institutions that appeal to the intellectual life. It must beautify its streets, encourage the construction of handsome buildings and maintain perfect sanitary conditions. In other words, the Coming City is the Artistic City.

—*Riverside Daily Press*, December 3, 1900

The agricultural growth of Fair Oaks attracted the development of other community services. Reminiscences in *Fair Oaks and San Juan Area Memories* indicate that Fair Oaks experienced a boom at the end of the 19th century and early part of the 20th. A bridge, first built in 1901, crossed the American River and the Southern Pacific Railroad Company built a railway and station to service the community. Along Main Street, a variety of stores and services arose. Shoppers could stop by the blacksmith's shop to watch the smith shape shoes and fit them to the plow horses. Customers could visit Leonard Shelton's combination post office and general store to mail letters while picking up essential sundries. In the back of Clayton Vaughn's mother's home, one could even get a nice haircut at Fair Oaks' first barber shop. Lumber and tools were available at Charles H. Slocum's lumberyard or hardware store. In fact, Slocum also helped to start Fair Oaks' first bank in 1905 and ran a general store with W. Ralph Gore.

Fair Oaks grew at a steady pace throughout the small town's inaugural years, as a pharmacy, cemetery, and a number of small dry goods and grocery stores also opened. If little Johnny happened to catch a cold, Fair Oaks even had a medical doctor in R. N. Bramhall, who began his practice in 1902. The Murphy Building, built by Frances Murphy in 1901, served as a store building and public hall where Fair Oaks residents and visitors throughout the years have been able to buy groceries, visit a doctor, get a mouthful of ice cream, cut loose in the upstairs dance hall, buy hardware, or purchase some insurance. Today the Murphy Building attracts visitors and customers alike and has served the community for over 100 years.

As Fair Oaks continued to grow, it developed services to meet the changing times and technology. Residents wanting to visit the "big city" of Sacramento could pay for a ride on one of Fair Oaks' auto stage lines, choosing to cruise in Ollie Beauchamp's Rambler or Bill Stowell's Reo. Service and repair stations began to appear as automobiles became more predominant and affordable. Indeed, 1909 EMF or Ford Model Ts were repaired at Dewey Rice's Highway Garage, located where the current Oaks Hardware Store lies along Fair Oaks Boulevard.

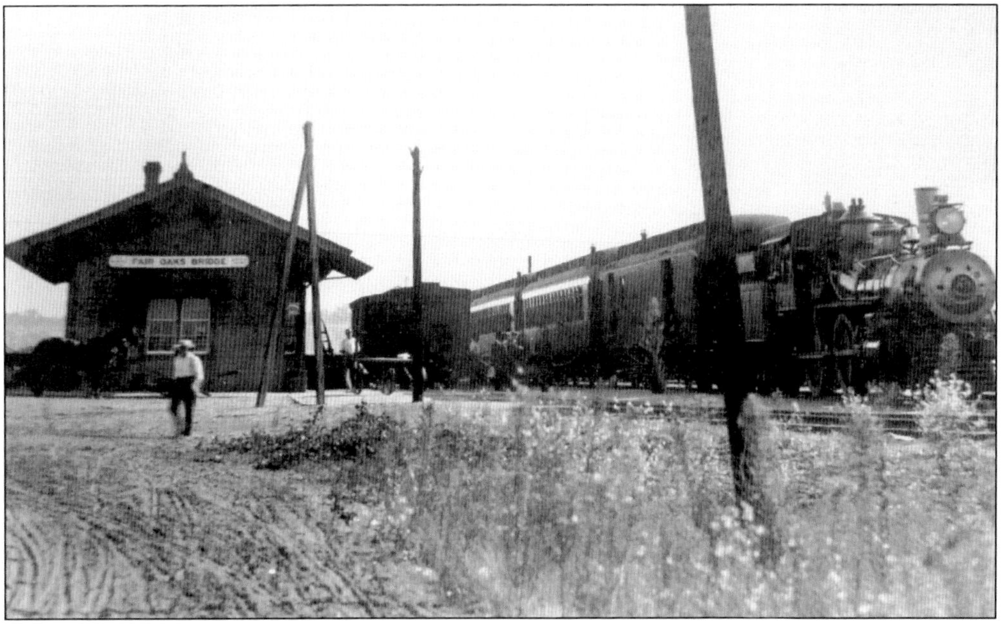

In the summer of 1901, the Southern Pacific Railroad Company built a railroad spur and station, originally called Fair Oaks Bridge Depot. The railroad spur helped the budding fruit colony grow and prosper as farmers and the local Fair Oaks Fruit Company could now ship fruit to local and out-of-state markets. The train ran only twice a day, leaving for Sacramento in the morning and returning around three in the afternoon. (Courtesy Fair Oaks Chamber of Commerce.)

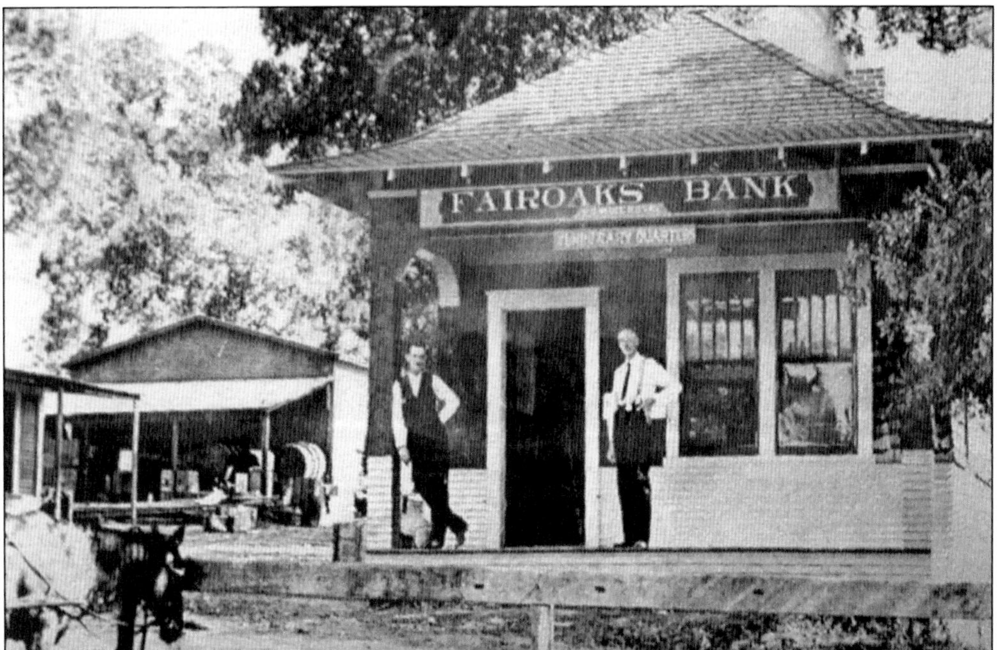

Fair Oaks' First Bank, cofounded by Charles H. Slocum and A. T. Hodge, opened in 1905, in "temporary quarters," to service the financial needs of the budding colony. The "temporary quarters" of the bank is pictured here around 1905. (Courtesy Fair Oaks Presbyterian Church.)

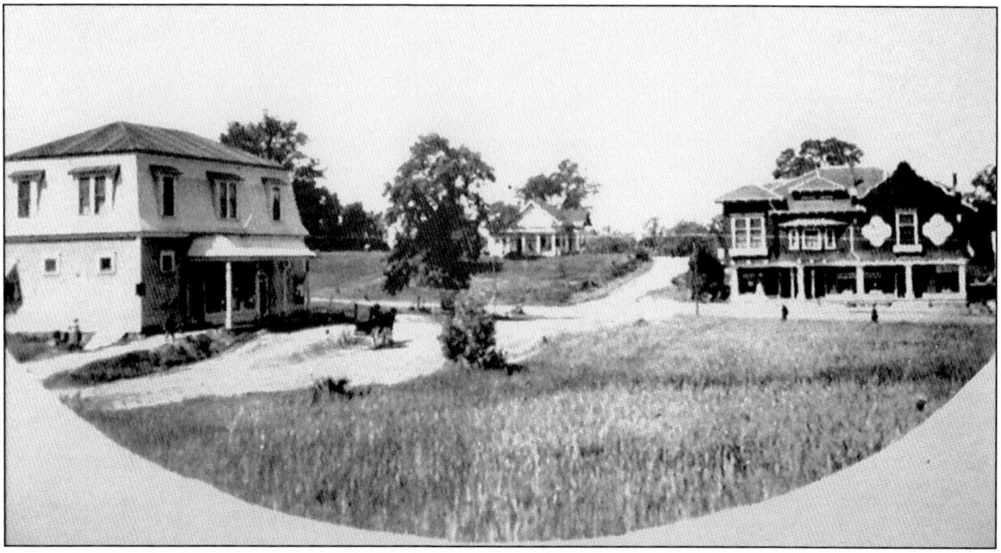

In 1902, Charles H. Slocum and W. Ralph Gore operated a small general store on the southeast corner of California and Howard (Fair Oaks Boulevard). It is pictured on the left, before it burned down in 1909. The house in the middle, referred to today as the California House, belonged to J. R. Johnston, and the far right building, the Murphy Building, served as a store building and public hall. (Courtesy Fair Oaks Presbyterian Church.)

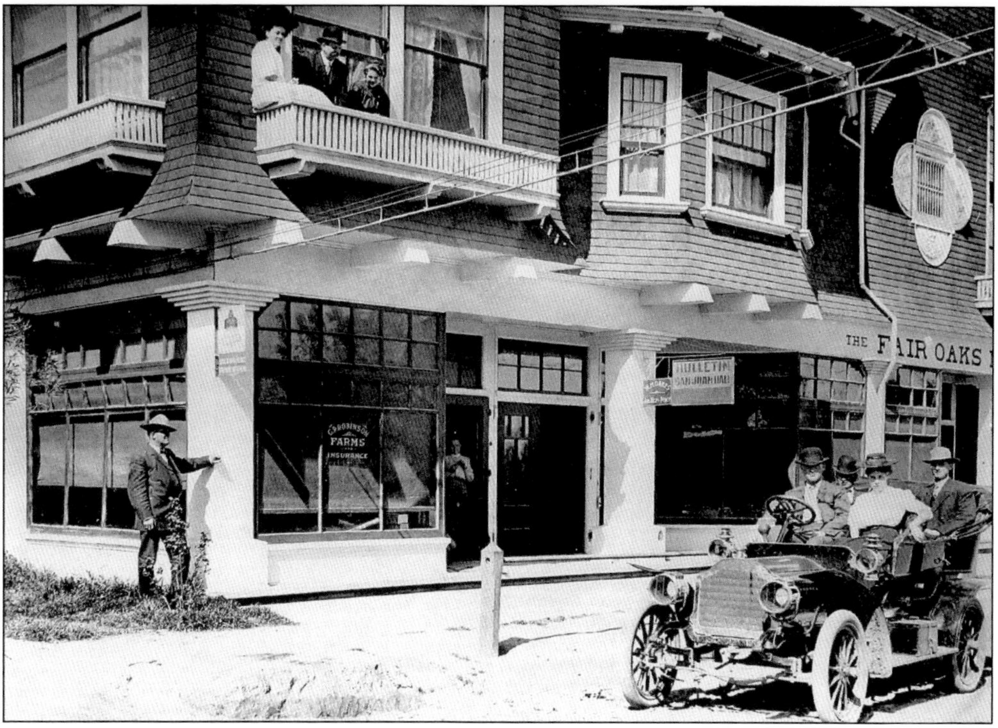

The Murphy Building (pictured here c. 1916), also known as the Mercantile Building, served as a store building and public hall where Fair Oaks residents and visitors have historically been able to buy groceries, visit a doctor, get a mouthful of ice cream, socialize, buy hardware, or purchase some insurance. (Courtesy Fair Oaks Chamber of Commerce.)

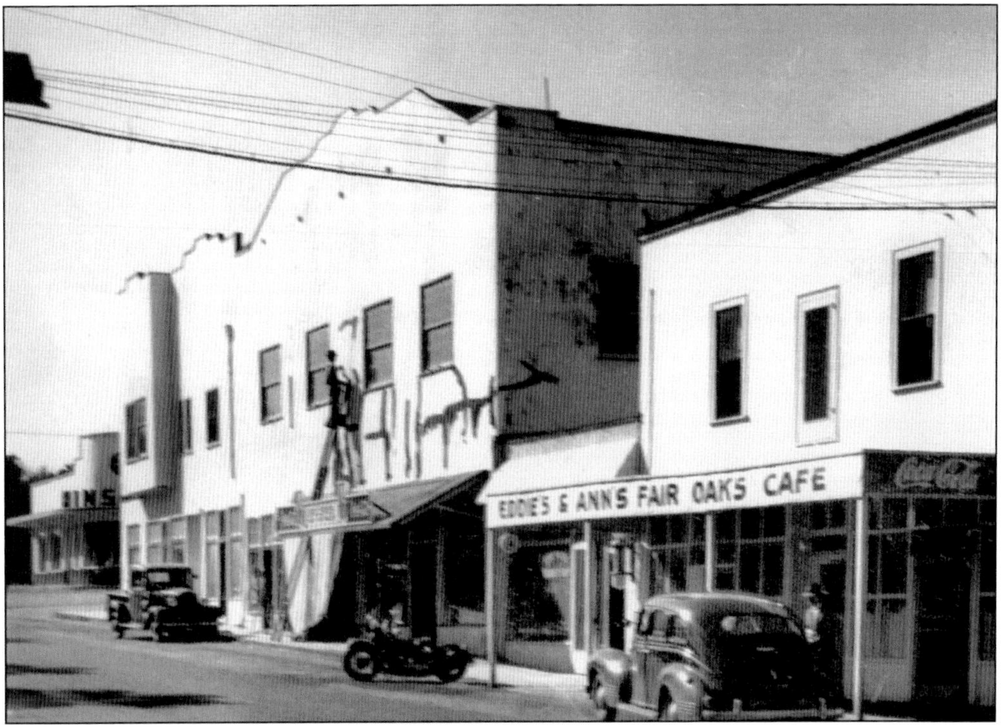

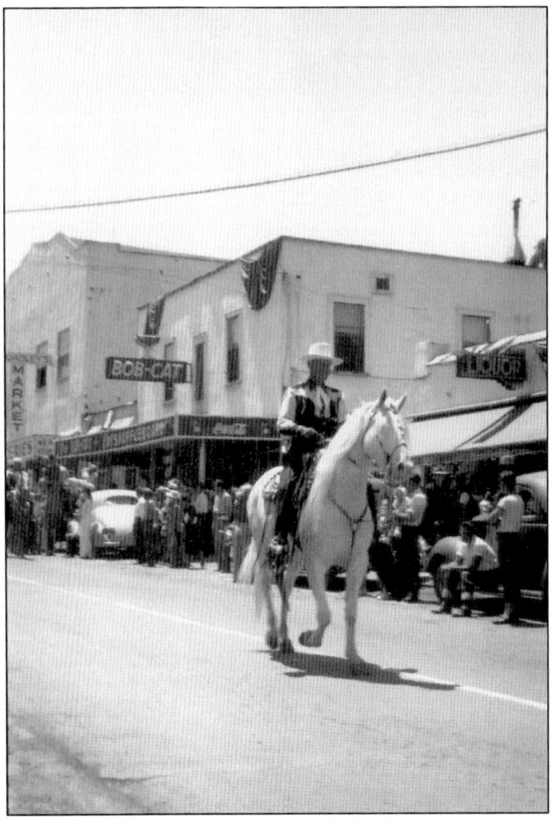

The Murphy Building, known today as the Murphy-Scott Building, now with a stucco facade, has served as a focal point of business throughout Fair Oaks' remarkable history. Other businesses, such as the Hinsey Store and Eddie's and Ann's Fair Oaks Cafe (modern day site of Stockman Club) opened for business nearby. At right, a parade gallops through downtown around 1950. (Above courtesy Dallas Bock; below courtesy Donald Kenmouth.)

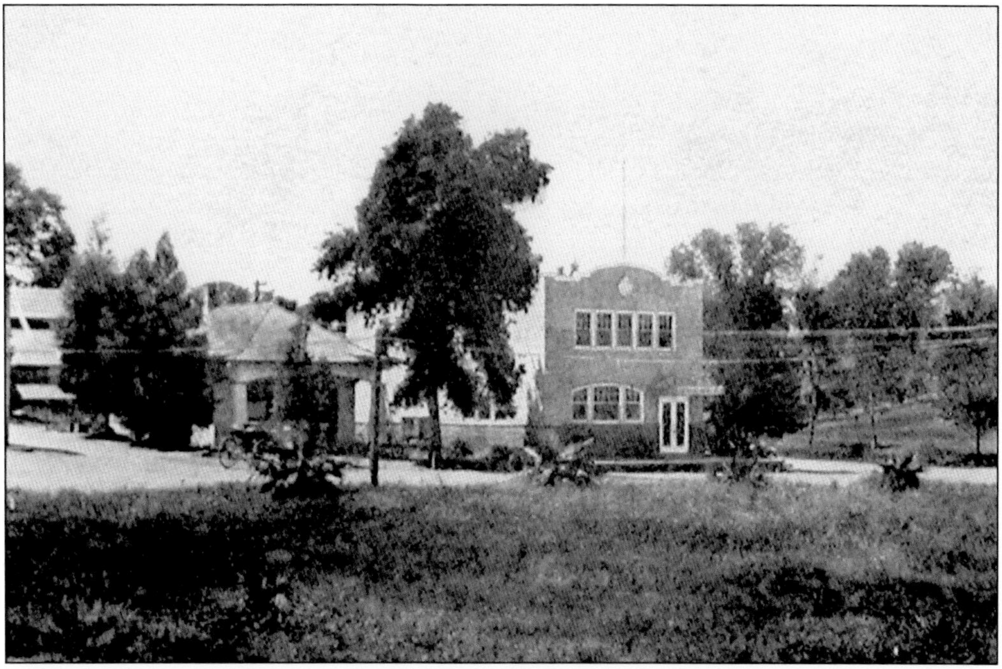

Fair Oaks' business district is pictured here *c.* 1910, with the Fair Oaks Bank's "permanent" building located in the middle. (Courtesy Fair Oaks Presbyterian Church.)

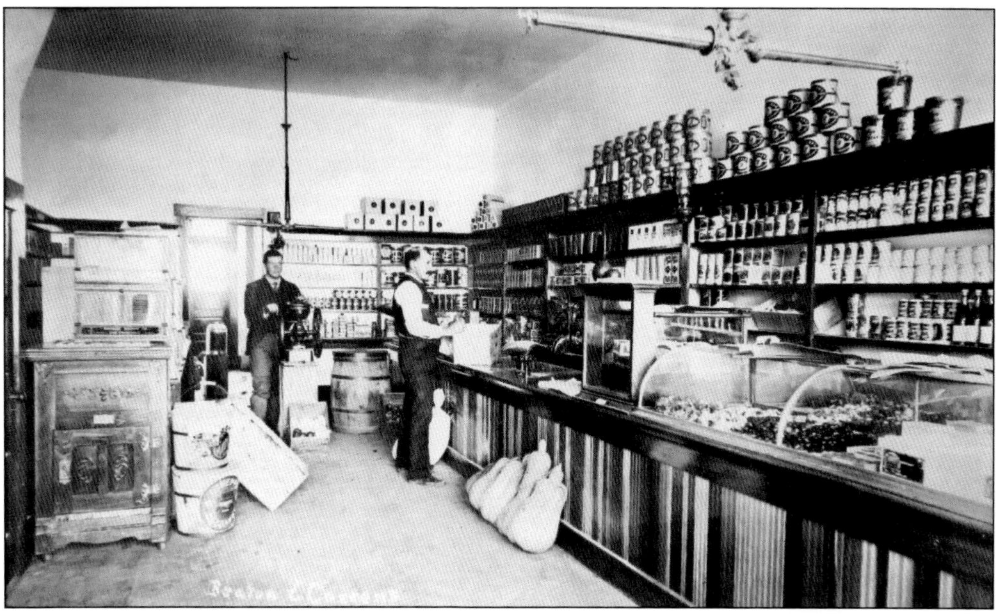

This image provides a rare glimpse inside the Slocum-Gore Store, *c.* 1900, where Fair Oaks residents and visitors were able to purchase many of the sundries and groceries of the day. (Courtesy Fair Oaks Chamber of Commerce.)

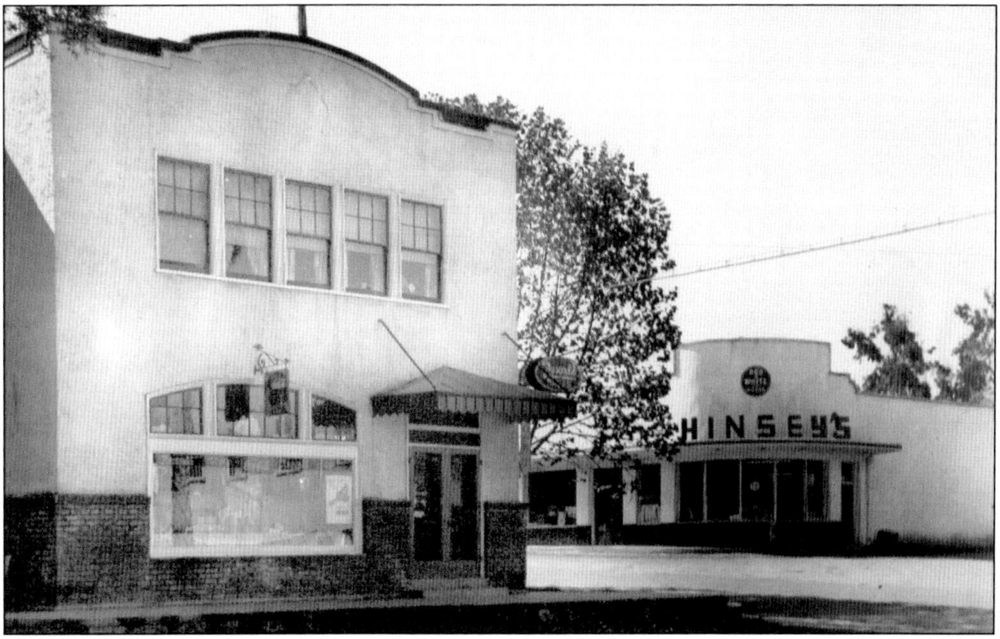

In 1909, Fair Oaks' first bank relocated from its temporary quarters to a permanent block building on the corner of California and Howard. The structure later housed, among other things, a drug store in the 1950s. The Hinsey Store, also known as the Red and White Store, across the street, sold groceries and still stands today as an antique and craft store (seen below). (Above courtesy Fair Oaks Historical Society; below courtesy Paul J. P. Sandul.)

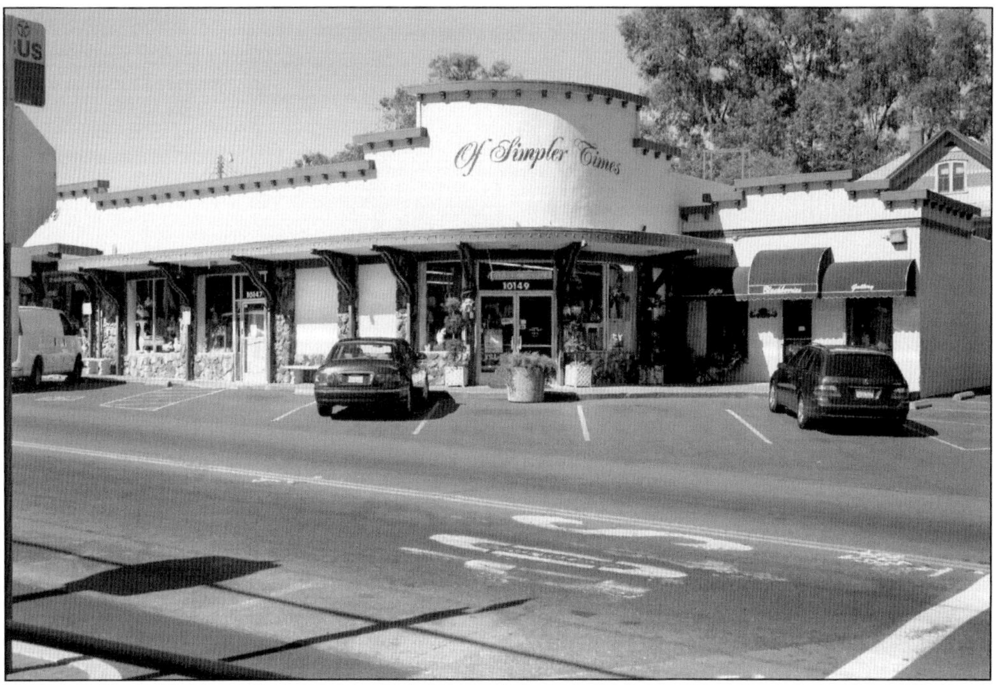

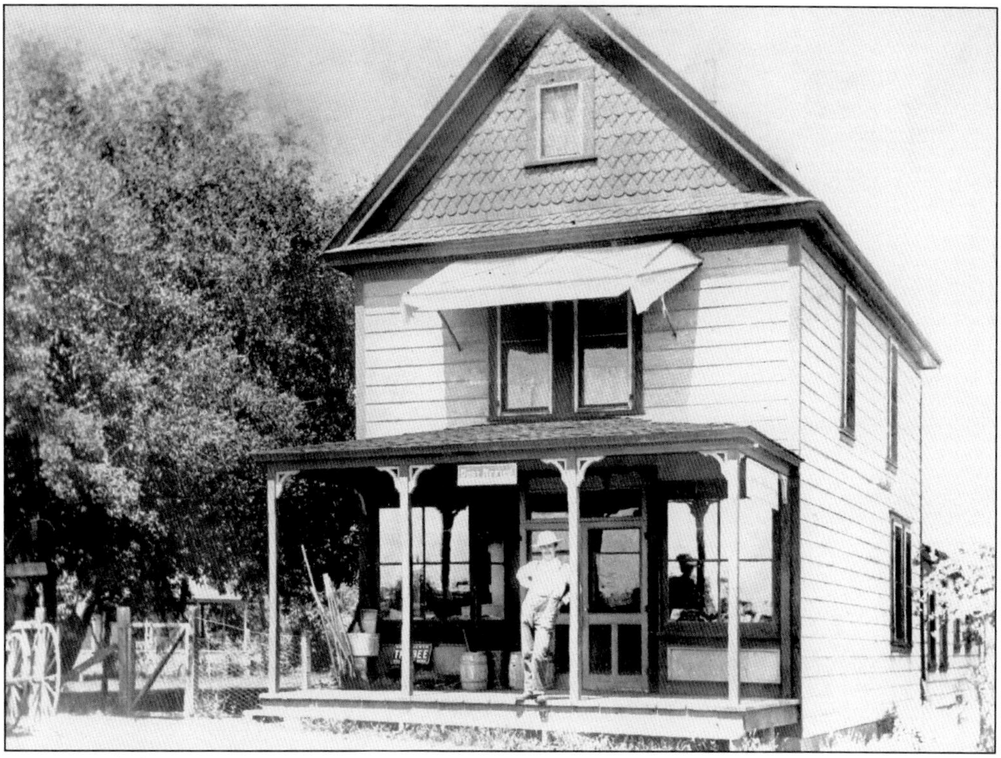

Leonard Shelton opened Fair Oaks' first store and post office in 1896 on the southeast corner of California Avenue and Main Street. Above, Shelton's store is pictured in 1896 before the construction of an addition (shown below) around 1900. (Above courtesy Fair Oaks Chamber of Commerce; below courtesy Fair Oaks Presbyterian Church.)

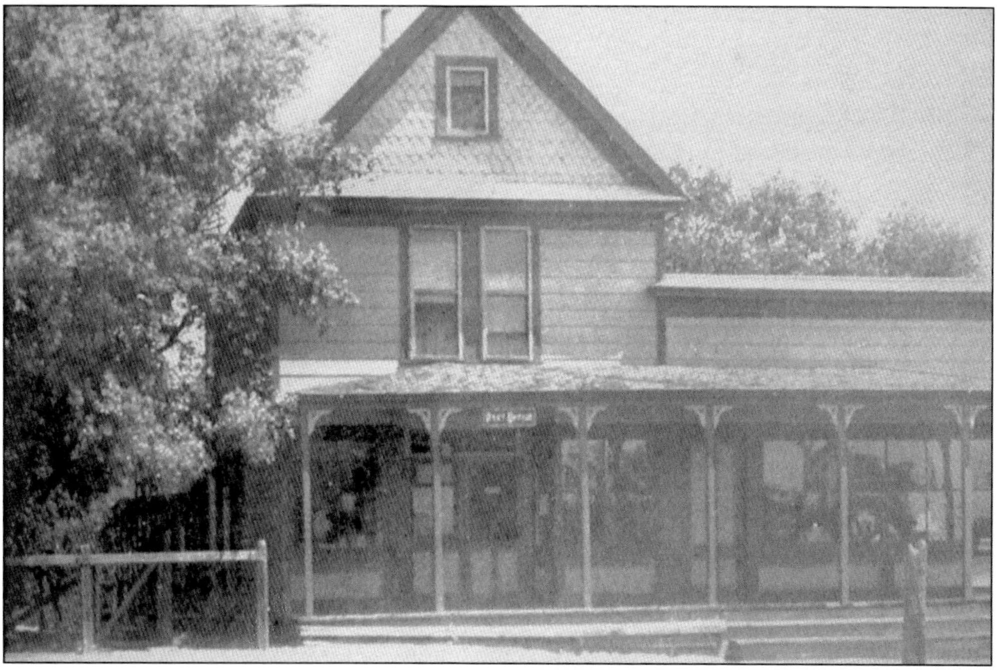

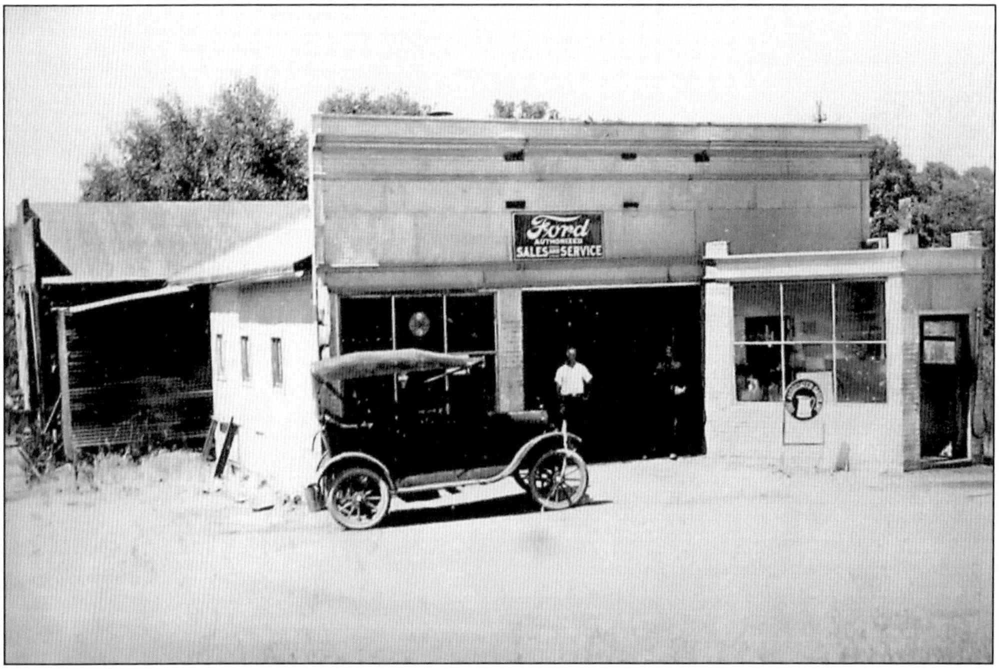

As technology advanced and automobiles became more affordable, service stations began to appear in Fair Oaks. Sim Green and Al Williams opened the Ford Agency on Entrance Street (shown above, 1910s) and Dewey Rice opened his Highway Garage on Howard Street (modern day Fair Oaks Boulevard) where the Oaks Hardware Store stands today. The Highway Garage is shown around 1900 below. (Above courtesy Fair Oaks Historical Society; below courtesy Fair Oaks Chamber of Commerce.)

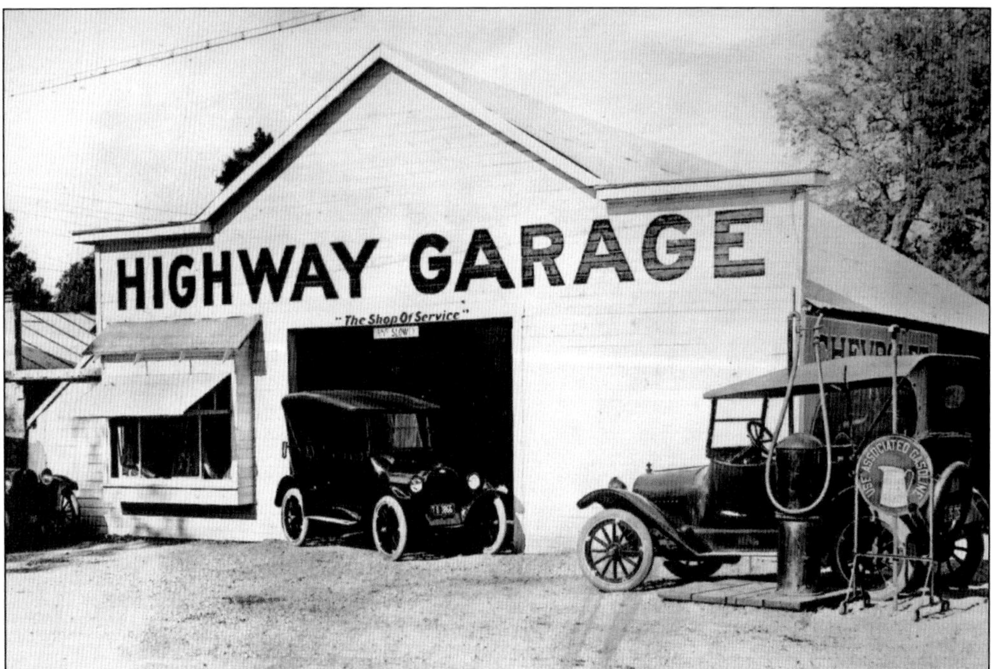

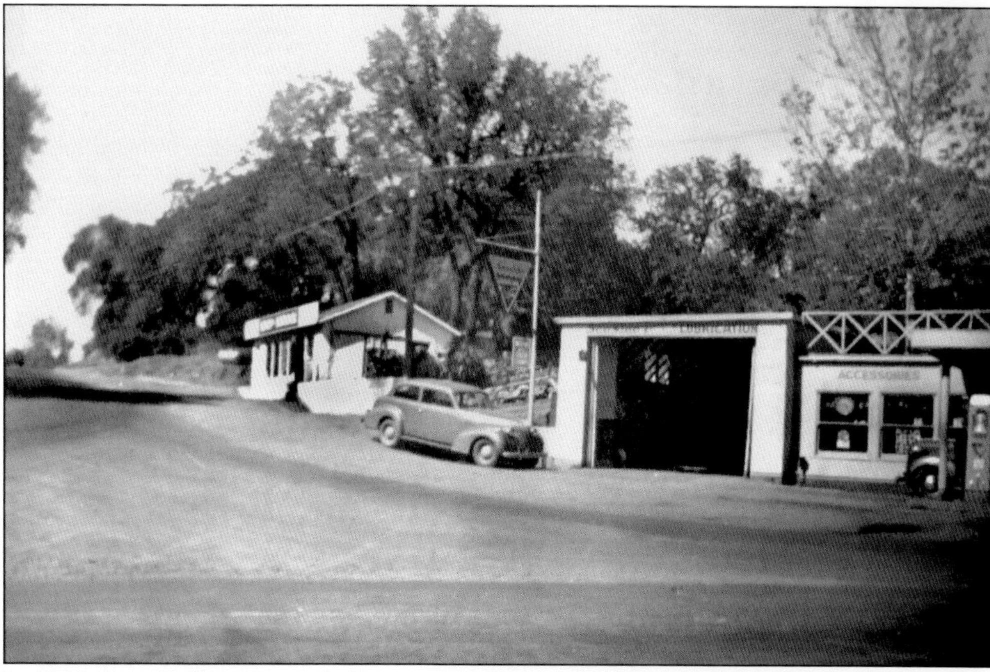

In 1946, Pete Codina operated this service garage and Chevron gas station on the corner of Fair Oaks Boulevard and Howard Street, where the current Marshall and Wilson Buildings now stand. (Courtesy Hugh Gorman.)

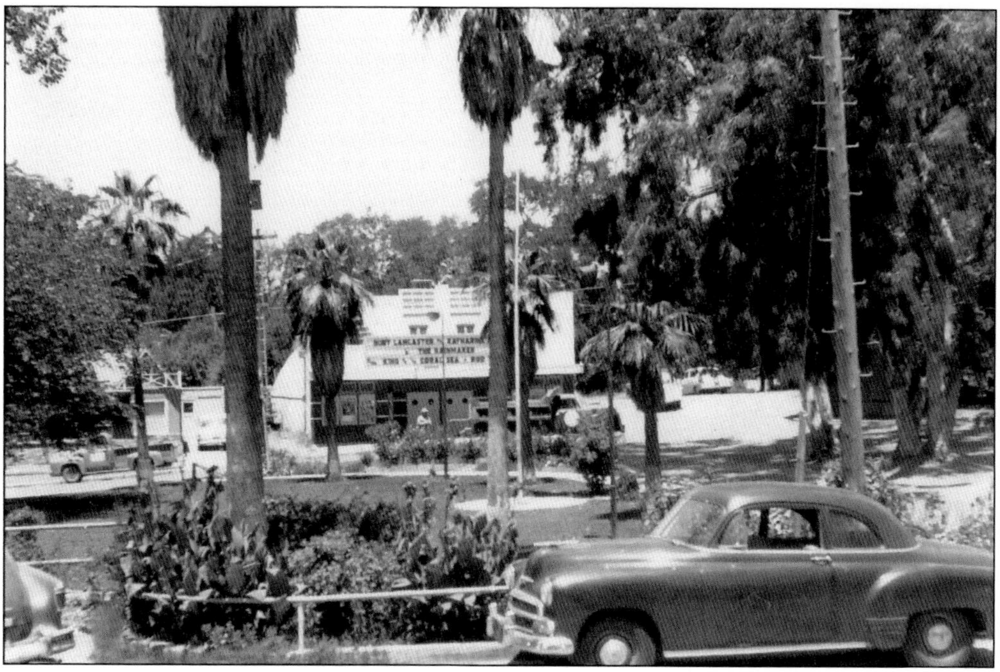

This view of the Fair Oaks Plaza, taken in 1956 on California Street looking north, illustrates the unchanging beauty of the plaza for nearly 50 years. Across from the plaza on Park Drive is the old Fair Oaks Theatre, which still stands, featuring the *Rainmaker* with Burt Lancaster and Katharine Hepburn. (Courtesy Donald Kenmouth.)

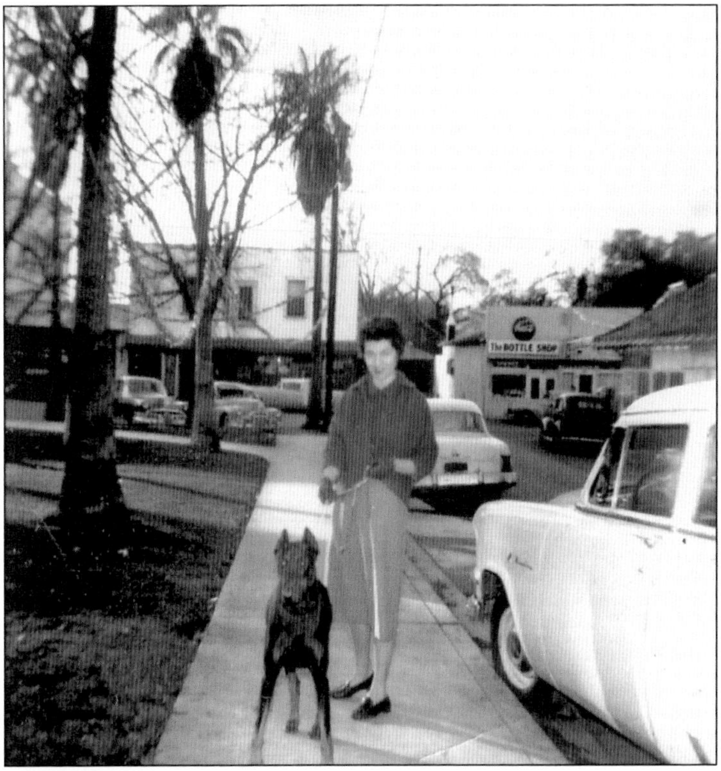

Many Fair Oaks residents and visitors have enjoyed strolls through Park Plaza. This is believed to be Mrs. Leo Malek walking her dog along Park Drive around 1956. Behind her, note the business district where Stockman Club and the Fair Oaks Coffee and Deli are today. (Courtesy Donald Kenmouth.)

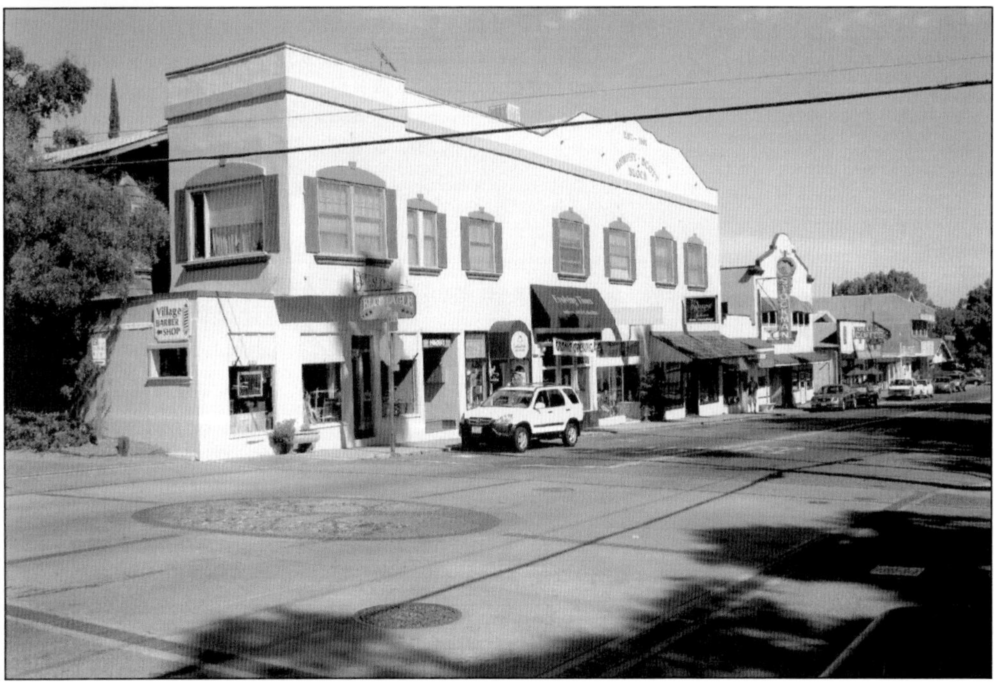

The modern Fair Oaks' downtown village area is still a thriving hub of activity and is a favorite stopping point for tourists and residents alike in search of, among other things, antiques and a good brew. (Courtesy Paul J. P. Sandul.)

Four

GIVE ME SHELTER

The strength of a nation lies in the homes of its people.

—Abraham Lincoln

Private property ownership, particularly home ownership, is a defining feature of Western civilization and is often considered a sacred right of Americans. At the local level, "home" is both a place and a process. It is the impetus for creating community. One's interest in the activities of others increases as concern grows for the value of individual property holdings. The property owner eventually comes to see that his personal future begins to be bound to the development of an ever expanding area. Thus, a "we feeling" is created that can also be defined as community.

In Fair Oaks, the process of community building through private home ownership began with the advertising of the Fair Oaks Development Company. This 1900 advertisement clearly established the creation of community as a goal for Fair Oaks real estate development:

> The evidences of social life will rapidly multiply within the next few years, not only through the influx of new purchasers. But also because a number of present owners, as yet non-residents, are only waiting till their trees mature and the new improvements develop, to build. Many of the Chicago businessmen, belonging to the Chicago–Fair Oaks Association . . . have architects' plans already prepared for their Fair Oaks homes. One of them is now completing a $6,500 house.

Often the most salient characteristics of any community are the homes in which its citizens reside. Indeed, sociologists and urban geographers contend that the urban landscape is an architectural container that constrains and directs spatial decisions, imparts personality to place, and plays a major role in the creation of positive and negative images of places that can affect the future character of a community's urban landscape. In other words, the homes of Fair Oaks have helped to foster its unique and wonderful personality that continues to make it a popular destination for tourists and settlers alike.

The American dwelling has naturally captured the popular imagination of most Americans given that they are as simple as four walls and a roof but as complex as the American spirit which they symbolize. Homes are the territorial core of each and every American family—why else proclaim that home is where the heart is? The home is where each individual, each family has exclusive jurisdiction. The home is where one finds personal space in a country—a world—that is constantly changing. It provides identity, security, and stimulation in an increasingly assimilating and remote society. The homes that follow illustrate the individuality of the various home owners, but collectively, they give us a sense of the character and feel that have created community in Fair Oaks.

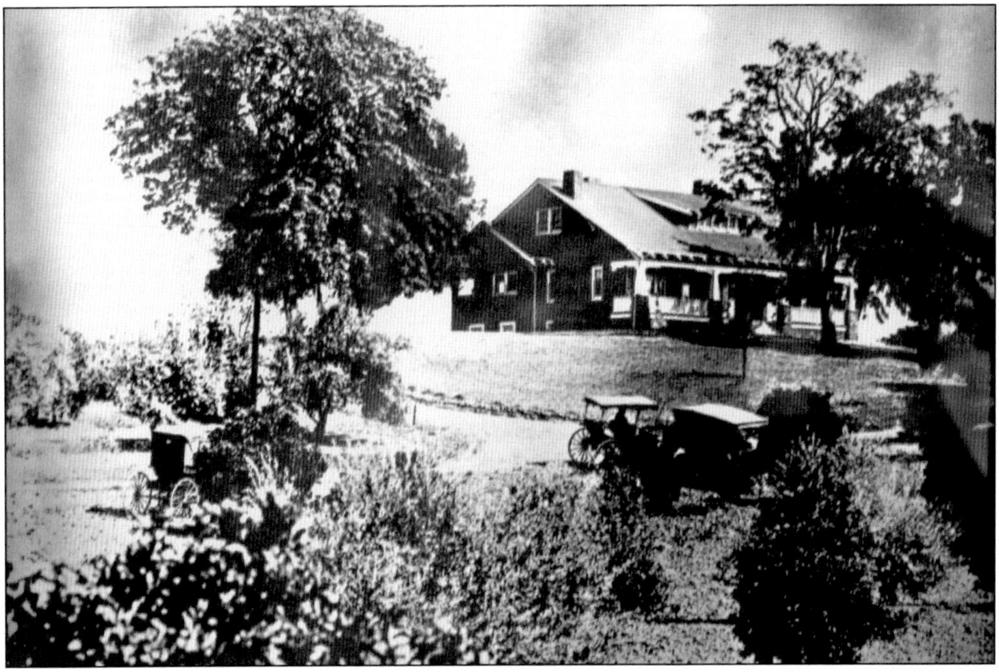

Early pioneers quickly cast their lots and built houses, such as this *c.* 1910 home owned by the Ruggles. (Courtesy Fair Oaks Historical Society.)

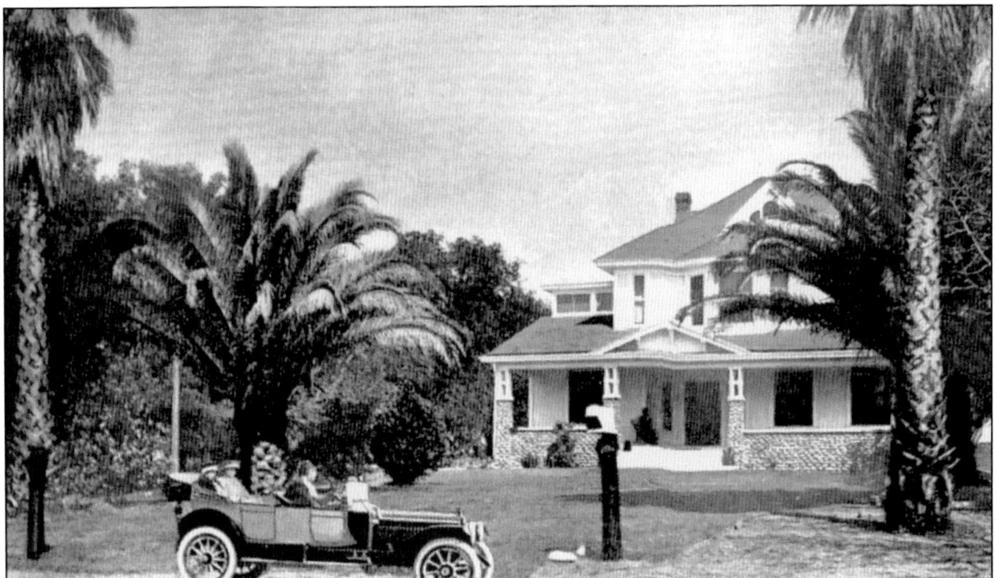

Built around 1900 on Sunset Avenue, the Cunningham house (seen here around 1915) still stands as beautiful today as it did then. John H. Cunningham owned this American Folk–style house with Craftsmen, Prairie, and Queen Anne elements. Cunningham, an original colonist from Minnesota, had the house built by another early settler, Joseph Broadley, after the original house on the site burned down in 1898. Cunningham, a founding shareholder of the Fair Oaks Fruit Company and its first director, purchased the land from James W. Wilson of the Howard-Wilson Publishing Company. (Courtesy Diana Lennon.)

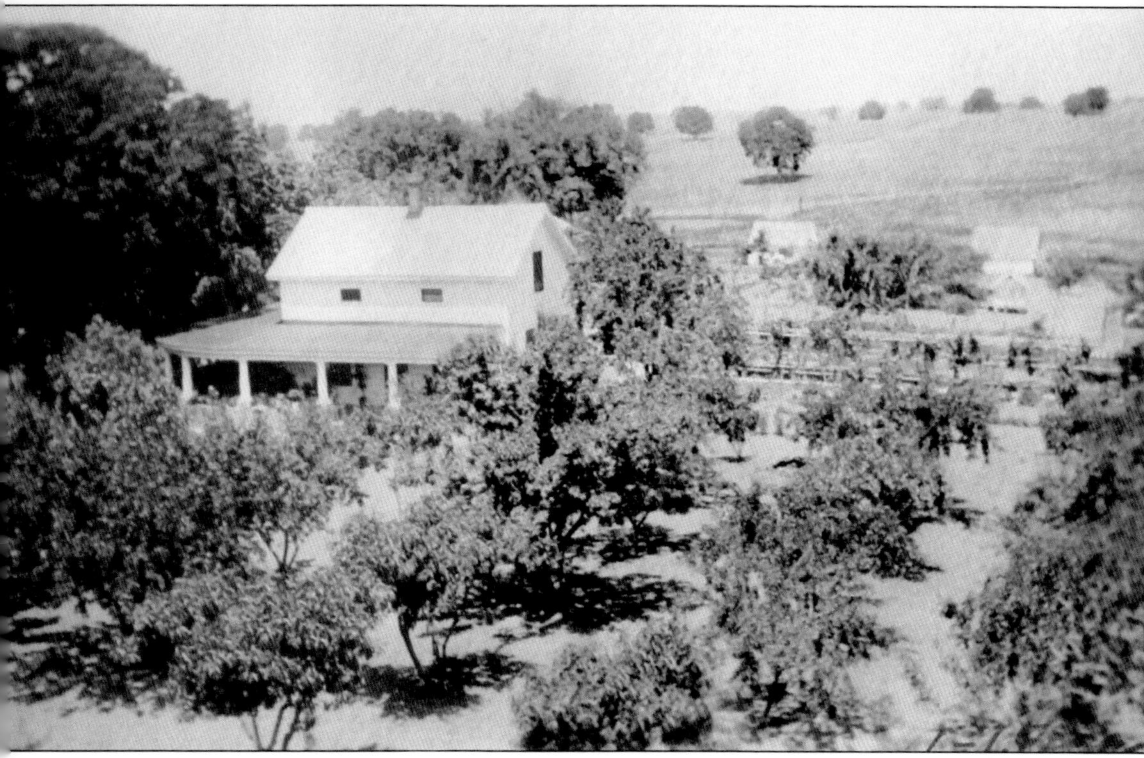

The Dewey farmhouse (seen here in 1915) still stands today off Winding Way near Dewey Drive. Originally built as a modest one-story house by Jacob Heintz in 1874, it slowly grew over the years after Harry Dewey married Bertha Heintz and took over the vast orchard and house in 1896 upon Jacob Heintz's death. (Courtesy Eileen Dewey Thomas.)

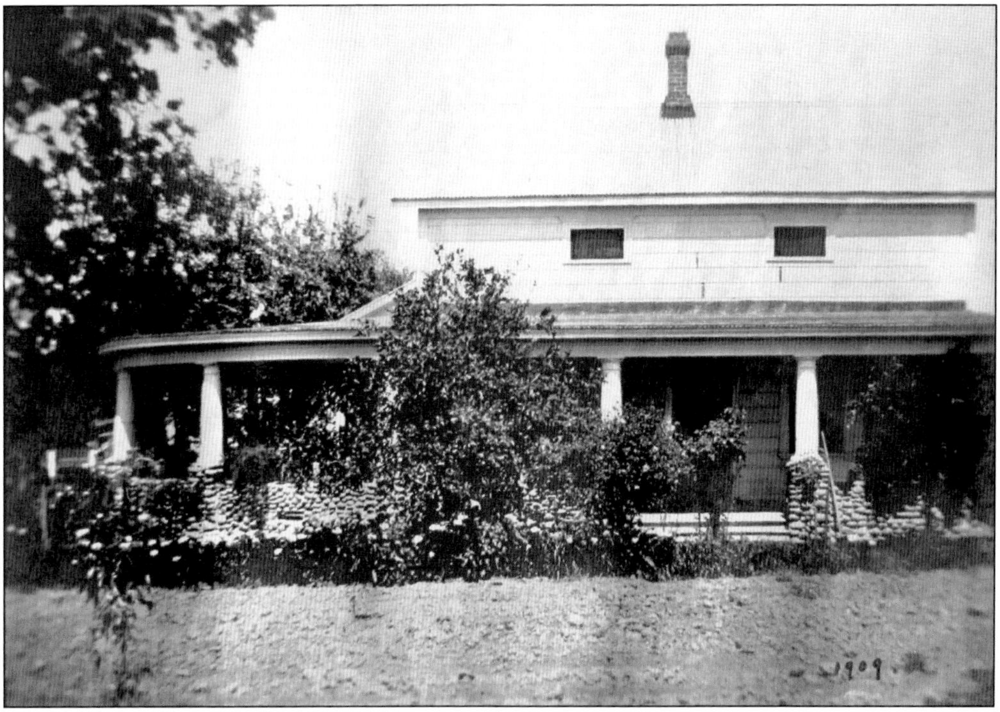

This close-up of the Dewey house in 1909 shows the huge wraparound Craftsmen–style porch that Joseph Broadley built for the family. (Courtesy Eileen Dewey Thomas)

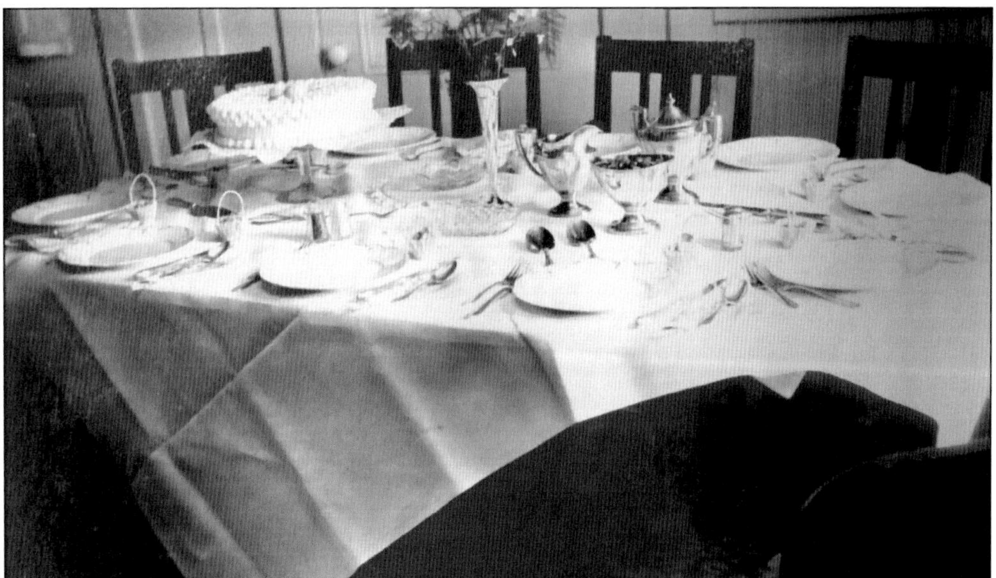

Whenever they could, or whenever the occasion called for it, Fair Oaks families, like families scattered throughout the United States, set out their finest china, tableware, and silverware, as seen in this Dewey family picture, *c.* 1910. (Courtesy Eileen Dewey Thomas.)

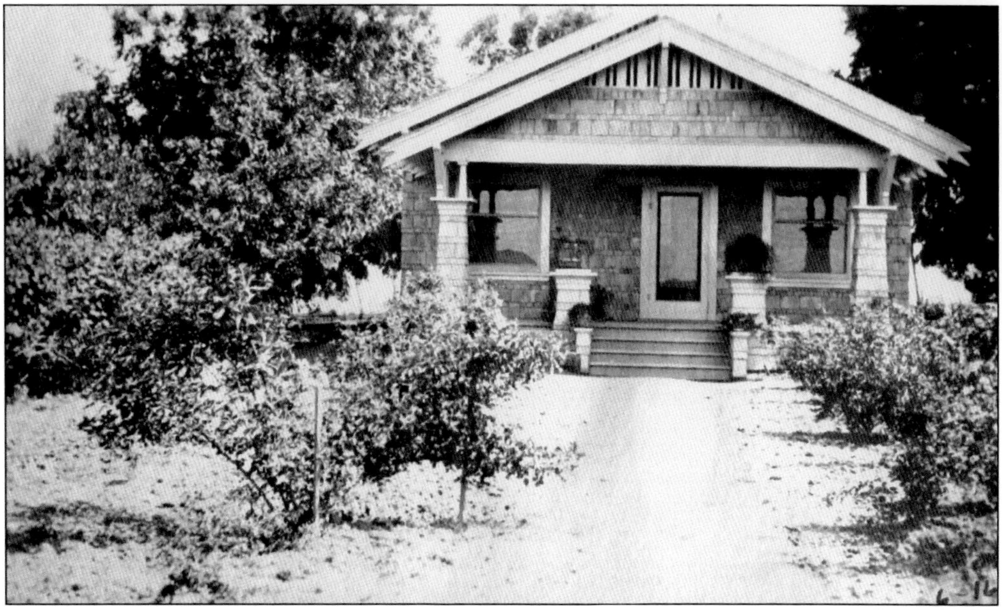

By 1910, the Bungalow-style house became one of the most popular and fashionable houses in the United States. This bungalow house, owned by the Dewey family, still stands today adjacent to the larger house shown on the previous page. (Courtesy Eileen Dewey Thomas.)

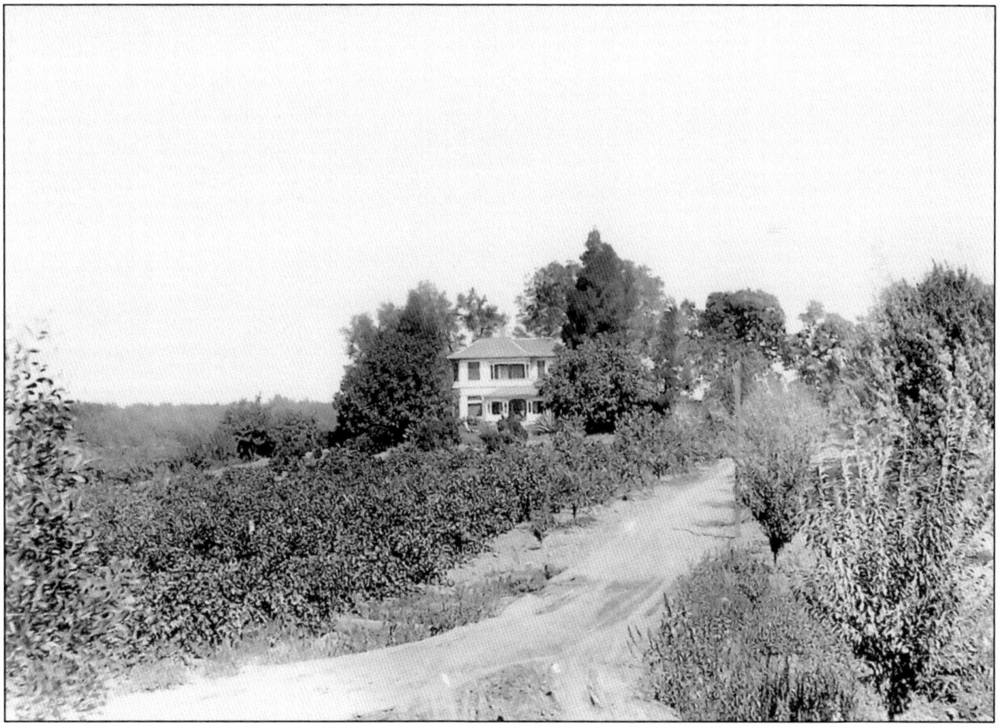

The Broadley home, located along Sunset Avenue between Chicago and Kenneth Avenue, was built in 1898 by Joseph Broadley. The house lodged the family for 40 years until Joseph's death in 1938. The vast amount of land seen here was then subdivided and the house torn down. (Courtesy Jim and Delores Broadley.)

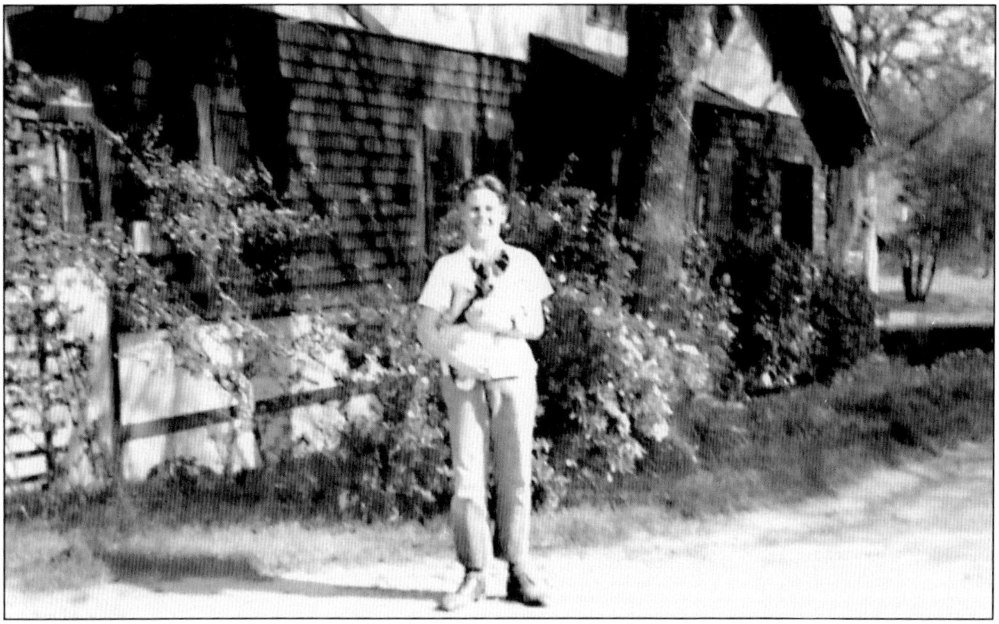

Built in 1923 by J. Murray Broadley, Joseph Broadley's son, this home still houses the Broadley family. In 1922, Harold Murray, J. Murray's brother, purchased the old Fair Oaks Hotel. J. Murray then bought the hotel from his brother and used the wood to construct the house that still stands along Main Street. Here J. Murray's son Jim is outside the house in the late 1930s. (Courtesy Jim and Delores Broadley.)

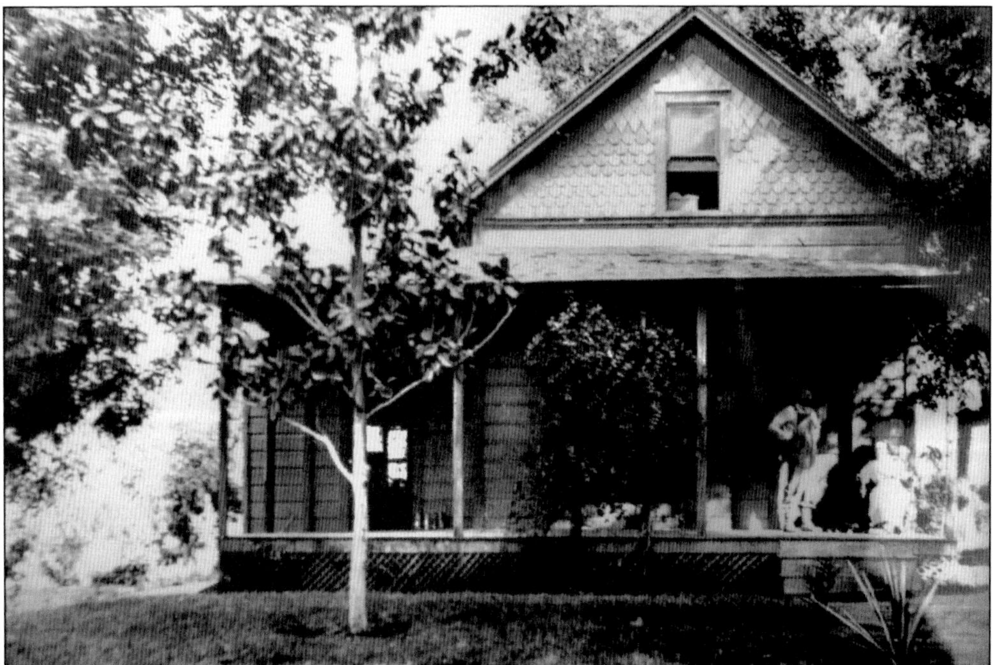

Built in 1895 by Neils Monson near the corner of Winding Way and Kenneth Avenue, this modest home was one of the first houses built in Fair Oaks. Munson reportedly had the first wedding in Fair Oaks when he married Helena Roediger in 1897. (Courtesy Fair Oaks Historical Society.)

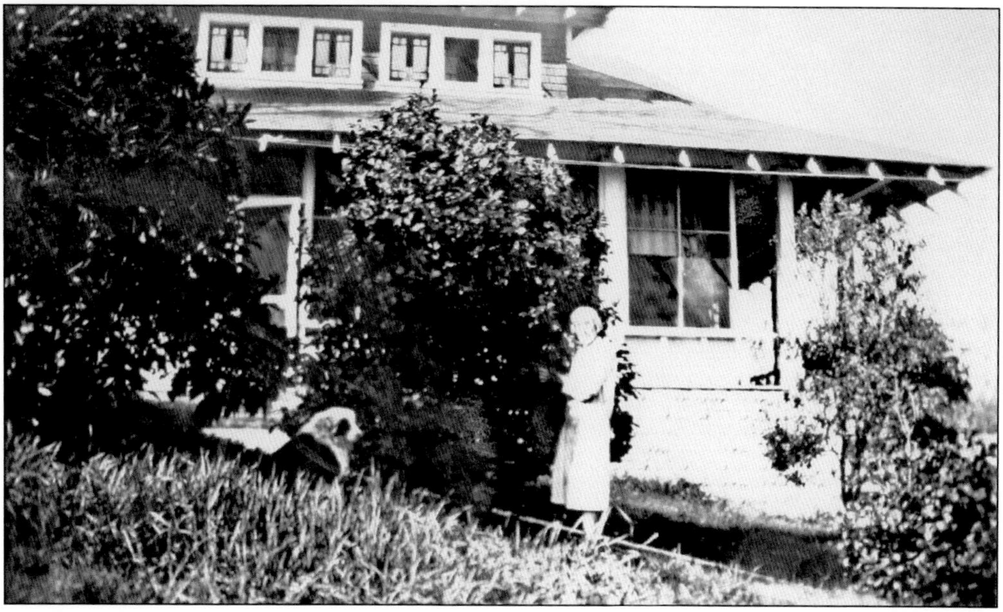

The Hinsey house (shown both above and below, *c.* 1925) sat upon a one-acre tract on the hill above Sunrise Avenue and Fair Oaks Boulevard. This elaborate Craftsmen house, built in 1910, accommodated the family of W. W. Hinsey and his wife, Carrie, shown above with the family dog Jack. Hinsey moved to Fair Oaks in 1898 and eventually became the general manager of the Fair Oaks Fruit Company, as well as a founding member and first president of the Fair Oaks Chamber of Commerce. (Courtesy Linda Morris.)

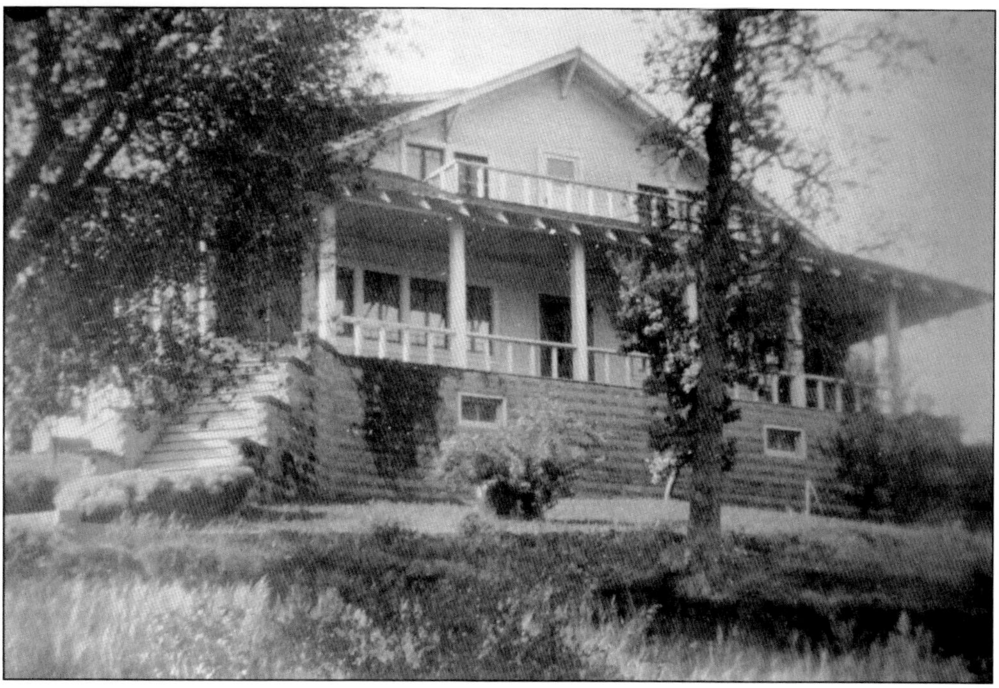

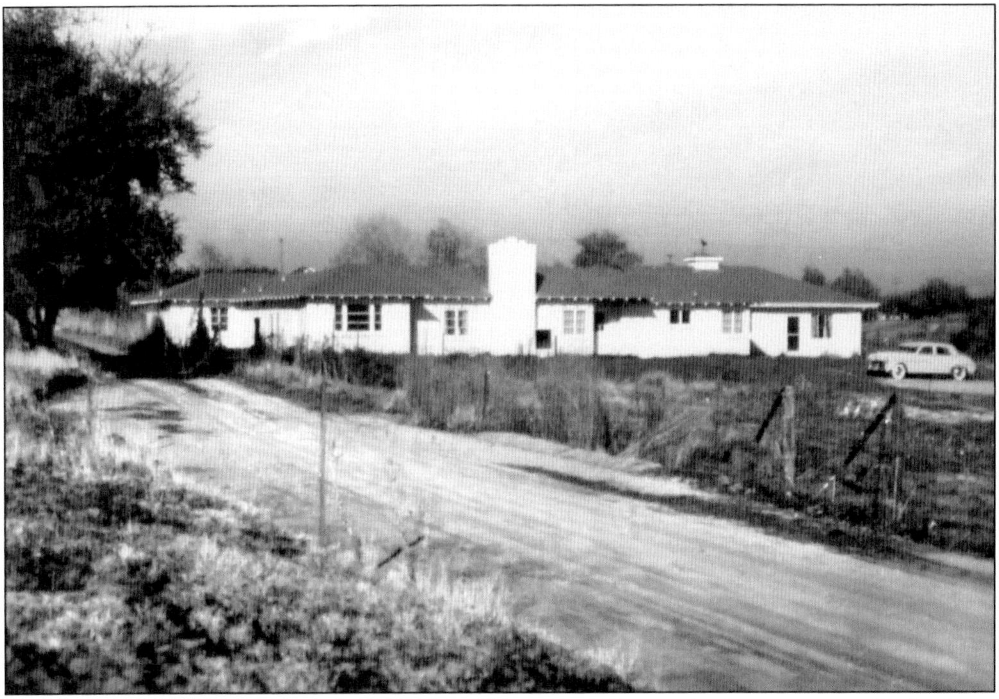

The Gallatin house, situated on Winding Way near Abernathy Lane, originally built in 1946, expanded to this ranch house in the 1950s. George Gallatin, who had moved from Michigan, opened a real estate and insurance business off of Winding Way. (Courtesy Jim and Delores Broadley.)

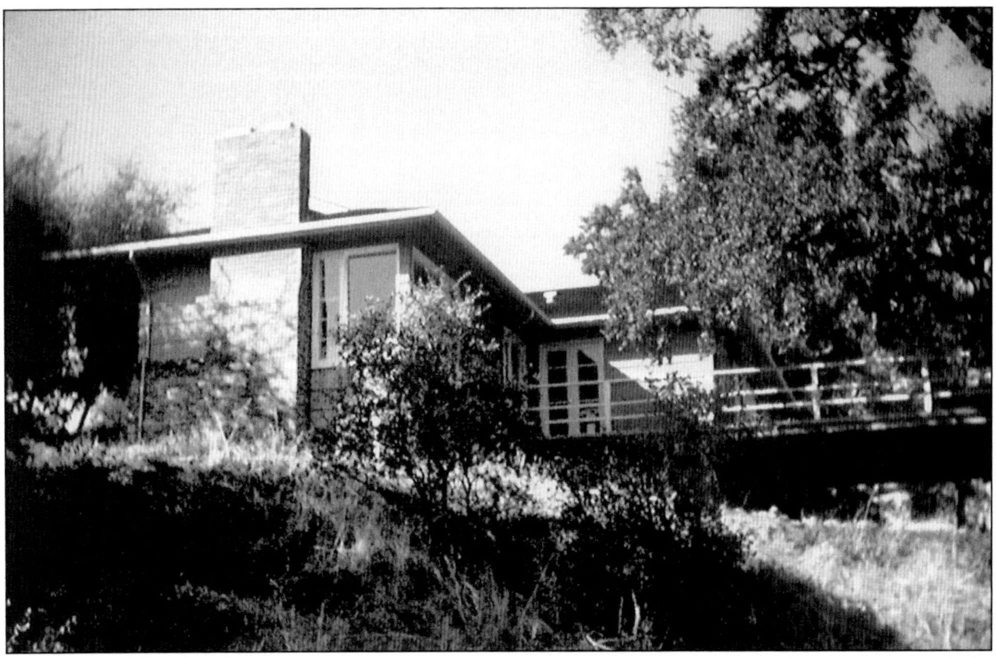

William Scott Campbell, lived in this Craftsmen house from 1938 to 1942. (Courtesy Fair Oaks Presbyterian Church.)

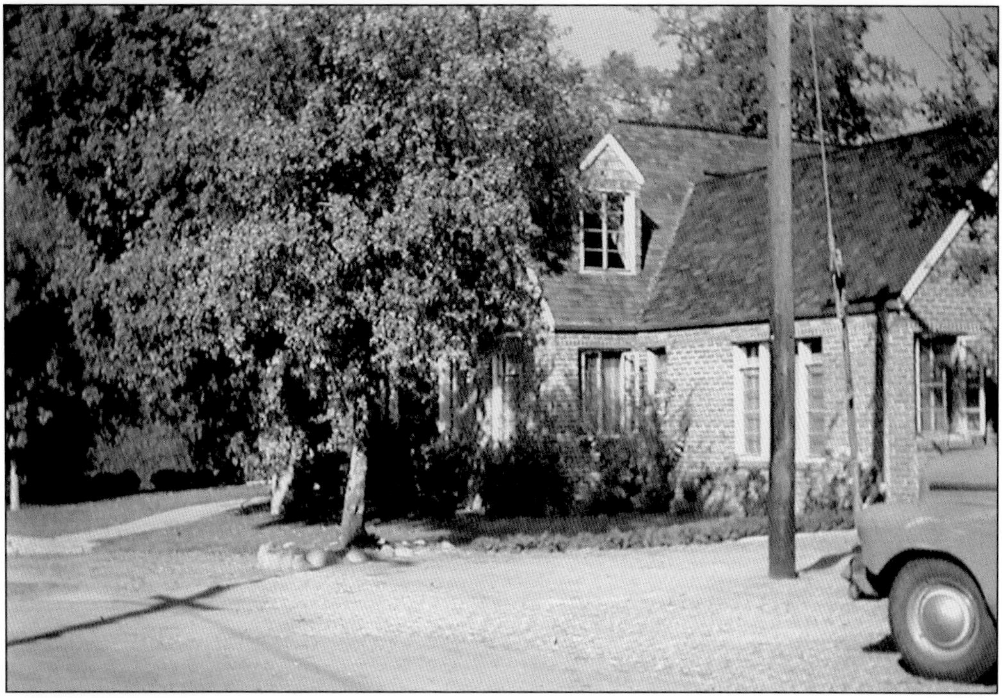

This beautiful Tudor–style brick house, *c.* 1945, was built on Villa Court near Howard Street, west of Sunrise Boulevard. (Courtesy Fair Oaks Presbyterian Church.)

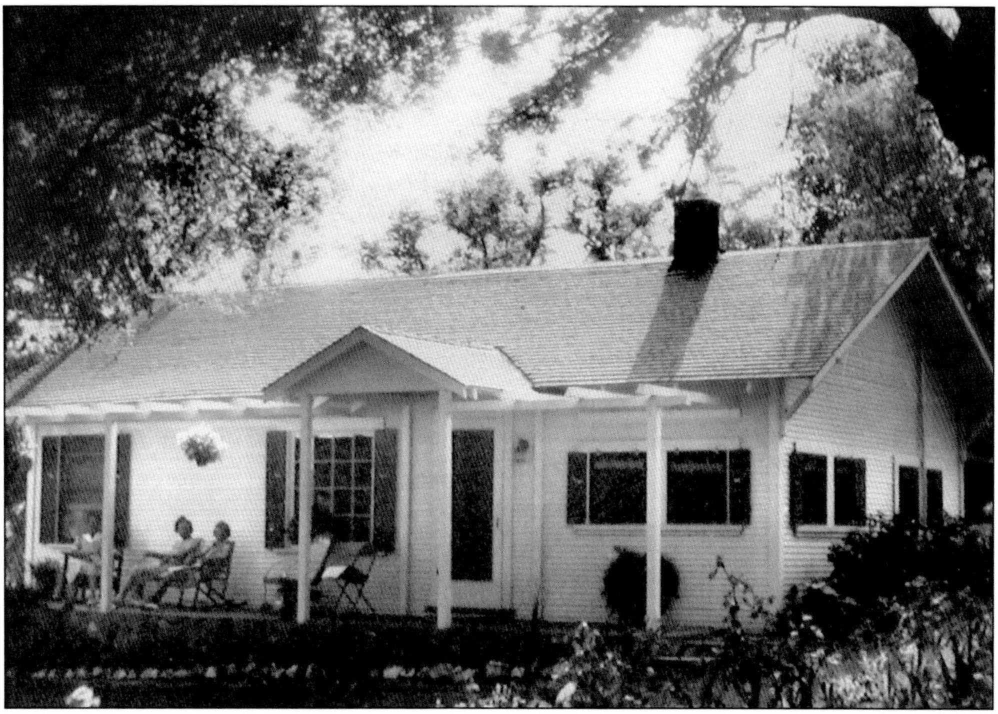

The house pictured here, *c.* 1945, was the home of Lon and Velma Ruppel, who ran an insurance and real estate business in Fair Oaks. (Courtesy Fair Oaks Presbyterian Church.)

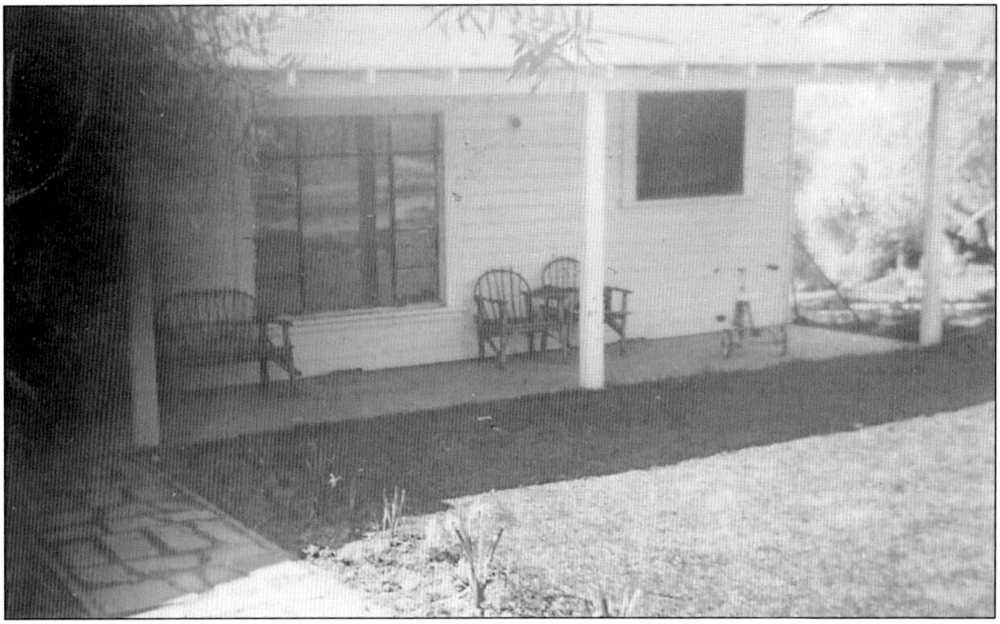

This simple house was built by Bob Wood in 1946 on Fair Oaks Boulevard. Bob added onto it every time his wife, Jimmi (Margaret), had a child—they had five in Fair Oaks and six in all! Bob eventually built eight houses behind this small house to use as rentals and the lot was renamed, and is still known as, Bob Lane. Unfortunately when Fair Oaks Boulevard was widened to four lanes in 1959, the Woods lost their first home in Fair Oaks. (Courtesy Sherry Lynn Wood.)

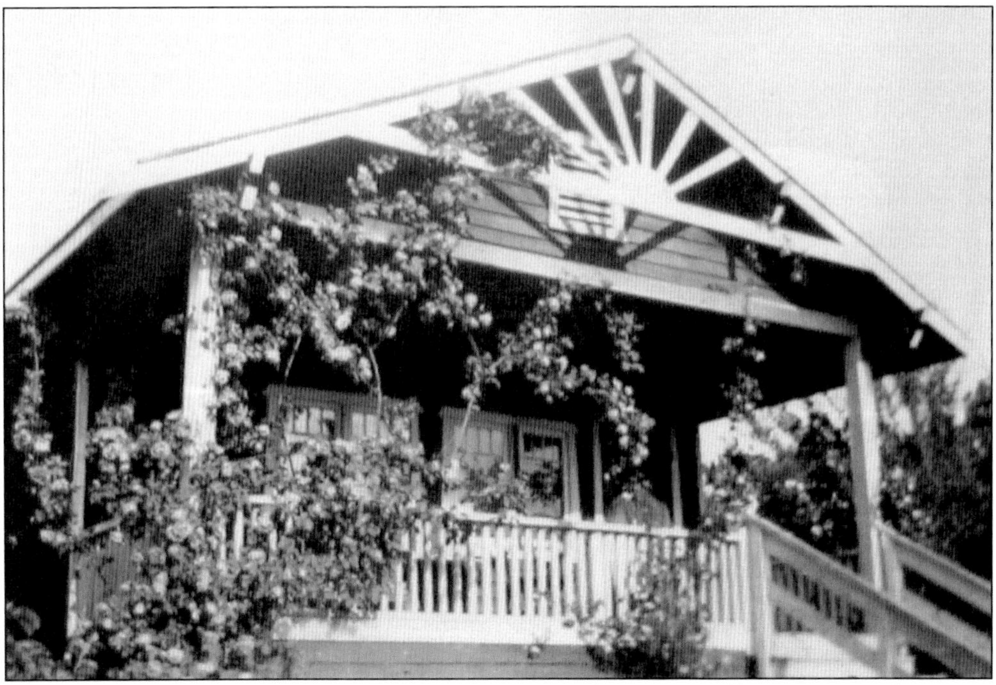

Built in the 1930s, the first prefabricated house in Fair Oaks was owned by Sim Green. (Courtesy Fair Oaks Historical Society.)

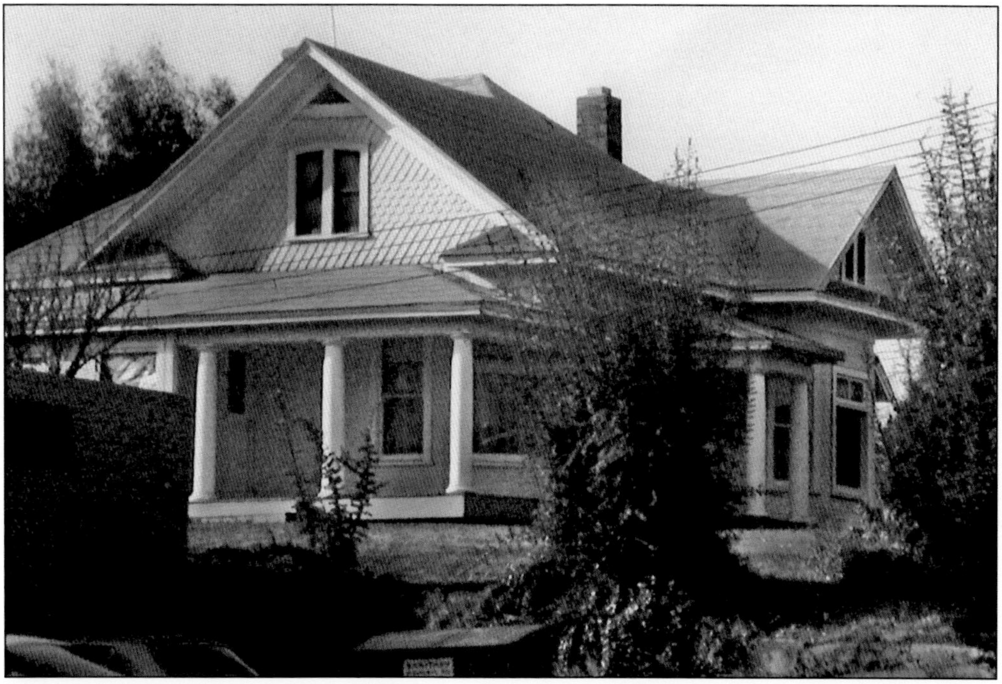

The Leedy home, shown here in 1930, sat on the corner of Madison and Hazel. Leedy also built homes and structures for other Fair Oaks residents, including the Hammonds and the Saunders. (Courtesy Fair Oaks Presbyterian Church.)

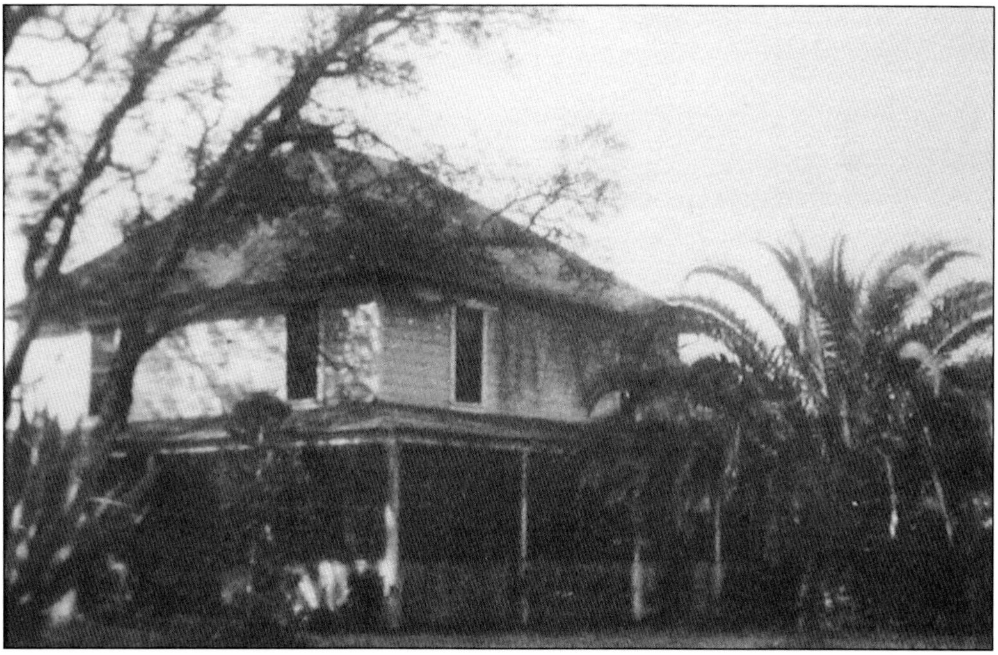

Among the many early farmhouses in Fair Oaks was the large Conkey house, shown in this 1978 photograph. (Courtesy Fair Oaks Presbyterian Church.)

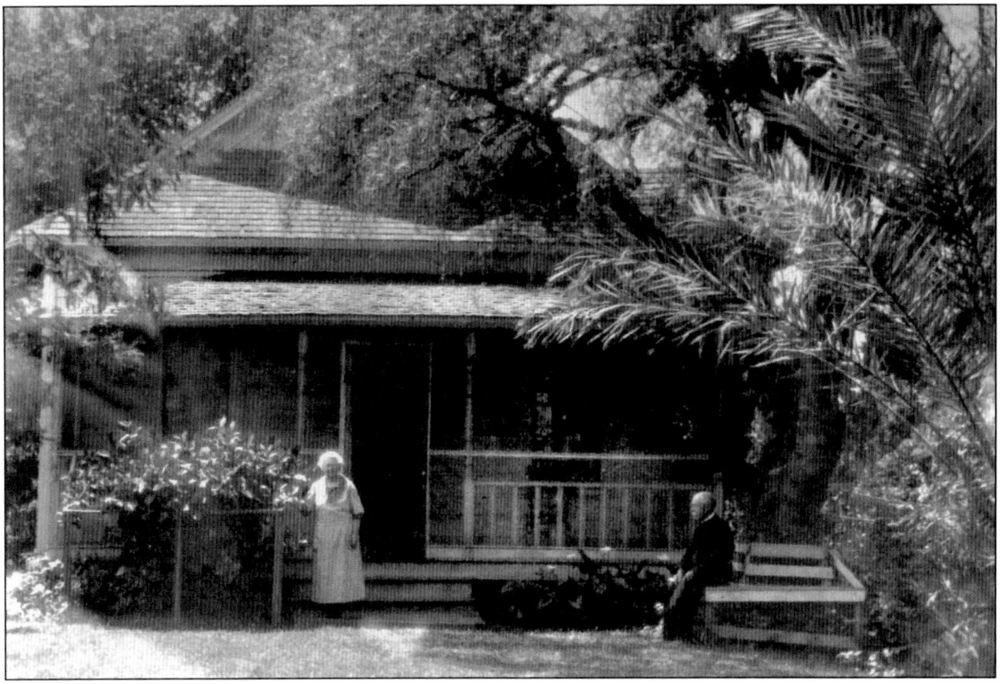

Frank and Mary Vincent, who came to Fair Oaks from Kansas in 1906, moved into this home on Sunset Avenue in 1907. The family stayed in the home until the mid-1950s. (Courtesy Fair Oaks Historical Society.)

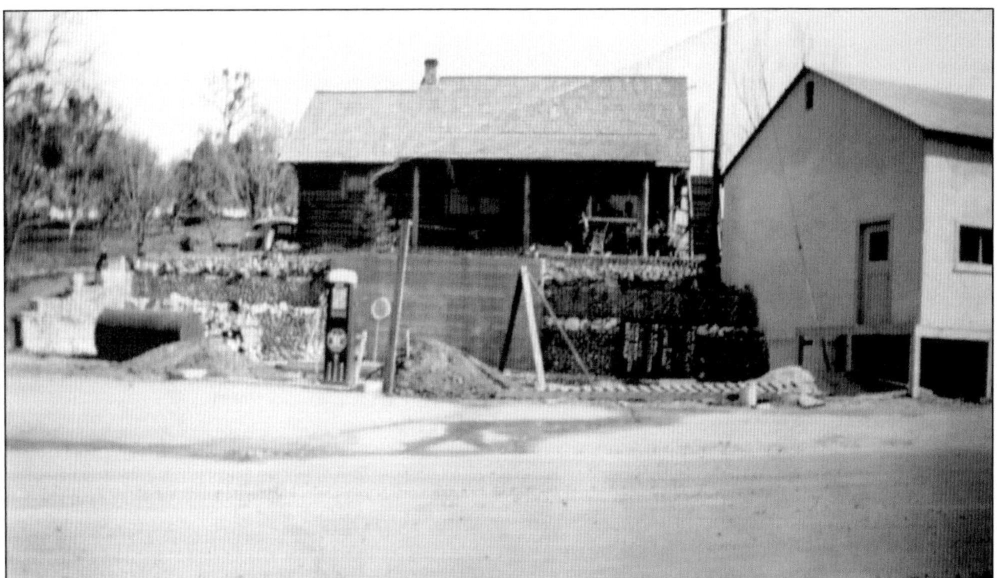

Jack "Pop" Wilson built this log cabin in the 1920s just above his own service station on the corner of Fair Oaks Boulevard where the Marshall and Wilson Buildings stand today. (Courtesy Hugh Gorman.)

Five

FACES OF FAIR OAKS

A man finds room in the few square inches of his face for the traits of all his ancestors; for the expression of all his history, and his wants.
—Ralph Waldo Emerson, *Conduct of Life*

History is undoubtedly sprinkled with the legacies of a few unique and courageous individuals: writers, artists, explorers, statesmen, etc. To honor their legacy, the public is often inundated with their images. Indeed, the most commonly recognized American presidents and heroes are the ones whose faces happen to be carved on a mountainside or placed prominently on money. Nonetheless, images of people, like homes, capture a spirit and moment that help to define an era and often succeed in making that moment or person seem more clear, real, and recognizable. To look upon the faces of those who came before is to glimpse into the one thing that makes the past the same for us all—our humanity.

The history of Fair Oaks is also sprinkled with the legacies of a few unique and courageous individuals. In browsing over the history of Fair Oaks names like Dewey, Broadley, Hinsey, Cunningham, Watkins, Holst, Buffum, and many others repeat over and over again. These are truly the "founding fathers" of Fair Oaks to whom all that reside here owe their gratitude and reverence. The images of these pioneers and early settlers help put a face on history.

It would be remiss, however, only to focus on the founding fathers. The images that follow help put a face on the community. Not only are there images of Fair Oaks settlers, farmers, and businessmen, but also of boys and girls who grew up in the community and of young men and women who were married and raised families here. The choices included here reflect the quality and quantity of images available to us. They give a clear but limited snapshot into the faces of Fair Oaks.

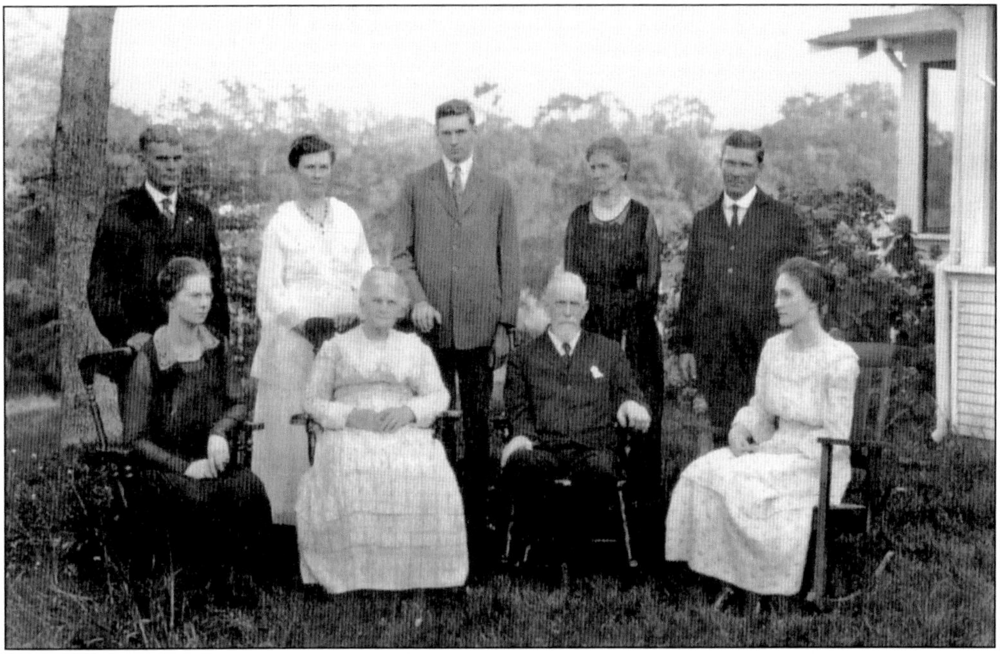

The Cunningham family joined together in front of their home to celebrate John and his wife's 50th wedding anniversary, *c.* 1910. John Cunningham, an original excursionist from Minnesota, served as the Fair Oaks Fruit Company's first general manager. (Courtesy Diana Lennon.)

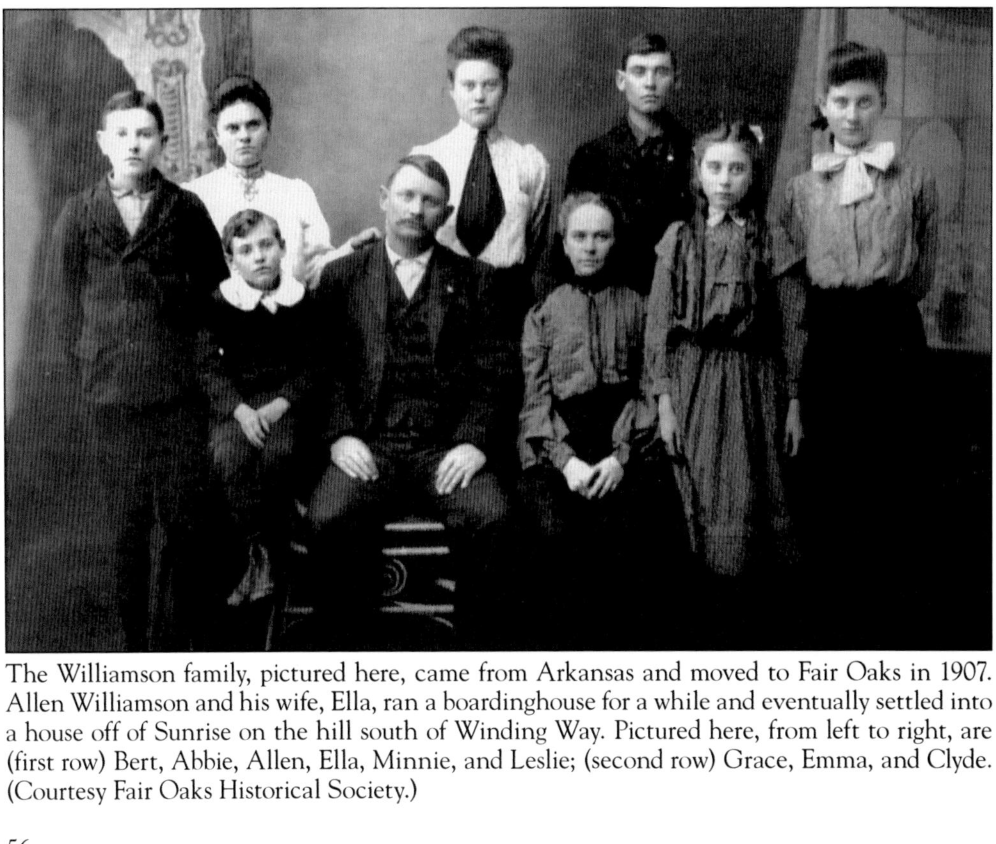

The Williamson family, pictured here, came from Arkansas and moved to Fair Oaks in 1907. Allen Williamson and his wife, Ella, ran a boardinghouse for a while and eventually settled into a house off of Sunrise on the hill south of Winding Way. Pictured here, from left to right, are (first row) Bert, Abbie, Allen, Ella, Minnie, and Leslie; (second row) Grace, Emma, and Clyde. (Courtesy Fair Oaks Historical Society.)

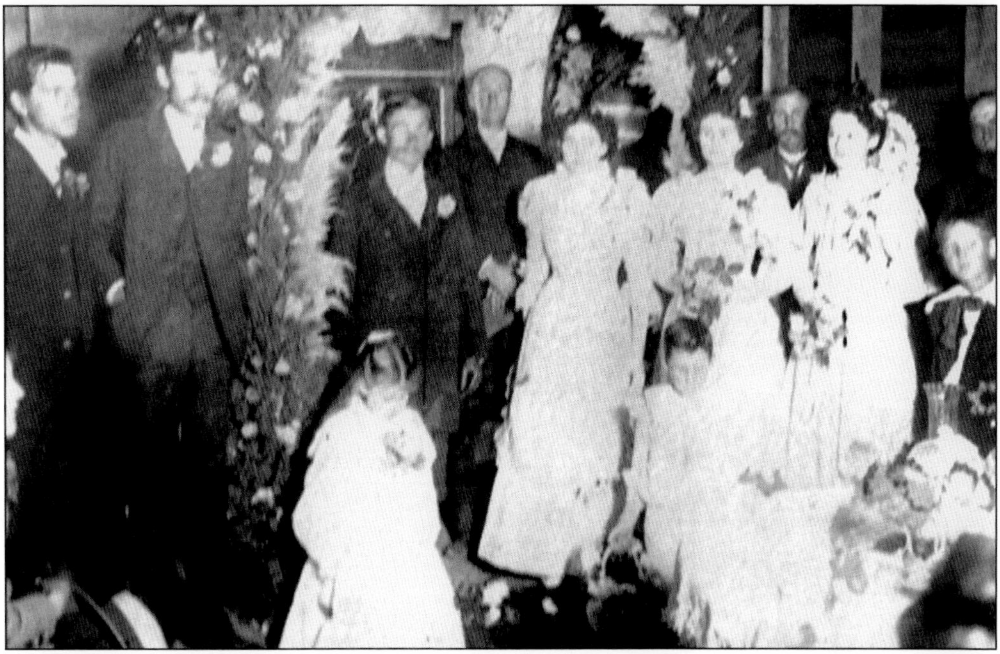

One of the first weddings in Fair Oaks took place on May 20, 1908, when Al Fowler and Edna Marshall (seen in the middle) married. Fowler, who arrived in Fair Oaks in 1902, worked as the foreman for the Fair Oaks Fruit Company's Olive Plant from 1913 to 1930. (Courtesy Fair Oaks Historical Society.)

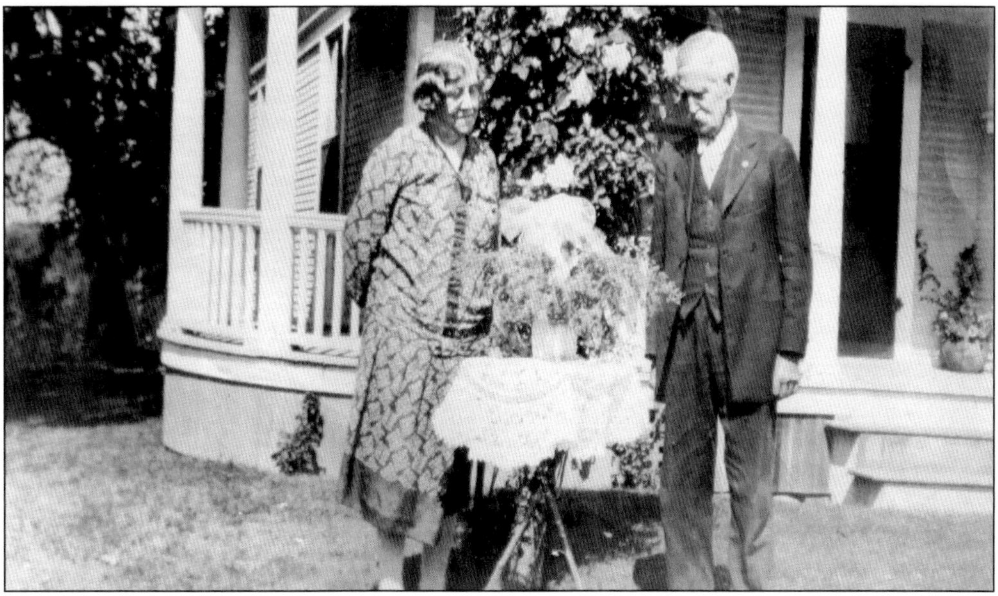

Uriah B. Watkins and Lena Watkins, pictured here in the 1930s, came from Kansas to Fair Oaks with the original excursionists and settled in the new colony in 1896. Lena, a retired schoolteacher, brought textbooks and operated a school out of the house. She also taught English to many Japanese immigrants and workers. Uriah, a farm equipment inventor and Civil War veteran, was active in the Methodist church and helped to acquire the bell that now sits atop the Fair Oaks Presbyterian Church on Fair Oaks Boulevard. (Courtesy Bobbi Mitchell.)

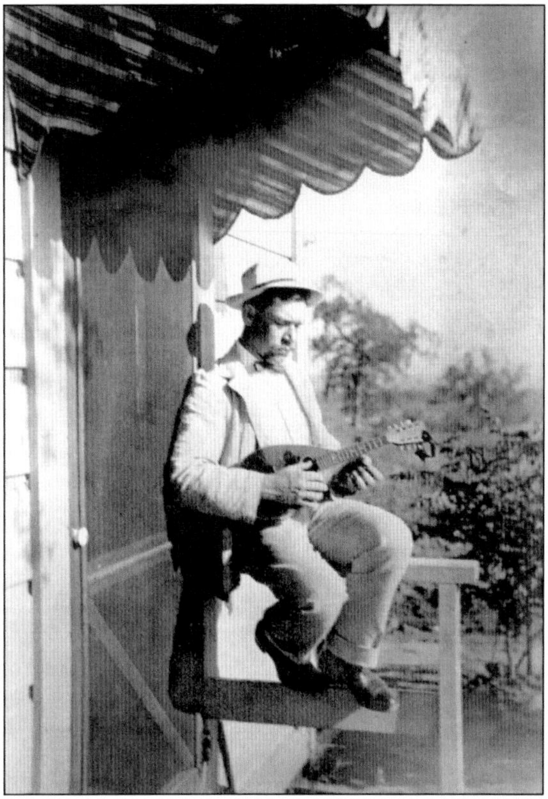

In 1900, Dr. Eugene H. Buffum came from Chicago to Fair Oaks with his father, Dr. Joseph C. Buffum, and his brother, Dr. J. H. Buffum. Dr. Buffum, one of the first physicians in Fair Oaks, helped organize the Fair Oaks Band with William Gregory. Dr. Buffum is shown here playing his mandolin. (Courtesy Fair Oaks Historical Society.)

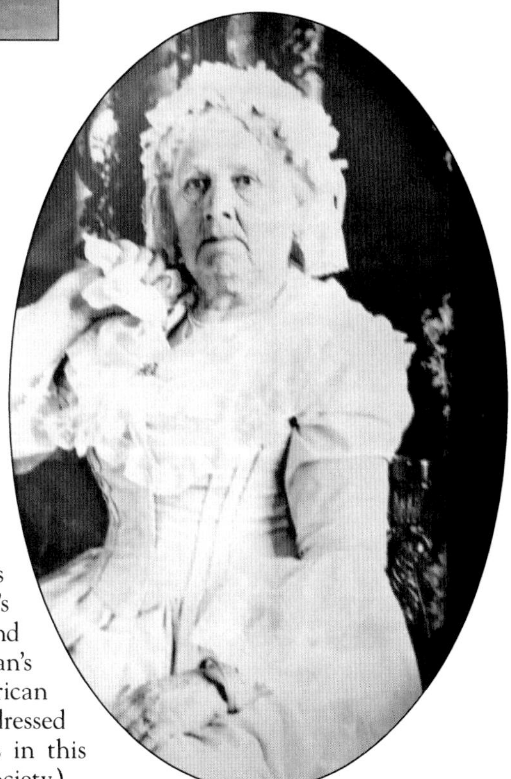

Dr. Buffum's wife, commonly referred to as Madame Buffum, organized The Woman's Thursday Club of Fair Oaks in 1902 and served as the club's first president. The Woman's Thursday Club often celebrated early American colonial celebrations, and the members often dressed like Martha Washington, as Mrs. Buffum is in this photograph. (Courtesy Fair Oaks Historical Society.)

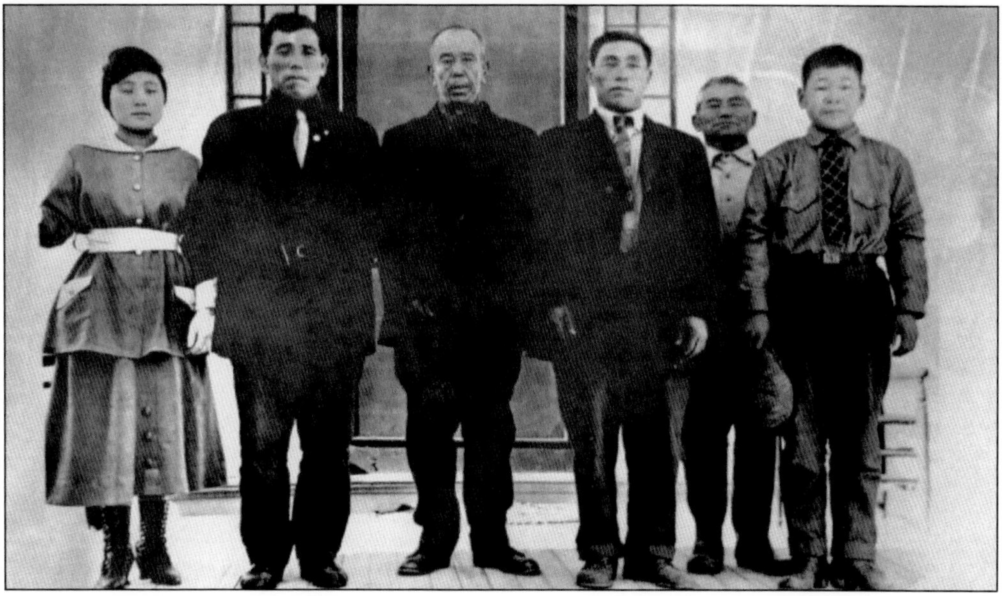

These unidentified Chinese immigrants worked as servants for the Buffum family. This extremely rare photograph shows that both men and women, young and old, came to Fair Oaks to find some sort of opportunity for work and a chance to carve out a better life. (Courtesy Fair Oaks Historical Society.)

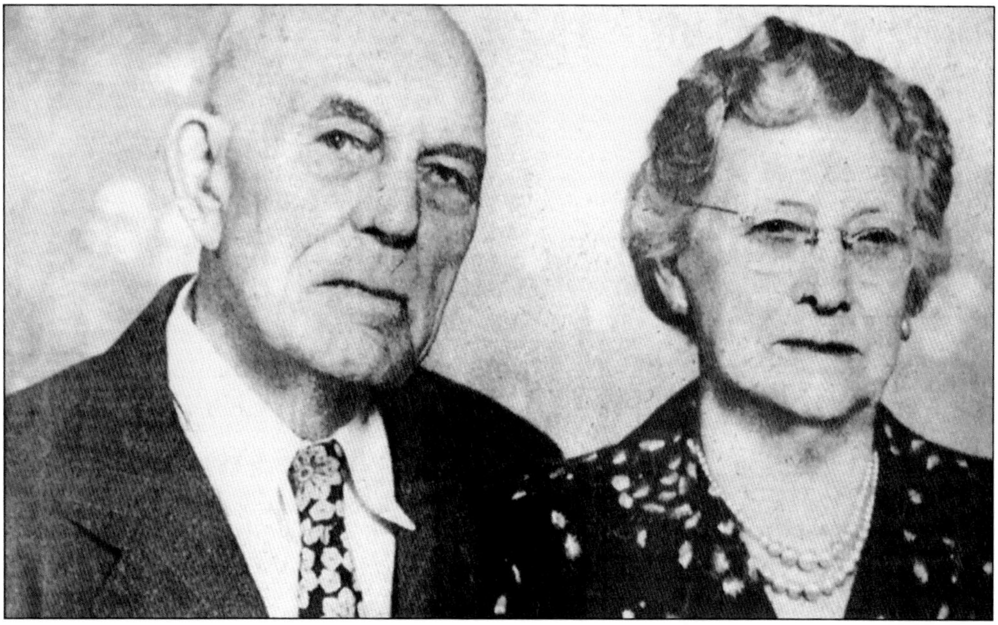

Inspired by the Howard-Wilson Publishing Company's booster ads in *Farm, Field and Fireside*, Mr. and Mrs. John E. Holst arrived in Fair Oaks from Minnesota on November 1, 1895—before the 165 original excursionists. The Holst's placed palm trees in front of their house, built just north of the Fair Oaks Elementary School on Fair Oaks Boulevard that are still visible today. John served as a clerk for the Fair Oaks school trustees for 41 years and was instrumental in building the first schools. The elementary school built in 1953 on Bannister Avenue was named after him. (Courtesy Fair Oaks Presbyterian Church.)

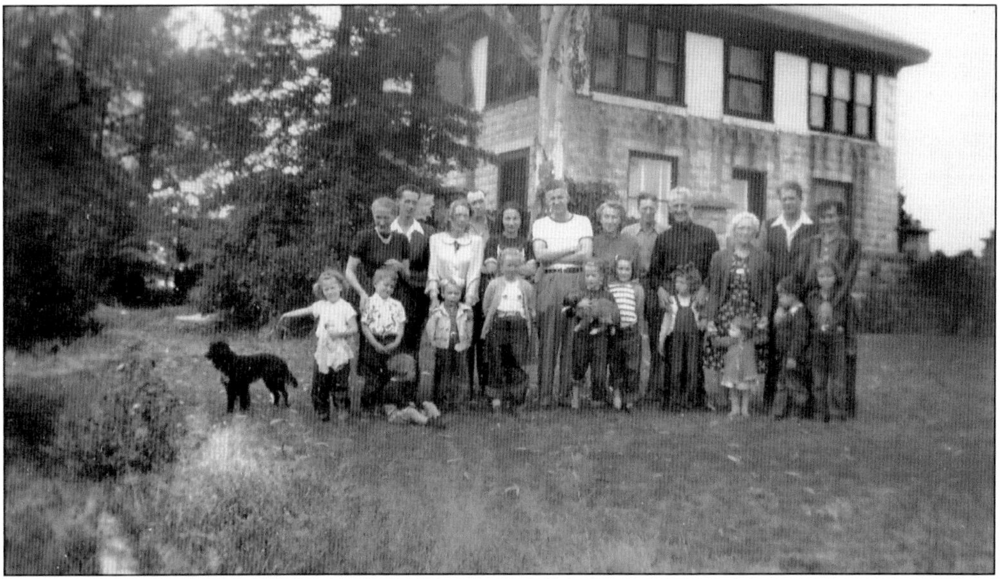

The Maleks, seen here with family and friends in the 1930s, lived near Kenneth Avenue in the old house of D. D. Dickson, an early settler to Fair Oaks. The family patriarch, Leo Malek, worked in construction and supposedly installed Fair Oaks' first pool, complete with beautiful tile, which is still used and enjoyed by the Kenmouth family. (Courtesy Donald Kenmouth.)

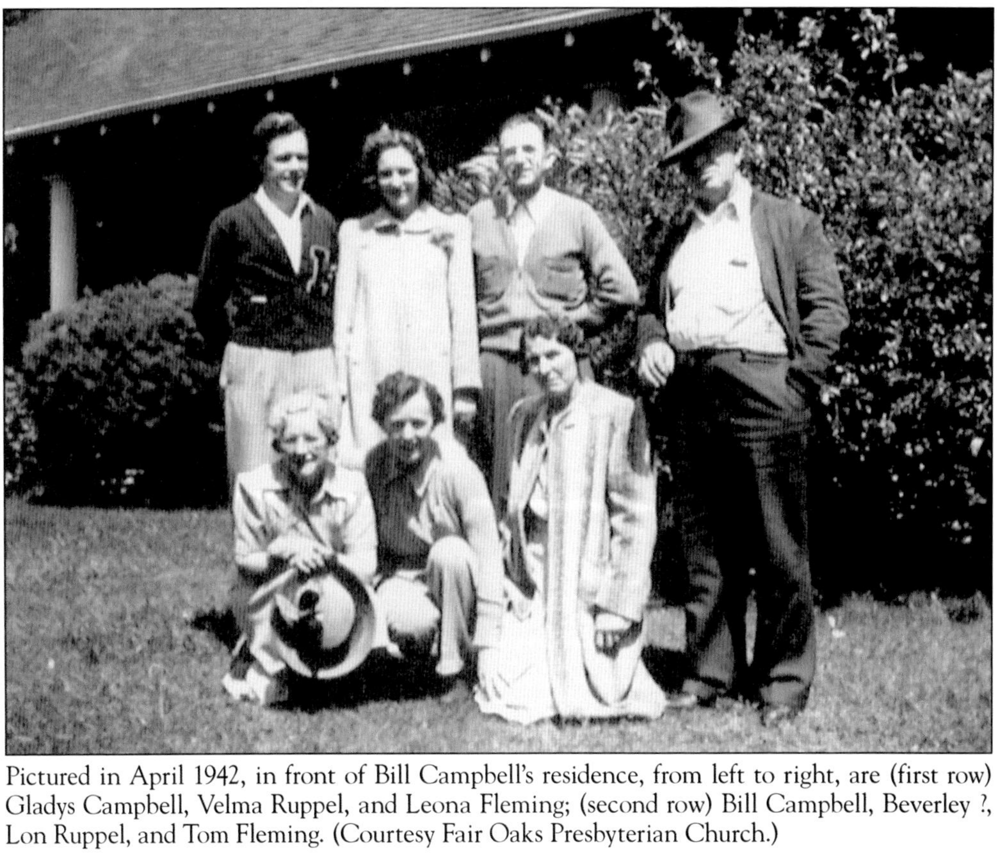

Pictured in April 1942, in front of Bill Campbell's residence, from left to right, are (first row) Gladys Campbell, Velma Ruppel, and Leona Fleming; (second row) Bill Campbell, Beverley ?, Lon Ruppel, and Tom Fleming. (Courtesy Fair Oaks Presbyterian Church.)

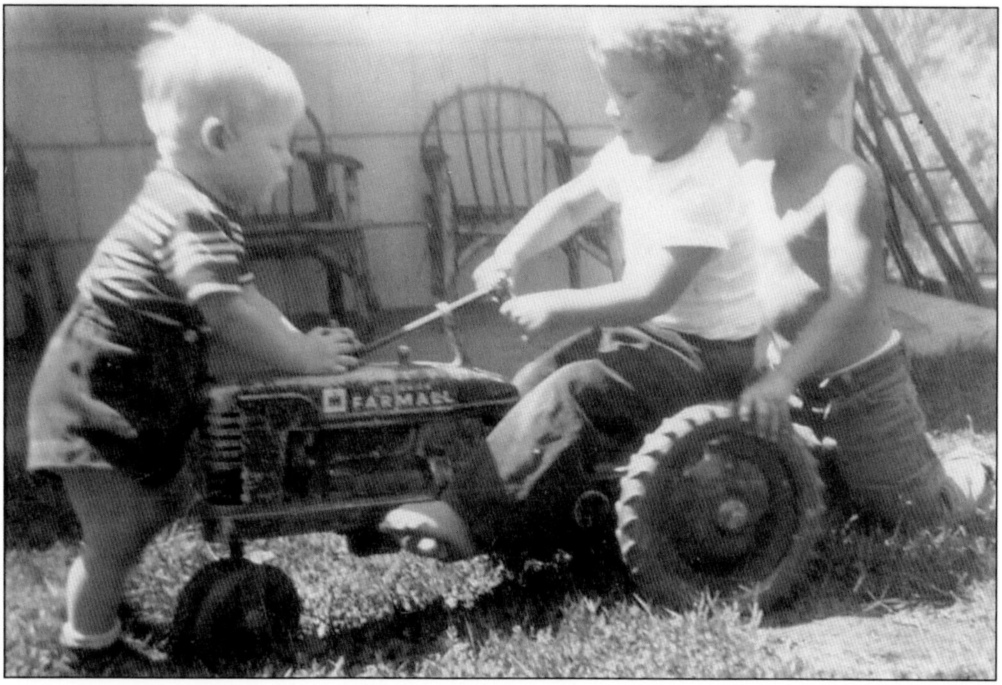

The Wood family children, seen here at their home on Fair Oaks Boulevard, enjoyed playing in the front yard. Pictured above in 1952, from left to right, are Rob, Sherry, and Ritchie Wood. Pictured below in 1949, from left to right, are Ritchie, Sherry, Tamara, and Missy the cat. (Courtesy Sherry Lynn Wood.)

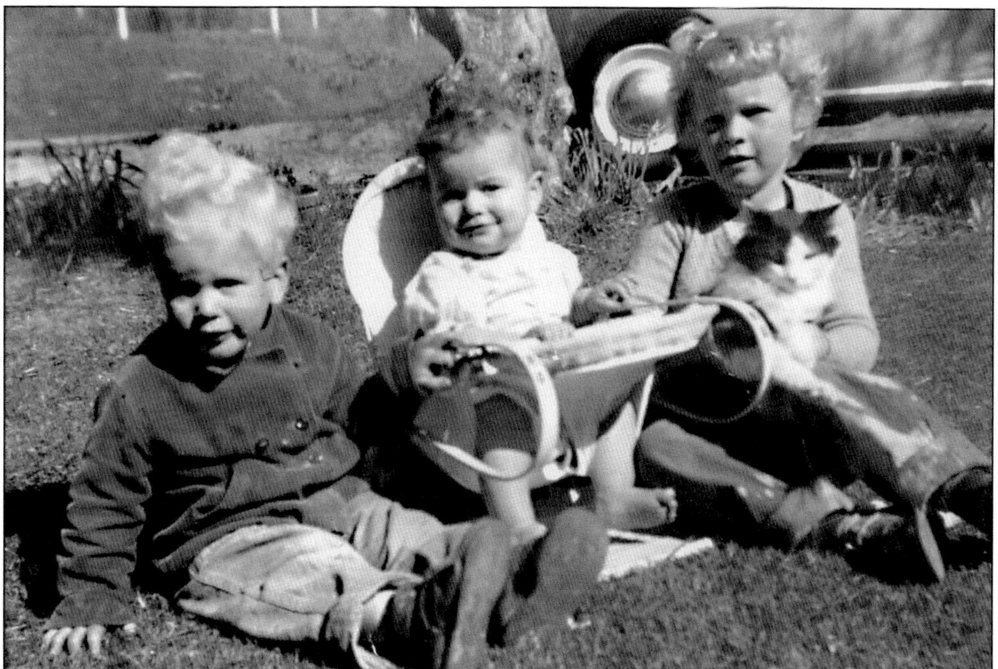

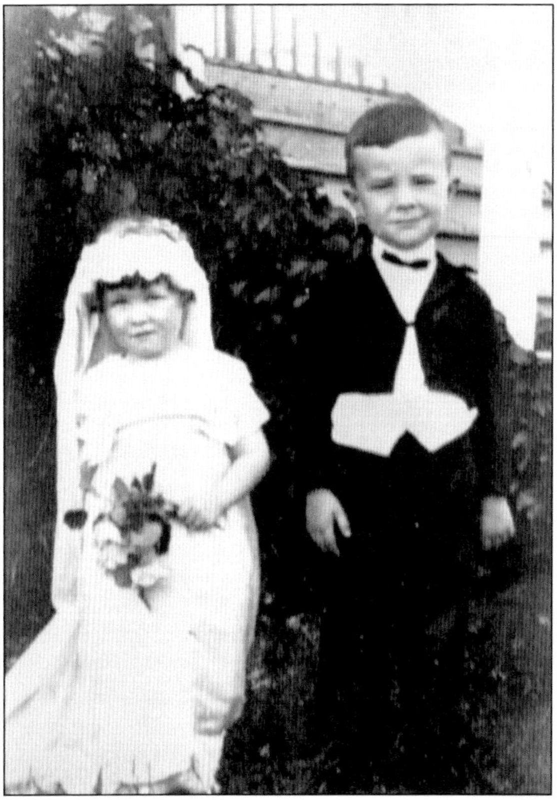

Betty Rose Green and Hugh Broadley posed for this "Tom Thumb Wedding" in the early 1900s. (Courtesy Fair Oaks Historical Society.)

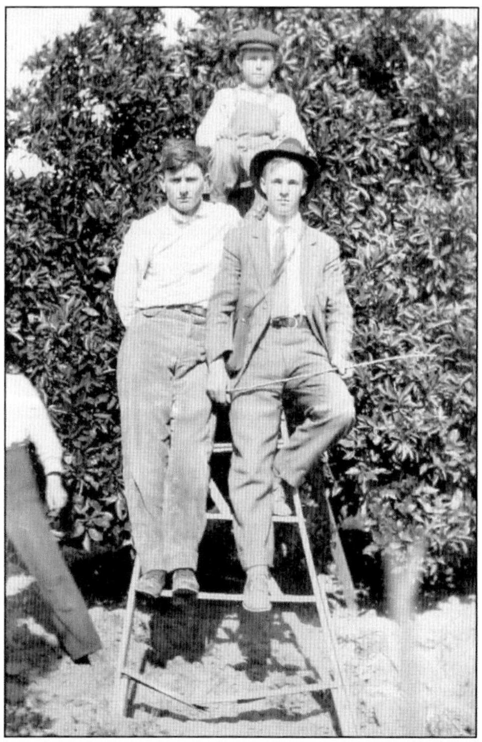

Vernon Munson, Sim Green, and Less Tall posed on top of a ladder in this 1920s photograph. The image captures the deciduous tress that flourished in Fair Oaks' earlier days. (Courtesy Fair Oaks Historical Society.)

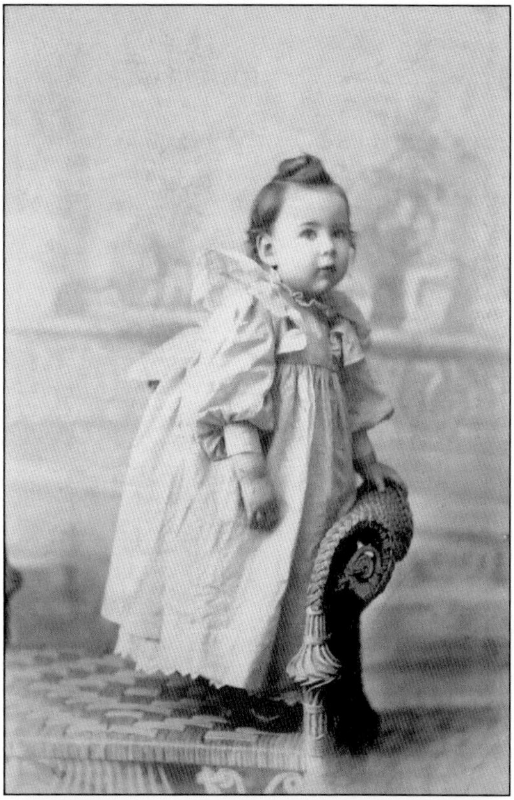

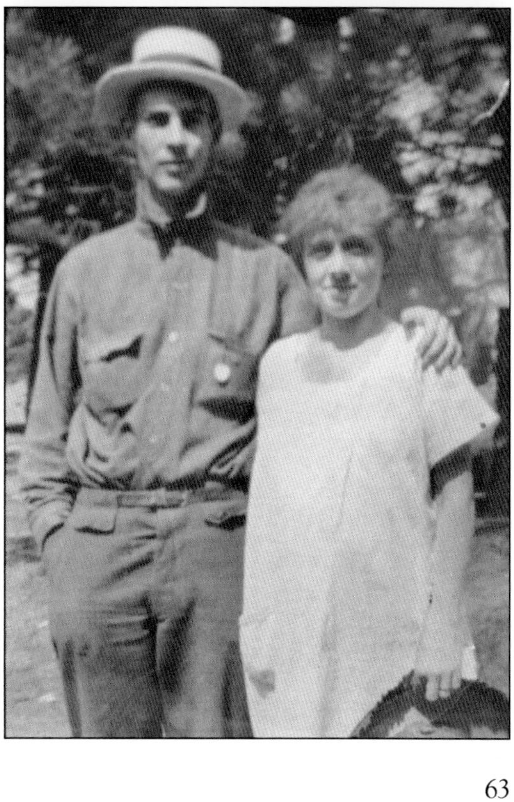

George Hinsey, shown above in 1896, was one of Walt and Carrie Hinsey's seven children who eventually made their homes in Fair Oaks. Below, in 1916, an older George Hinsey poses with his wife, Ilga Gregory. (Courtesy Linda Morris.)

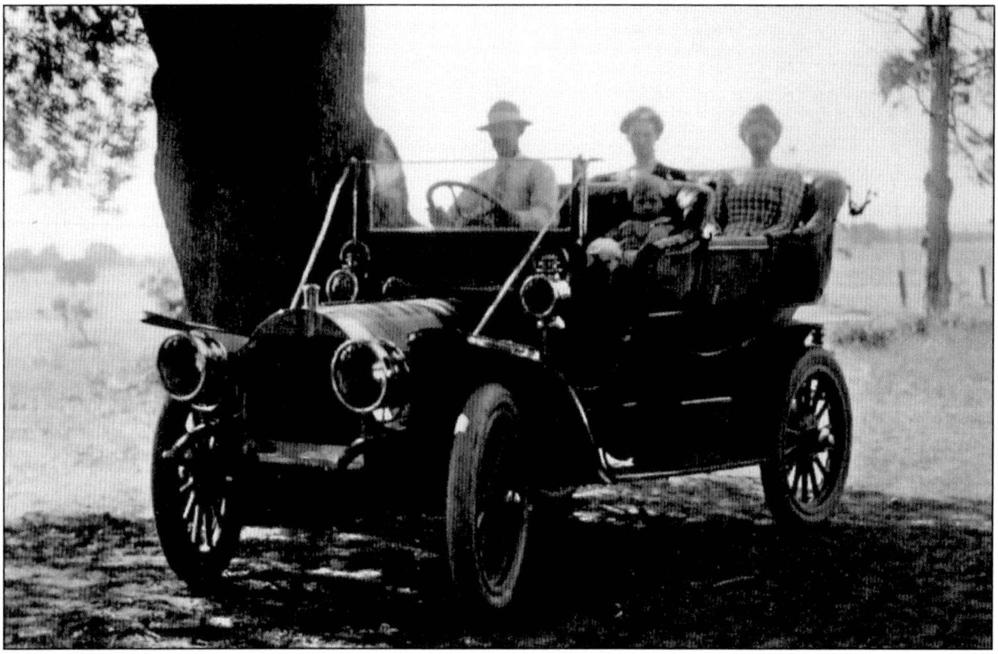

During the 1920s, the Beauchamp family is seen here in the family's Rambler. They used the car to run Fair Oaks' first auto stage for trips to the "big city" of Sacramento. In the front seat is Ollie with his son Earl and in the back seat are his daughters. (Courtesy Fair Oaks Historical Society.)

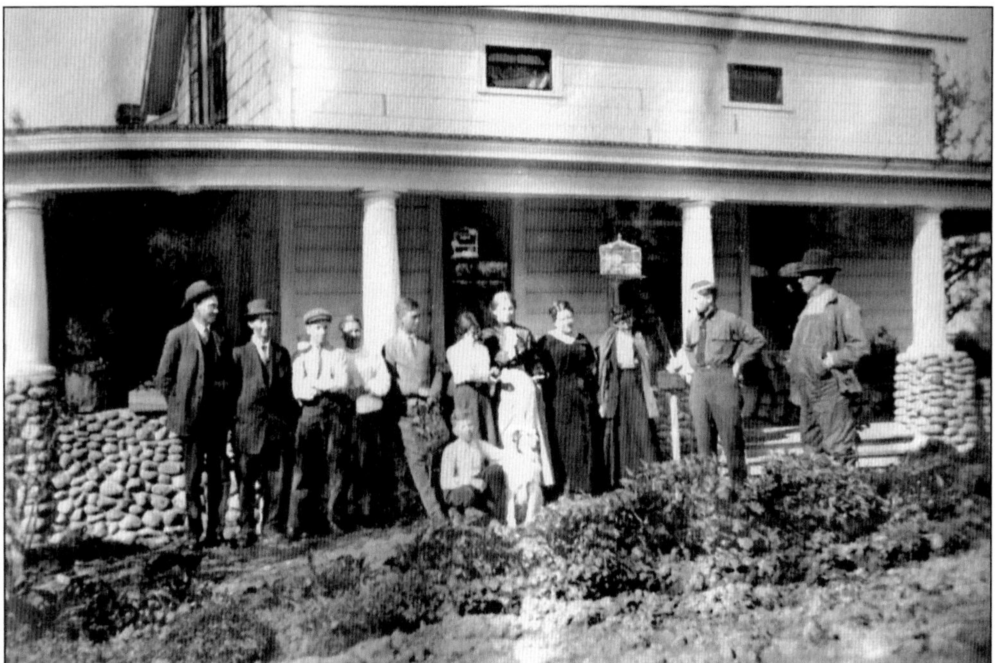

The Dewey family is shown here in the 1910s in front of their house on Winding Way. On the far right is Harry Dewey. Pictured, from left to right (starting with the fourth person), are Bertha, Harold, and Alta Dewey. The rest are unidentified. (Courtesy Eileen Dewey Thomas.)

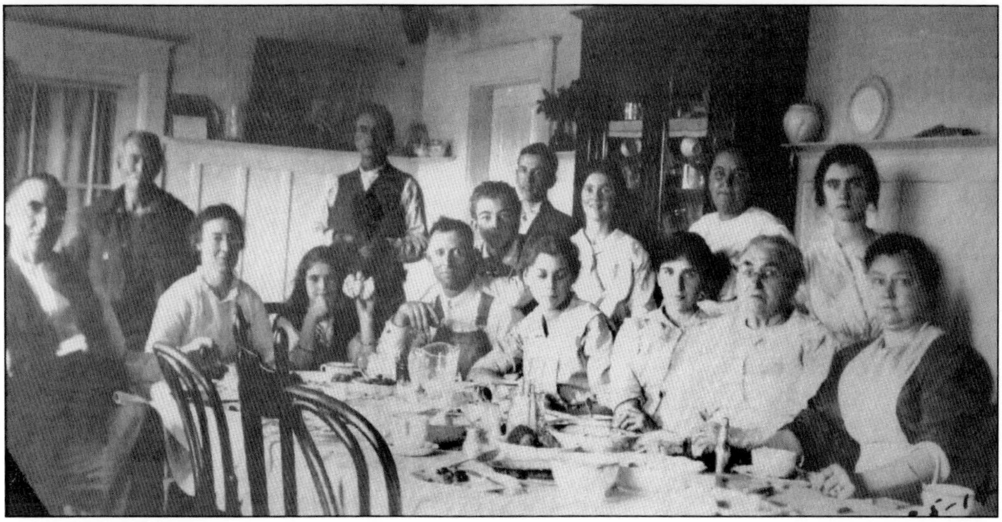

A rare 1914 glimpse inside the Dewey home shows the family sitting around the dinning table. Among those identified here are Harry Dewey, Jim Gee, Harold Dewey (standing), Drury DeMoss (sitting), Joseph Dewey (behind), Alta Dewey (sitting next to future husband Drury DeMoss), and Bertha Dewey. (Courtesy Eileen Dewey Thomas.)

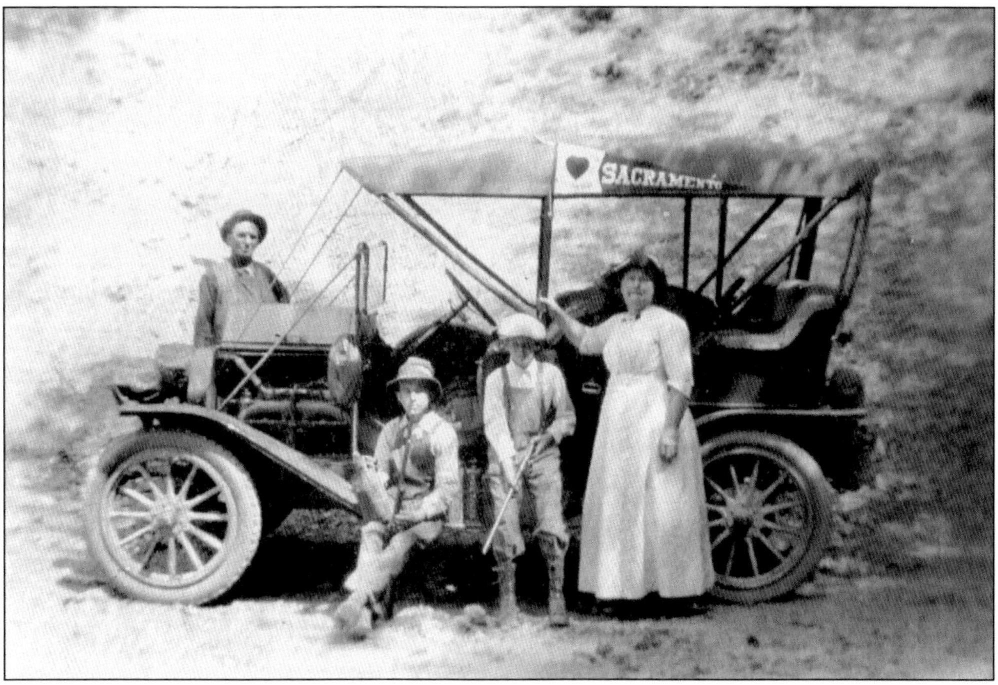

In the 1910s, Harry and Bertha Dewey pose in front of an unidentified car with two boys and their guns. (Courtesy Eileen Dewey Thomas.)

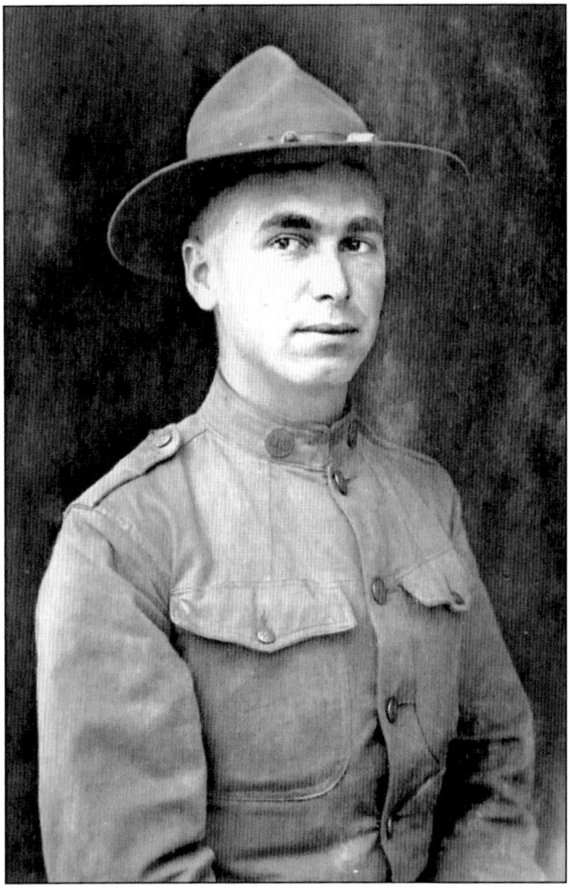

Harold Dewey, in uniform, trained in Los Angeles in preparation for World War I. Luckily Harold never saw action and returned home safely to the family. (Courtesy Eileen Dewey Thomas.)

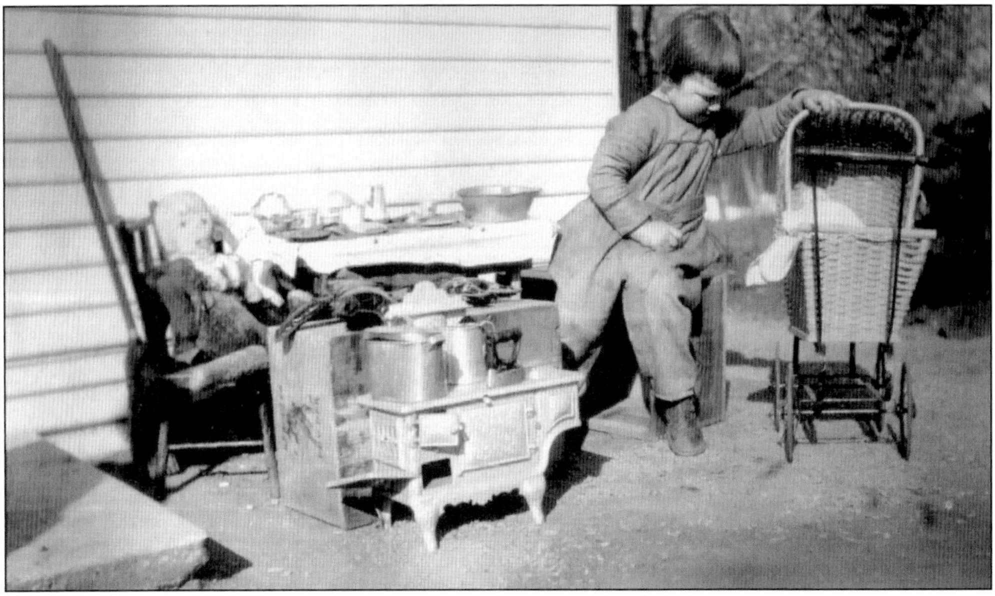

Ester Dewey, Harold's daughter, enjoyed playing with her toys during the 1910s in front of the family home. (Courtesy Eileen Dewey Thomas.)

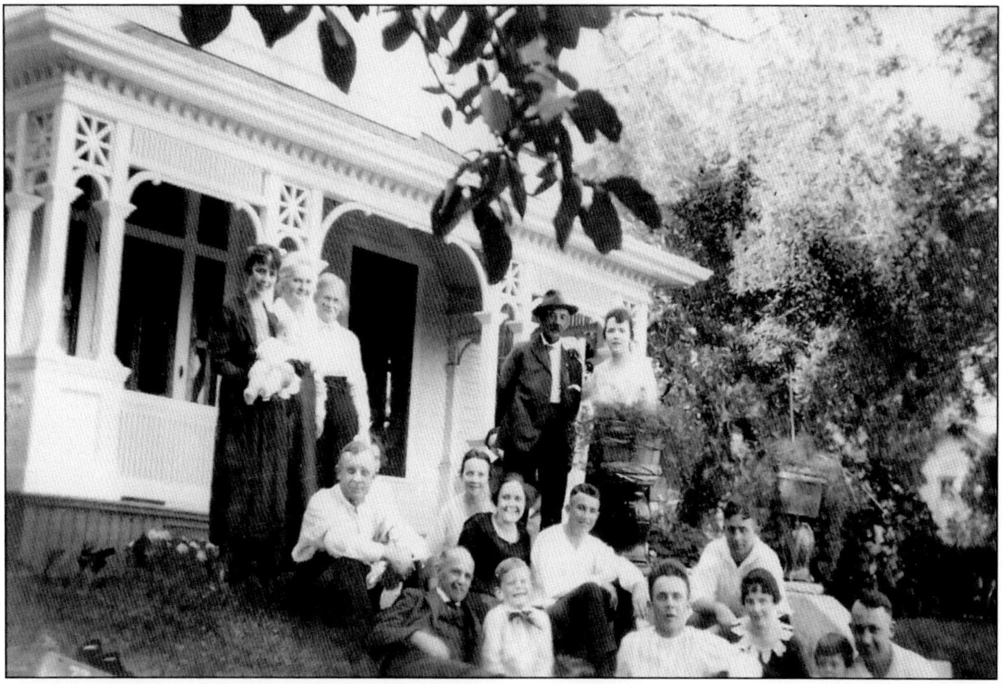

The Broadley family pose in front of their house on Sunset before they moved in 1938. Pioneer Joseph Broadley is pictured in the back row wearing a hat and his wife, Jane, is seen opposite on the left side, in the middle. (Courtesy Jim and Delores Broadley.)

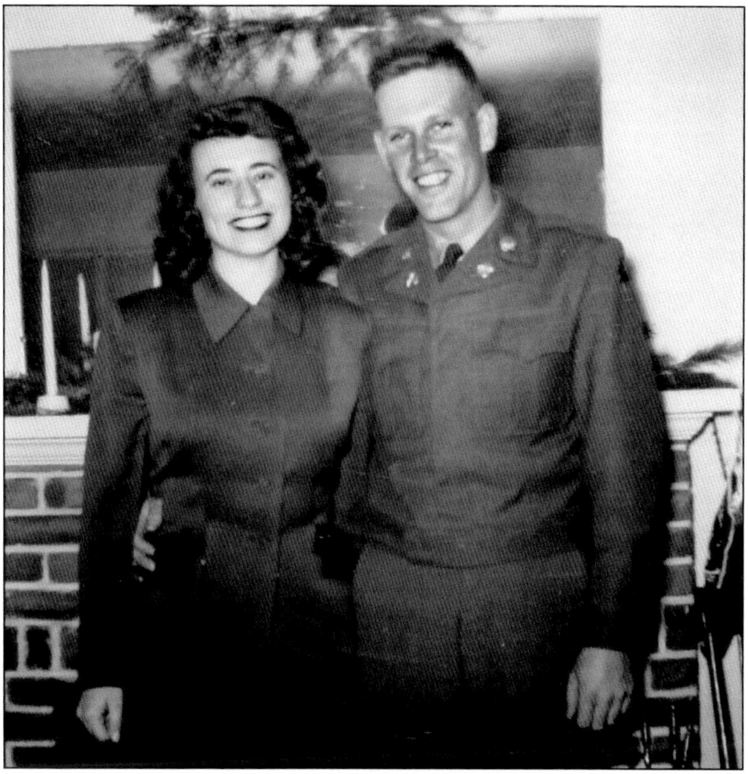

Jim and Delores Broadley pose in this 1951 photograph, with Jim dressed in uniform for battle in the Korean War. (Courtesy Jim and Delores Broadley.)

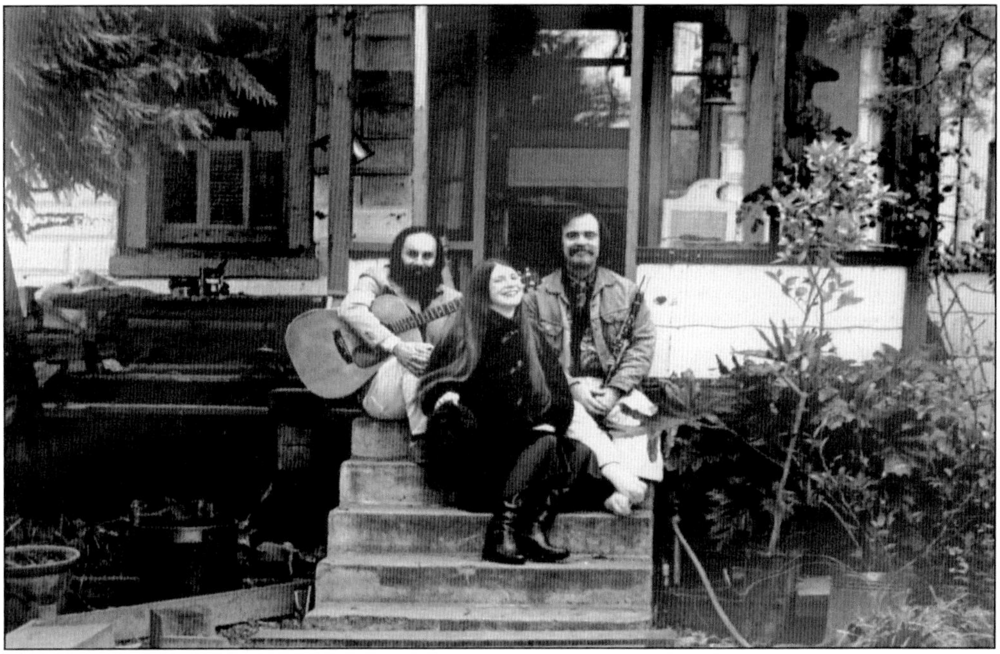

Paul Emery, Tom Schmidt, and Annie McCann, posing on the front steps of Hugh Gorman's place off of California and Temescal in 1977, formed a group that later became the Backwoods Jazz Band that played for Queen Elizabeth II in 1983 on her state visit to California. (Courtesy Hugh Gorman.)

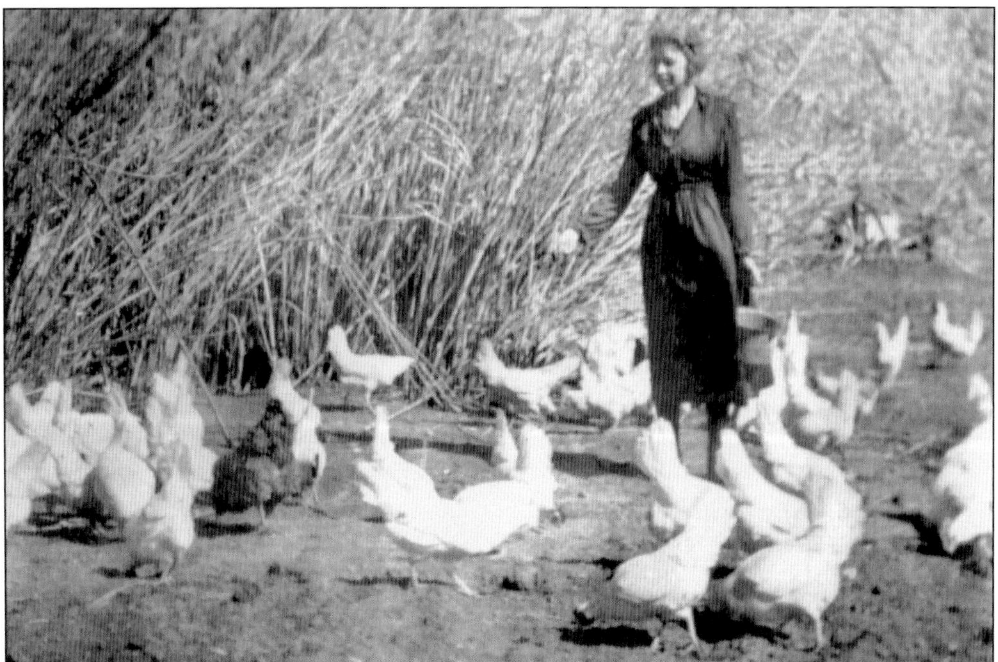

The beloved chickens in Fair Oaks, nationally known because of an article in the magazine *People*, have always been a part of life in Fair Oaks. The chickens are seen here with Alta Dewey in 1914. (Courtesy Eileen Dewey Thomas.)

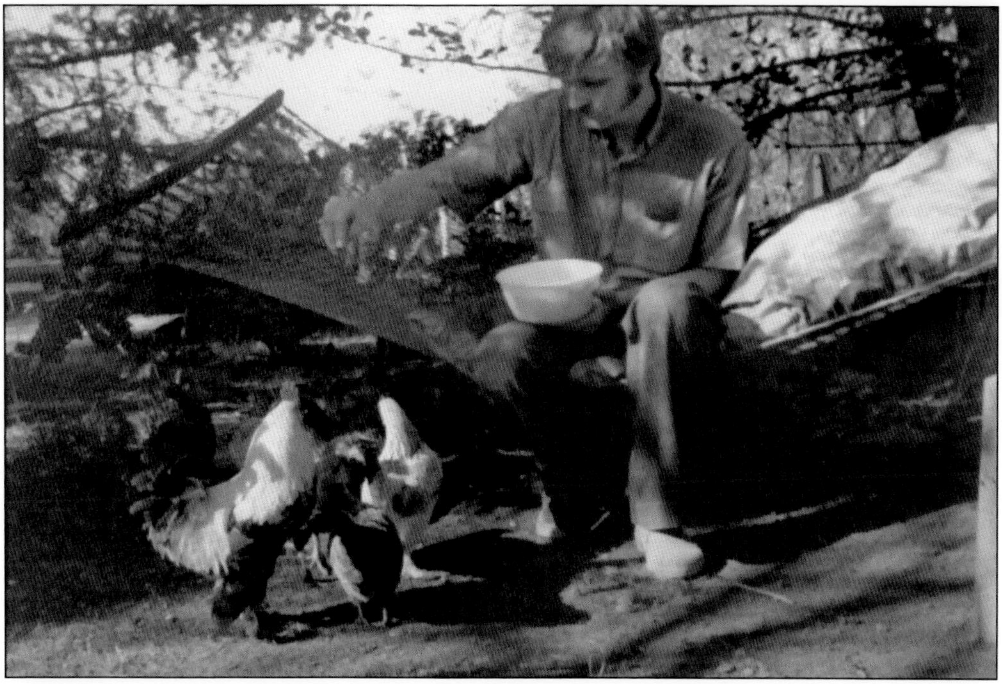

In 1977, Hugh Gorman, also known as the "Chicken Man," is seen above with his chickens. Hugh is responsible for introducing Fair Oaks' latest vibrant chicken population. Below is Mercury, the modern-day founding father and ancestor of Fair Oaks' beloved chickens and roosters. (Courtesy Hugh Gorman.)

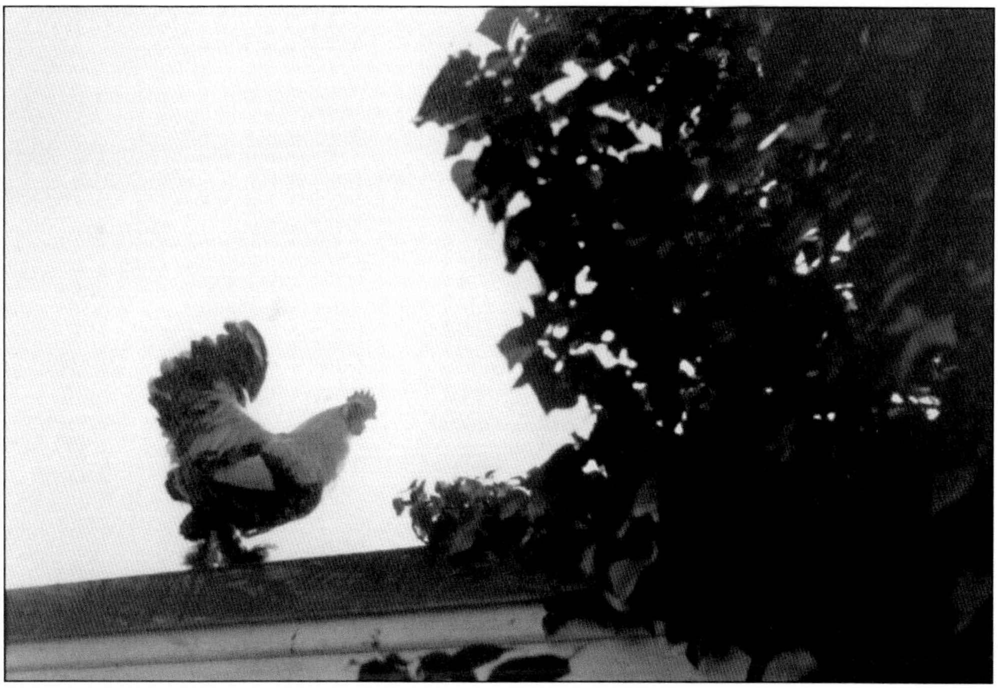

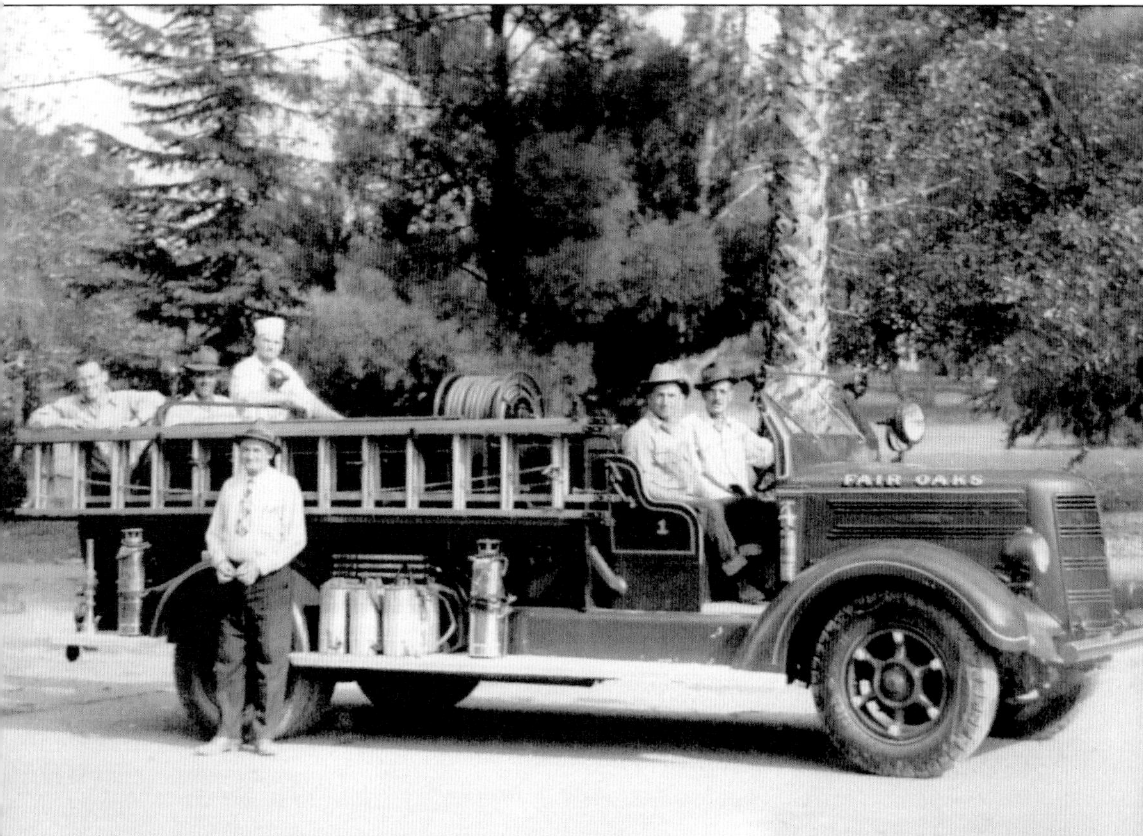

From 1938 to 1942, Fair Oaks had a volunteer fire department. For this photograph, some of the volunteers posed with their fire truck in front of the Fair Oaks Plaza. (Courtesy Fair Oaks Historical Society.)

Six

Reading, Writing, and Arithmetic

The good Education of Youth has been esteemed by wise Men in all Ages, as the surest Foundation of the Happiness both of private Families and of Commonwealths.

—Benjamin Franklin

As Benjamin Franklin so aptly stated, schools, libraries, and education are some of the most important institutions in any community. Education provides citizens with the tools and knowledge they need to understand their world and to be responsible and informed citizens. Education also provides people with the knowledge and awareness needed to promote tolerance and understanding among people. It helps to sustain the human values that contribute to individual and collective well-being. Yet schools and libraries do much more than just stimulate thought and disseminate knowledge and ideas, they too are centers for community building.

The history of schools and libraries in Fair Oaks reflects the history of schools in the West—they were needed, they were treasured, and they were attended! Some disagreement exists over where credit should go for the first school in Fair Oaks. Some accounts indicate that the first school opened in the Grange Hall at the foot of Main Street. The hall also housed a church and a social hall for such events as Saturday night dancing. Other accounts state that a school, called "Four Gables," instructed children in the home of Elmore Chase on Winding Way. Another school operated out of the home of Uriah and Lena Watkins. The community finally built a schoolhouse in 1898 at the corner of Watkins and Fair Oaks Boulevard. Growing out of this building by 1902, the town erected a second schoolhouse in what is today known as the Community Clubhouse. The original schoolhouse, rebuilt on Winding Way and Martsmith, served the east side of town to ease the length of travel for students farther away. Fair Oaks' third school replaced it from 1912 to 1920. Fair Oaks opened a high school in 1913 that was originally housed in the upper rooms of the second schoolhouse. Fair Oaks also constructed a brick school in 1928 that still stands on the corner of Winding Way and Fair Oaks Boulevard.

In 1908, the Fair Oaks Library Association formed. The library was housed in the basement of the Methodist church until 1912, when a library opened at the corner of Temescal and Main Street. The library then moved two more times—in 1961 to facilities on California Avenue and in 1967 to Bridge Street. In 1976, the Fair Oaks/Orangevale Community Library opened at its current location on Fair Oaks Boulevard near Madison Avenue.

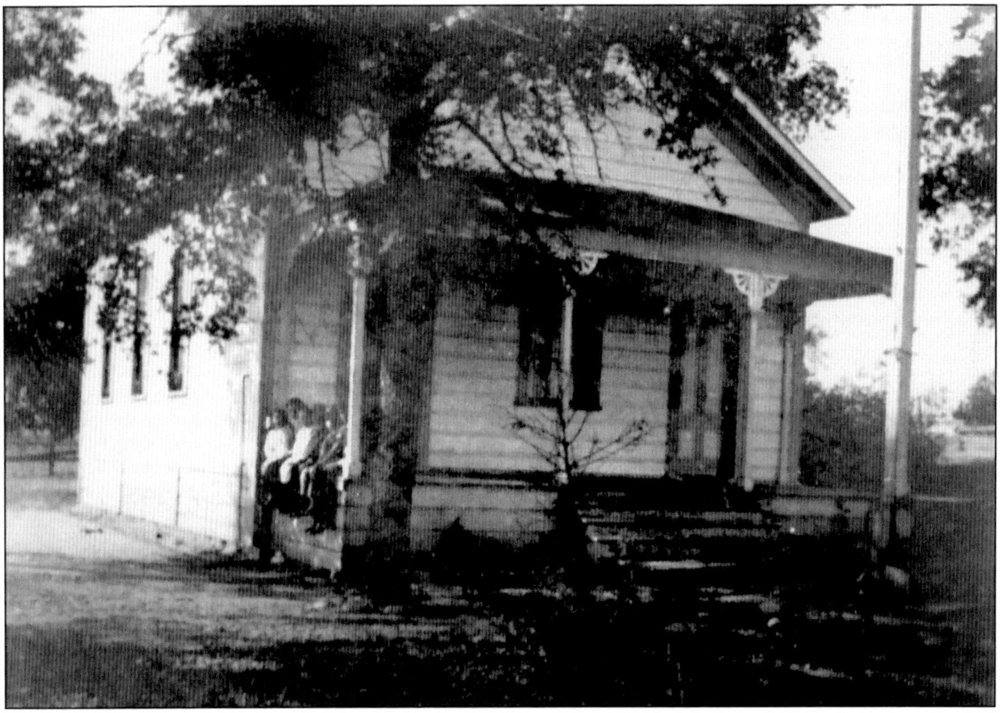

Built in 1898, Fair Oaks' first school was on the corner of Watkins and Fair Oaks Boulevard until it was torn down in 1902. (Courtesy Fair Oaks Historical Society.)

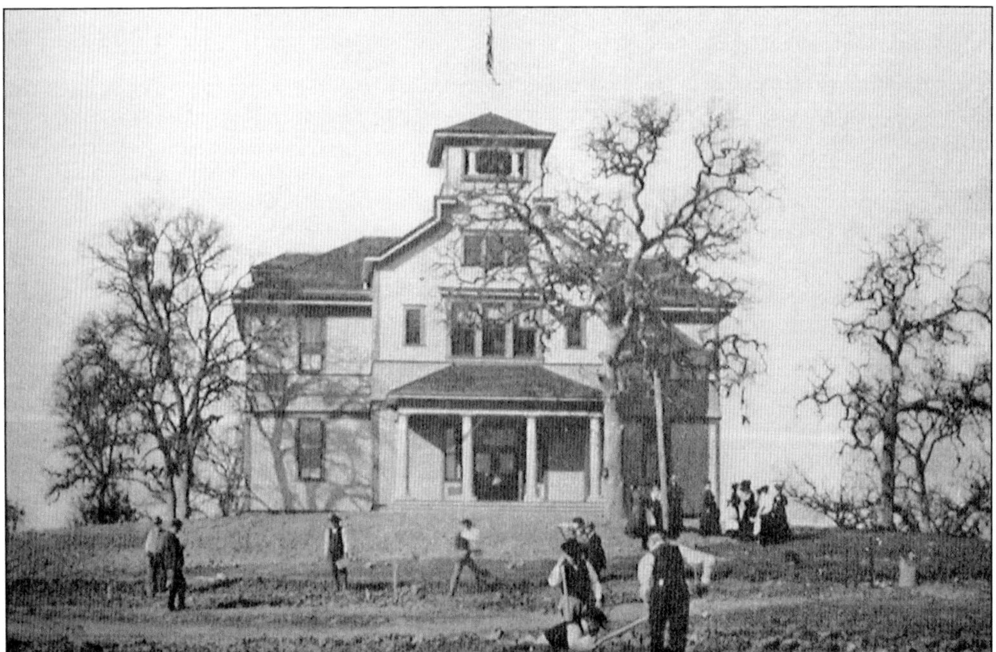

Fair Oaks' second school opened its doors on September 7, 1902, to service the growing population and needs of the community. Joseph Broadley contracted this two-story, four-room schoolhouse. In 1910, two more rooms were added. (Courtesy Fair Oaks Historical Society.)

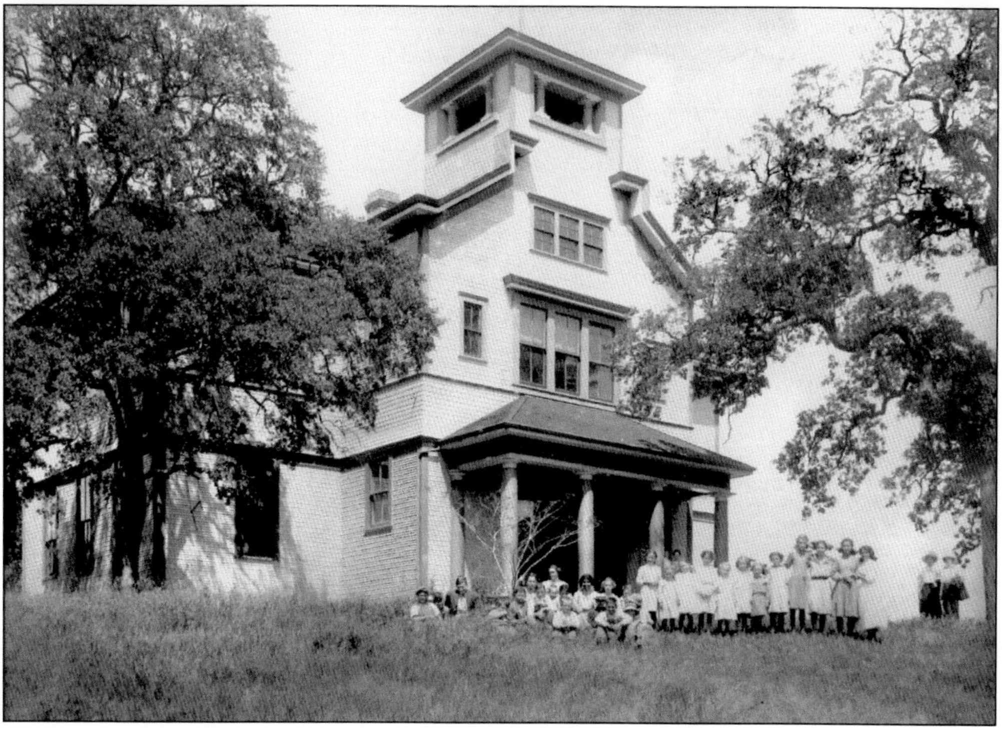

Two views of the second schoolhouse, c. 1905, show school children and teachers in front of the school (above), and the village in the background (below). (Above courtesy Fair Oaks Historical Society; below courtesy Linda Morris.)

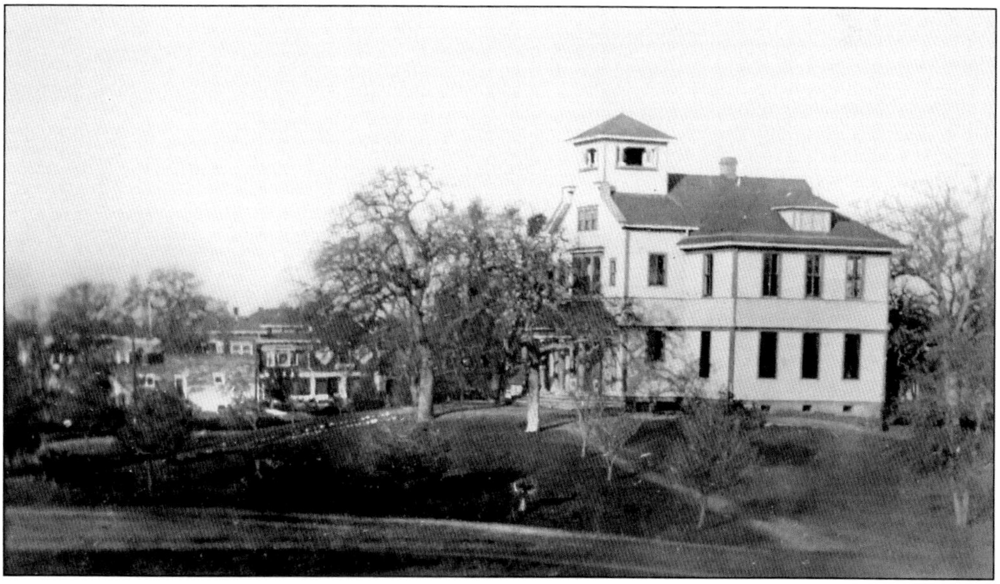

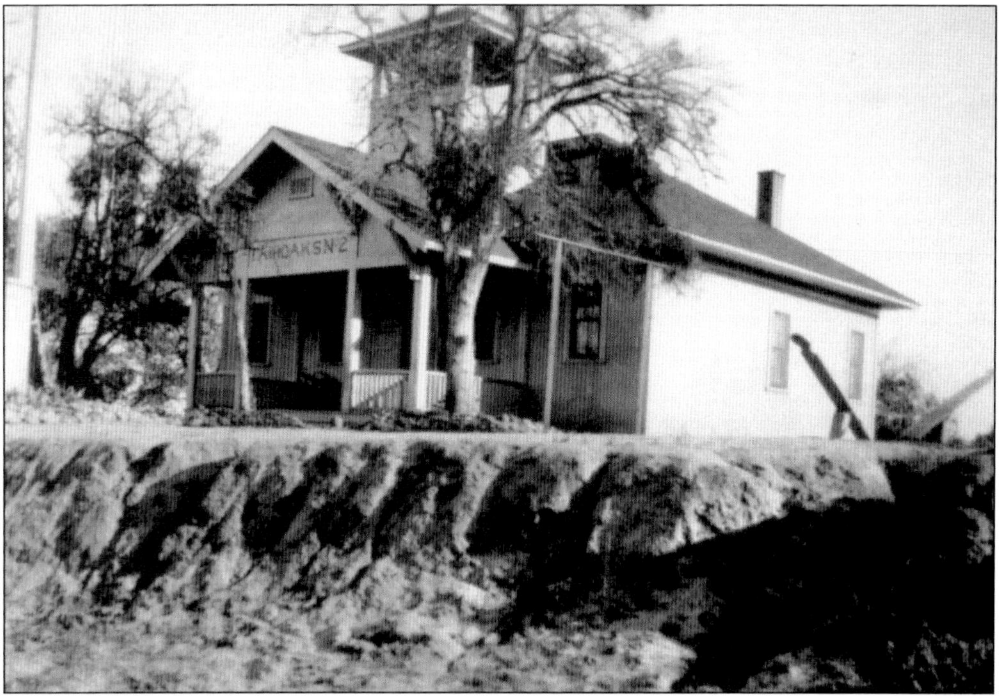

Fair Oaks' third school, which replaced the rebuilt first school, appeared in 1912 on the corner of Martsmith and Winding Way and helped in the education of Fair Oaks children until 1920. In 1903, the first class from the second school in Fair Oaks is seen posing below. (Courtesy Fair Oaks Historical Society.)

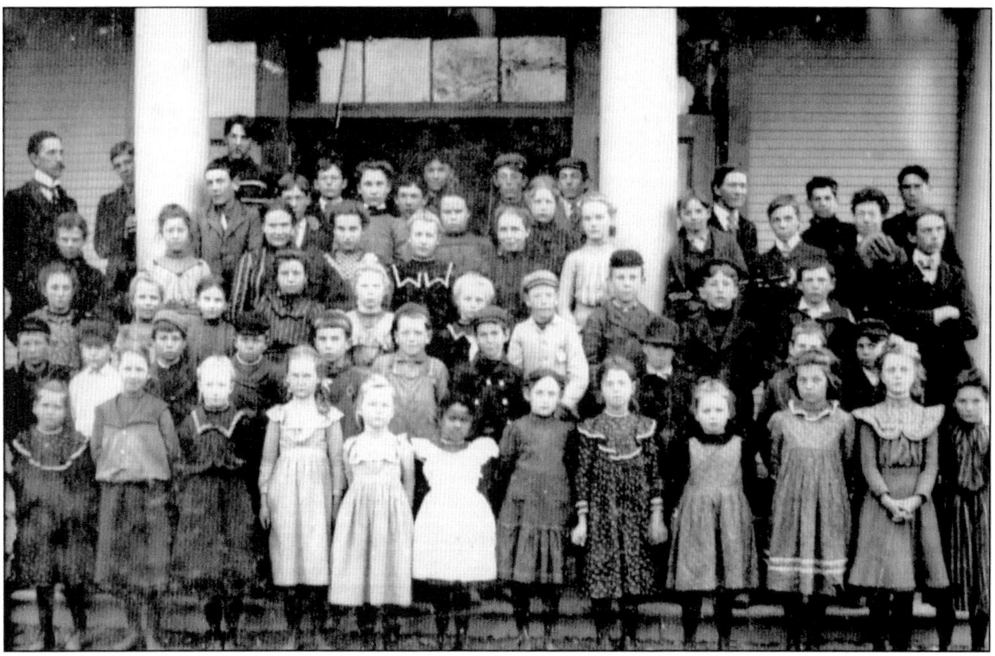

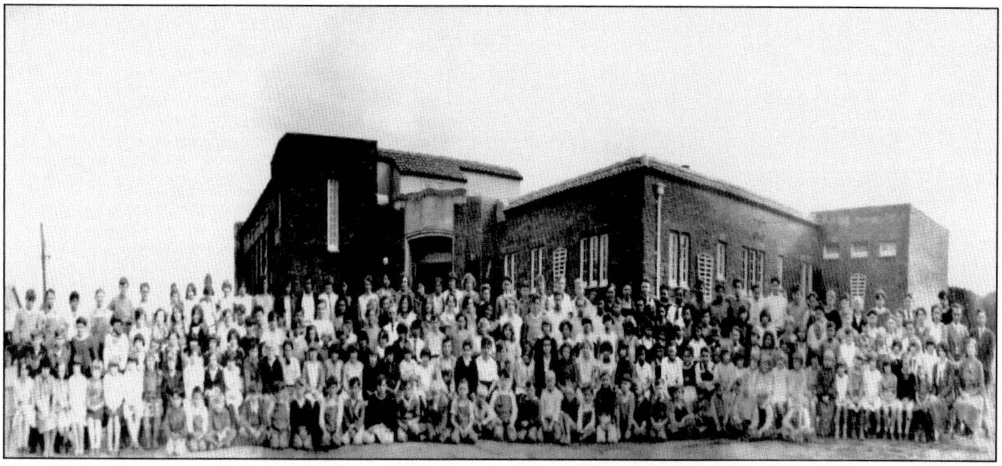

Fair Oaks Grammar School, built in 1928 for approximately $46,000, had a lunchroom, hospital room, large auditorium, offices, and other accessory rooms. Here the 1932 class is in front of the building located at the corner of Winding Way and Fair Oaks Boulevard. (Courtesy Fair Oaks Historical Society.)

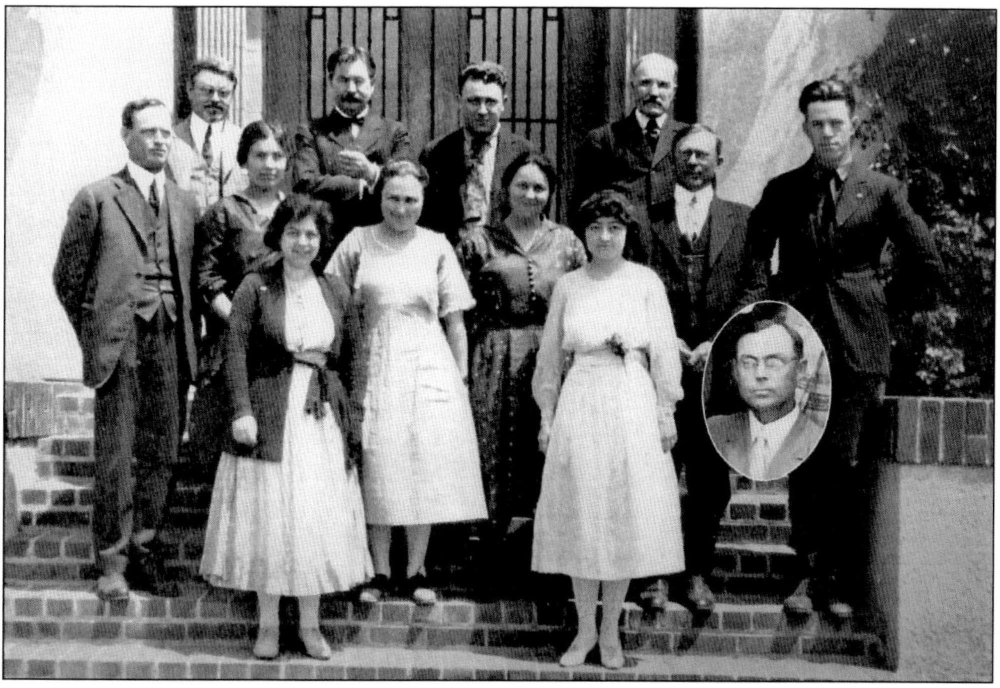

San Juan High School opened in 1913 to service the growing needs of the small community. It held its first high school classes in the upper rooms of the second schoolhouse. The 1922 faculty stands on the steps of the school. (Courtesy Fair Oaks Historical Society.)

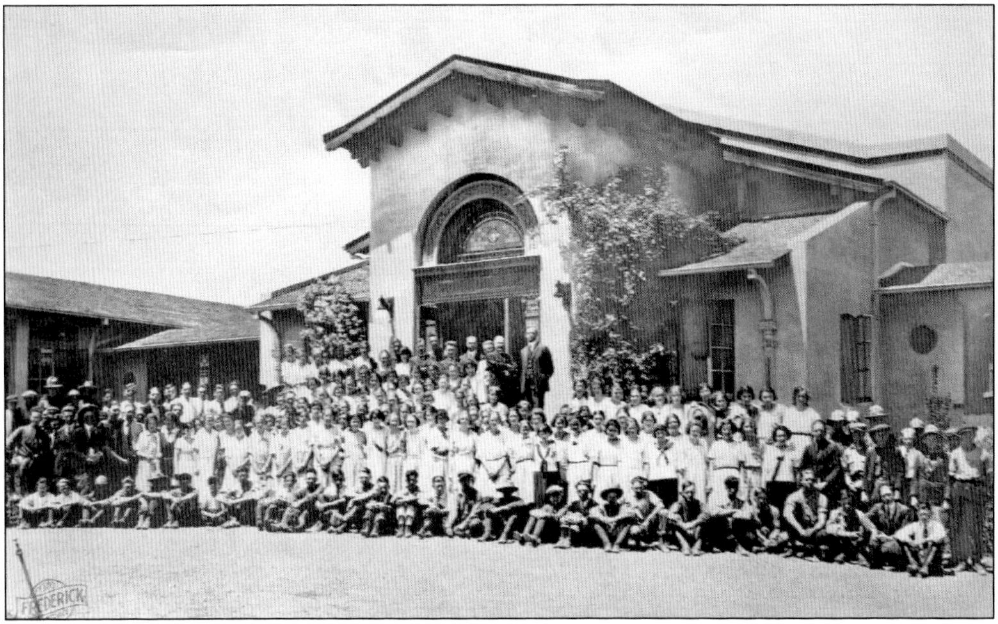

The 1922 San Juan High School class is in front of the school on Greenback Lane (above), while below, the orchestra and band practice on the grass. (Courtesy Fair Oaks Historical Society.)

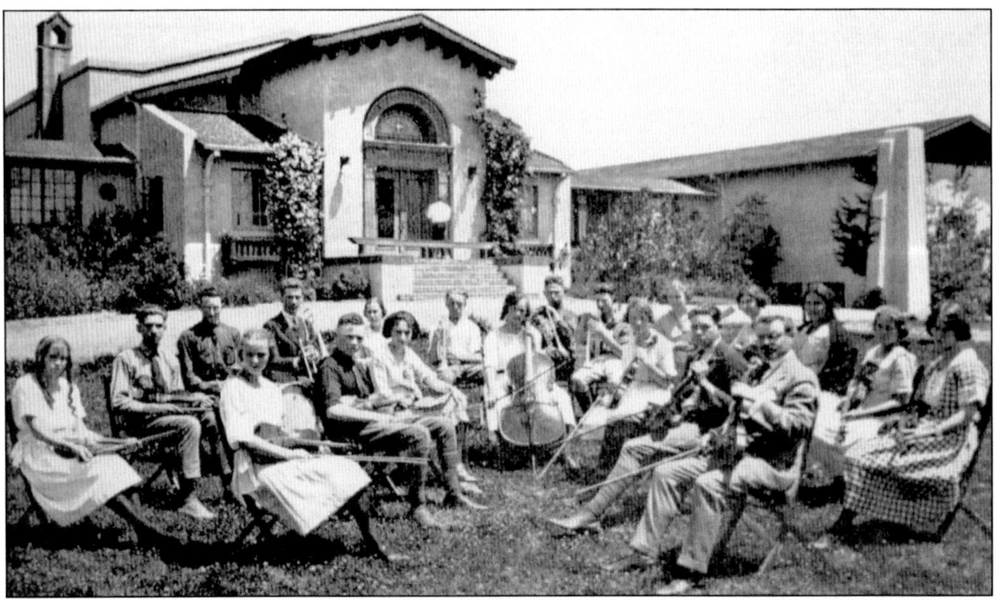

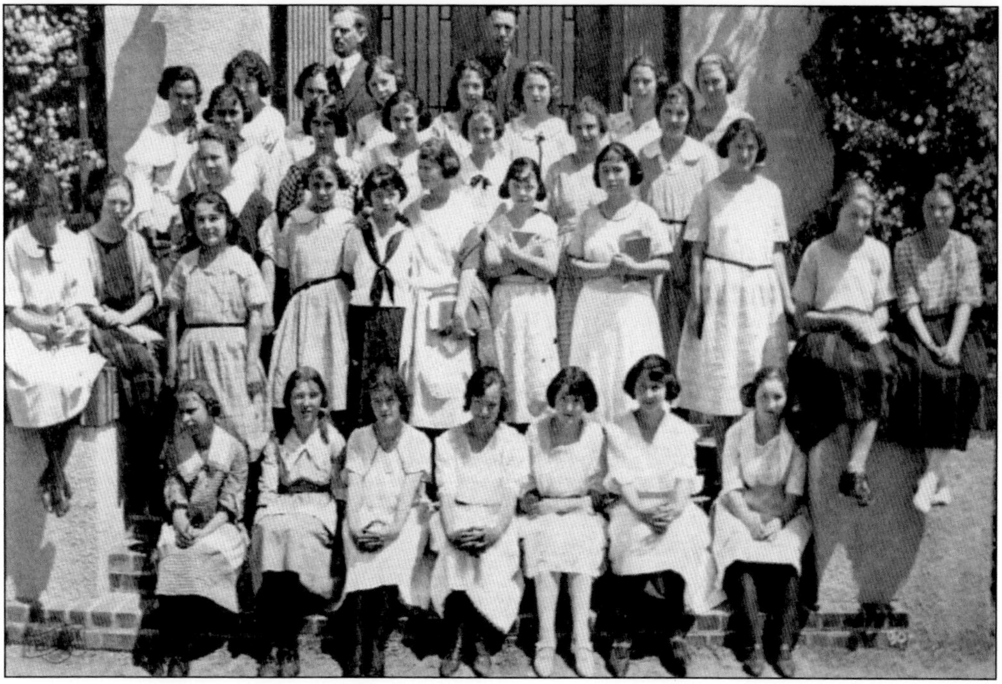

San Juan High School organized many school clubs and organizations, such as the cadets, orchestra, and athletic club. The 1922 agricultural club poses for a picture in the *Greenback Notes* yearbook. The 1942 Girls' League is pictured below. (Courtesy Fair Oaks Historical Society.)

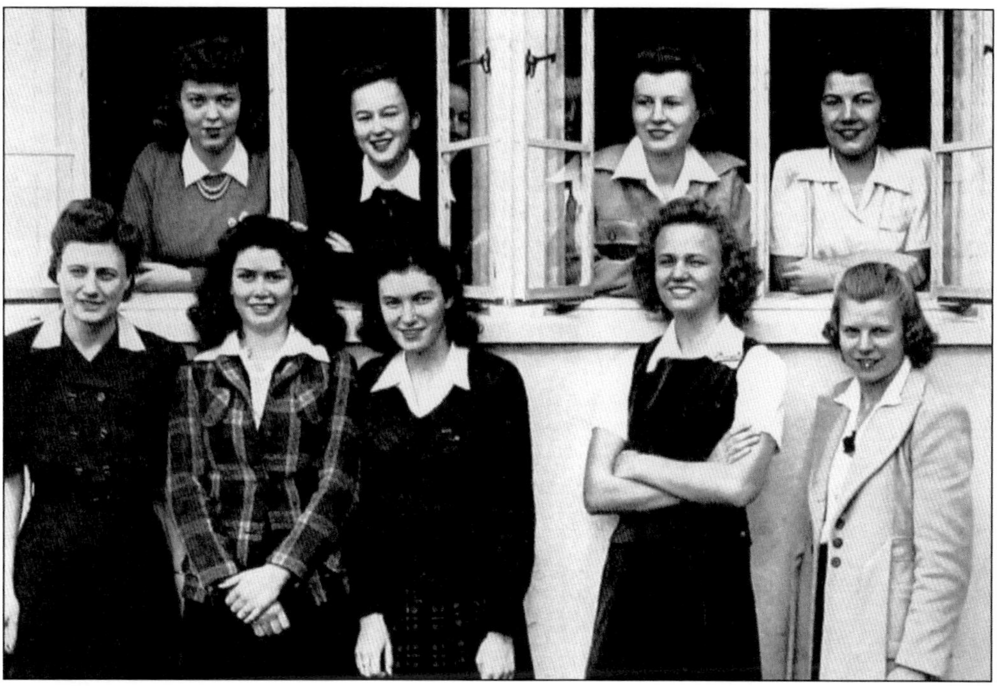

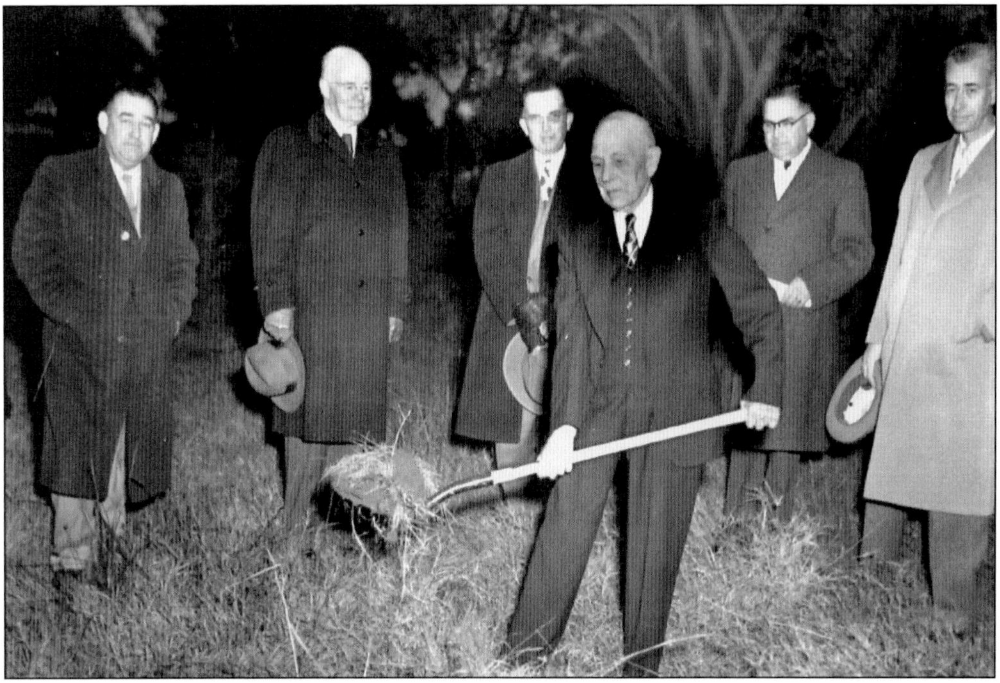

On December 16, 1952, John Holst shovels the first load of dirt during the groundbreaking for John Holst Elementary School. Below, in 1958, construction began on the Earl LeGette Elementary School. Earl LeGette works the shovel. (Courtesy Fair Oaks Historical Society.)

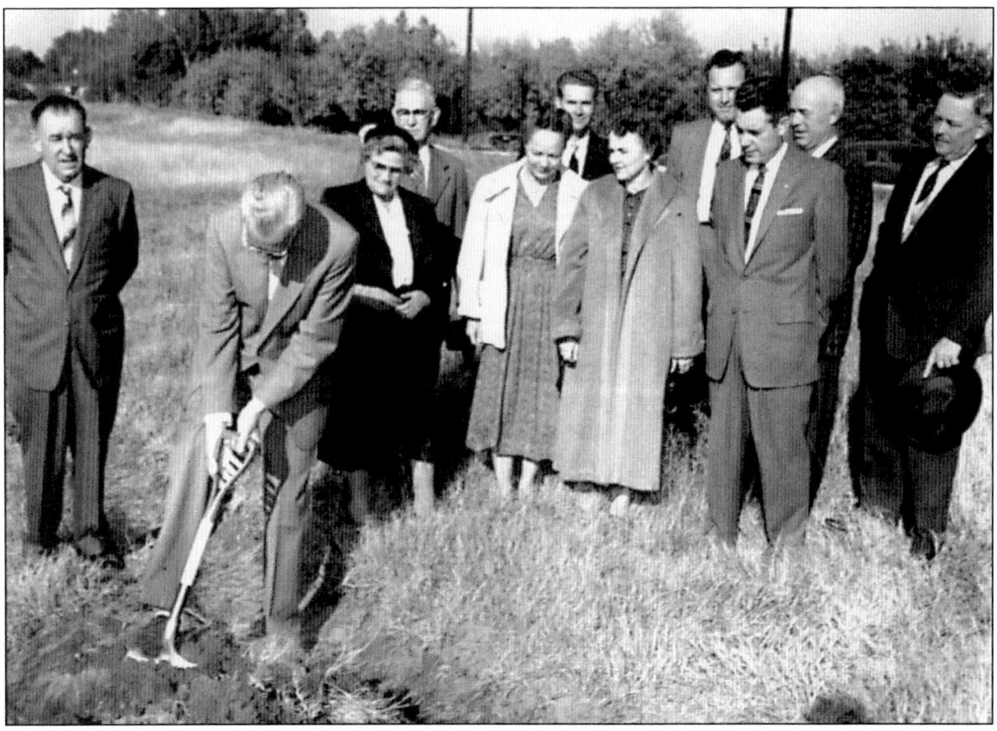

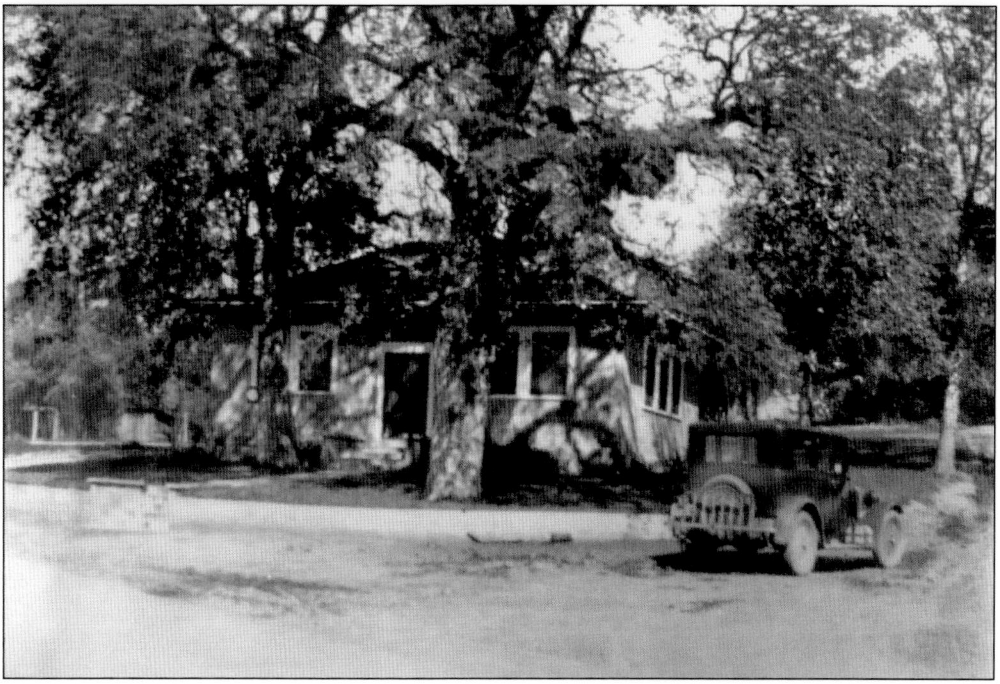

In 1908, the Fair Oaks Library Association created the community's first lending library in the basement of the Methodist church. Four years later, they constructed a permanent building pictured here in the 1930s or 1940s (above). The picture below captures a rare glimpse inside the old library. (Courtesy Fair Oaks Historical Society.)

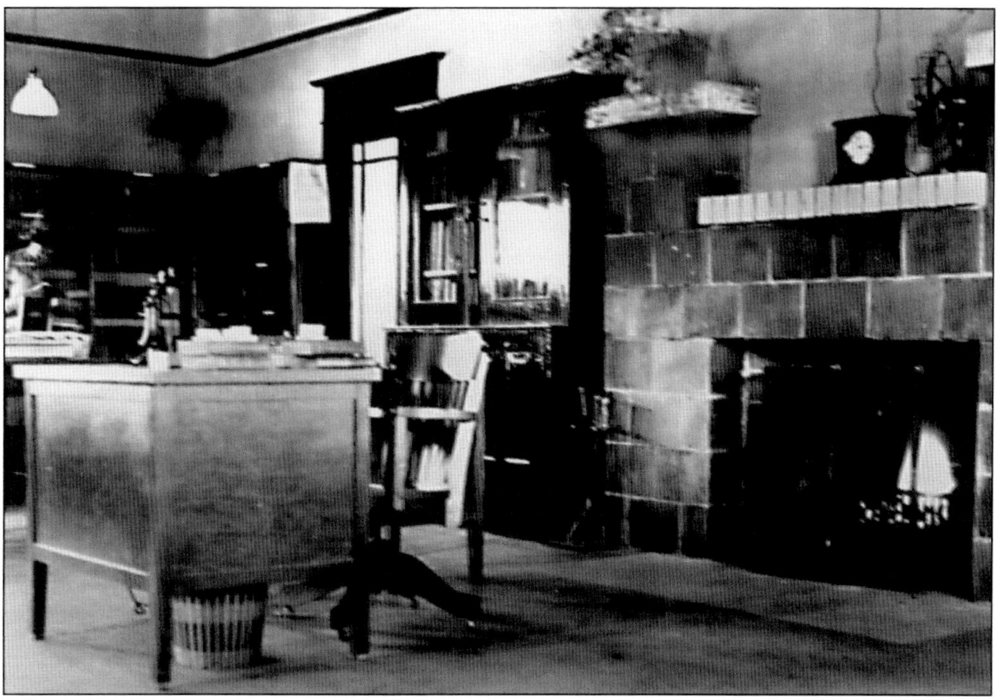

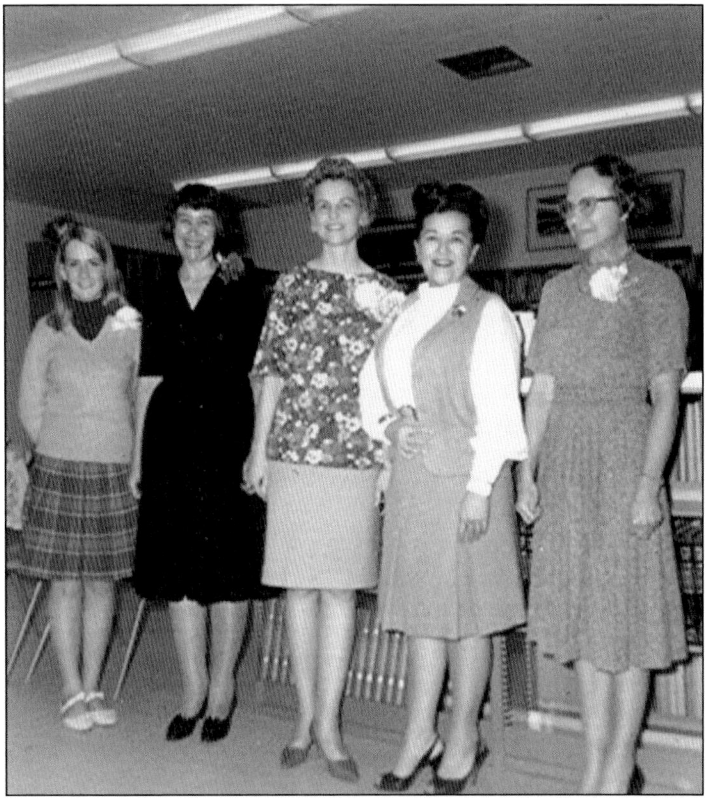

Caring librarians have helped to operate Fair Oaks' different libraries throughout the years, such as the five pictured at the library facilities off Bridge Street in the early 1970s. In 1976, Fair Oaks celebrated the opening of its new location and library, the Fair Oaks/ Orangevale Community Library. (Courtesy Fair Oaks/Orangevale Community Library.)

The Sacramento County Board of Supervisors

and

The Staff of the Sacramento Public Library

Cordially Invite You and Your Family

to the

Dedication of the New Fair Oaks/Orangevale Community Library

2:00 PM, Thursday, March 10, 1977

11601 Fair Oaks Boulevard, Fair Oaks, California 95628

Refreshments Will Be Served

Seven

The Soul of Fair Oaks

Yes, I love the Church; I love her sacred walls. How could I do otherwise?
—Martin Luther King Jr.

The importance of churches in the history of America is evident from the thousands of places of worship scattered across the American landscape today. Throughout American history churches have served local communities as houses of worship and local community centers. Citizens gathered to mingle and gossip. They also, however, gathered to exchange information about individuals, local events, and news from the state and nation. Churches served as places for the dissemination of democratic and rural values and as centers of community building.

Fair Oaks citizens could choose from numerous Christian denominations, including Methodist, Presbyterian, and Roman Catholic. According to John Holst and Stephen E. Kieffer in *Fair Oaks and San Juan Area Memories*, before churches were built in Fair Oaks, ministers from surrounding communities volunteered to come to Fair Oaks and preach. One such preacher, Rev. Fred Sheldon, helped to organize and construct Fair Oaks' first church, a Methodist one, in 1897. The Presbyterian church dates its roots in Fair Oaks to at least 1903 and, according to Al Fowler and Immer O. Rice in *Fair Oaks and San Juan Area Memories*, a Presbyterian church building appeared by 1907. In 1919, the two congregations of the Methodists and Presbyterians formed the Federated Church of Fair Oaks. They met and worshipped for over 30 years until the Presbyterian congregation split off to form a separate church in 1952. Eventually ground broke on November 22, 1953, at the current site of the church on Fair Oaks Boulevard. The Methodist congregation relocated to a building on Fair Oaks Boulevard near Pennsylvania Avenue.

On July 10, 1921, plans for Fair Oaks' first Catholic church were made as Auxiliary Bishop P. J. Keane dedicated a mission cross on a one-acre plot of land where Bridge Street and Grand Avenue intersect just north of the Old Fair Oaks Bridge. Thomas Kelly and John Barrett graded the land for the proposed mission church, which became St. Mel's Catholic Church, and on November 13, 1921, in one day, a small and modest chapel rose to serve the community of Fair Oaks. In 1923, improvements and additions were made. The little chapel on Bridge Street held its sanctuary doors open for nearly 40 years until Fr. William Horgan, the "building pastor," located a four-acre parcel on the southwest corner of Pennsylvania and Sunset Avenues in 1957. The new church celebrated its first Mass in May 1961 and, in 1963, the little chapel on Bridge Street was sold to a private party. It is used as a private residence today.

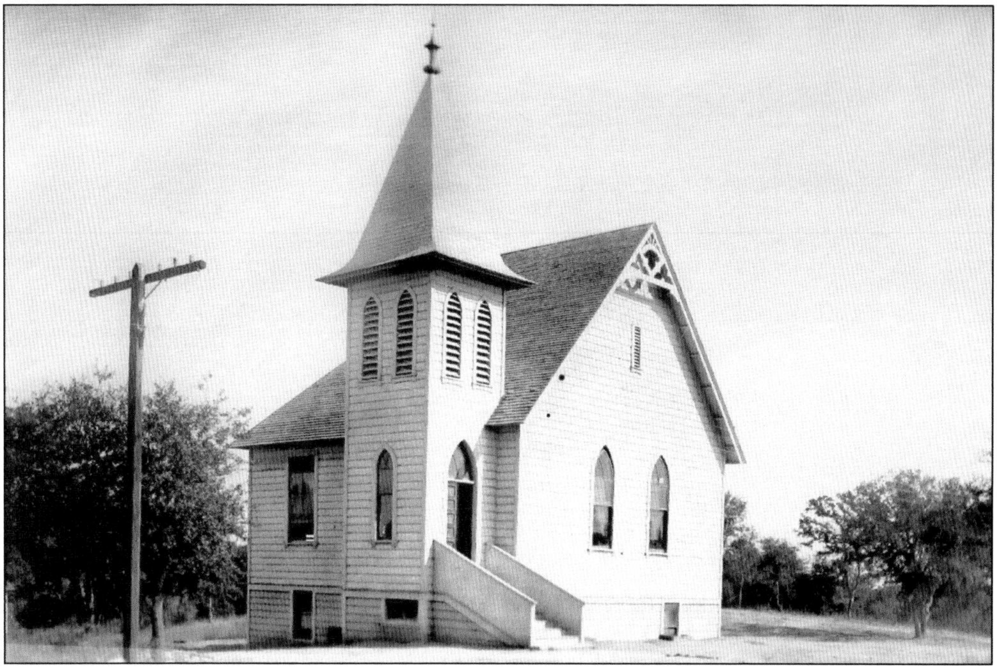

The Fair Oaks Methodist Church, Fair Oaks' first church, opened its sanctuary doors in 1897 on Watkins and Sacramento Street. (Courtesy Fair Oaks Presbyterian Church.)

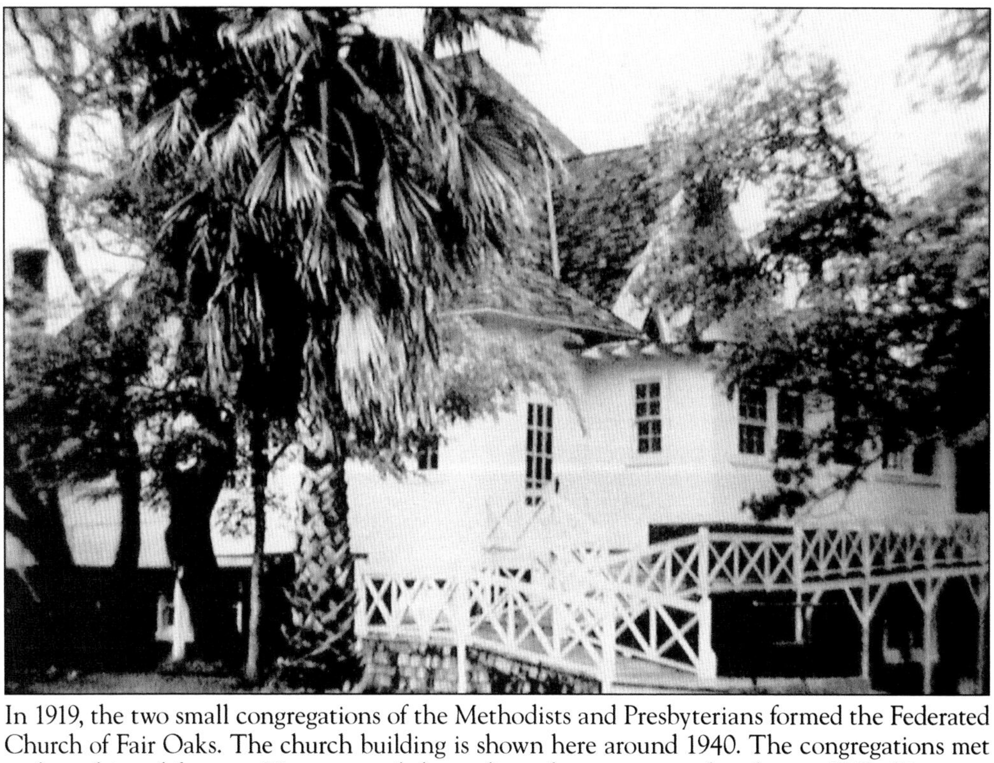

In 1919, the two small congregations of the Methodists and Presbyterians formed the Federated Church of Fair Oaks. The church building is shown here around 1940. The congregations met and worshipped for over 30 years until they split to form separate churches in 1952. (Courtesy Fair Oaks Presbyterian Church.)

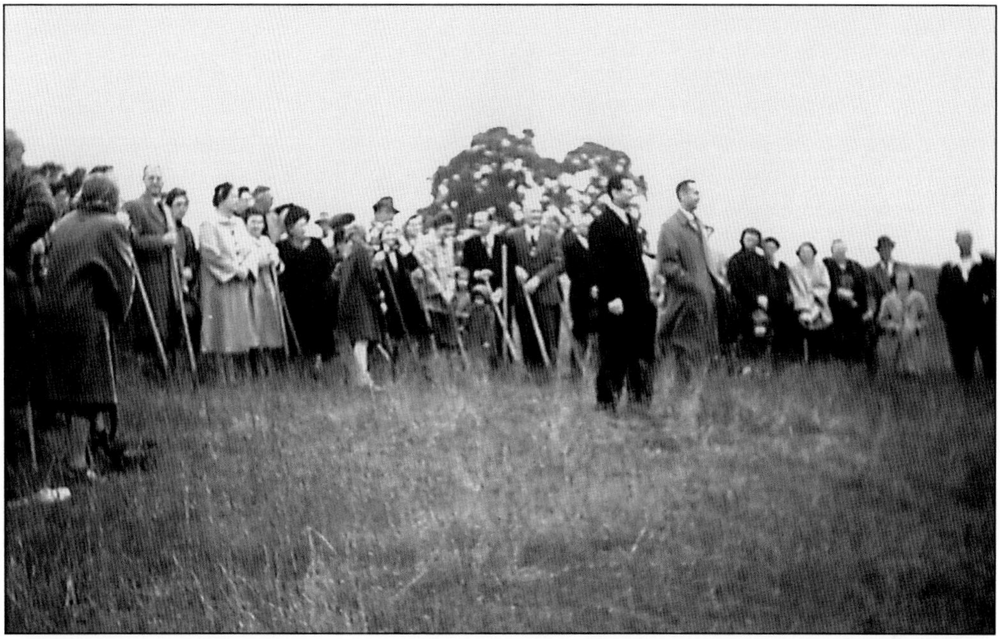

In 1953, the groundbreaking for the new Presbyterian church took place on its current site on Fair Oaks Boulevard near the Fair Oaks Park. (Courtesy Fair Oaks Presbyterian Church.)

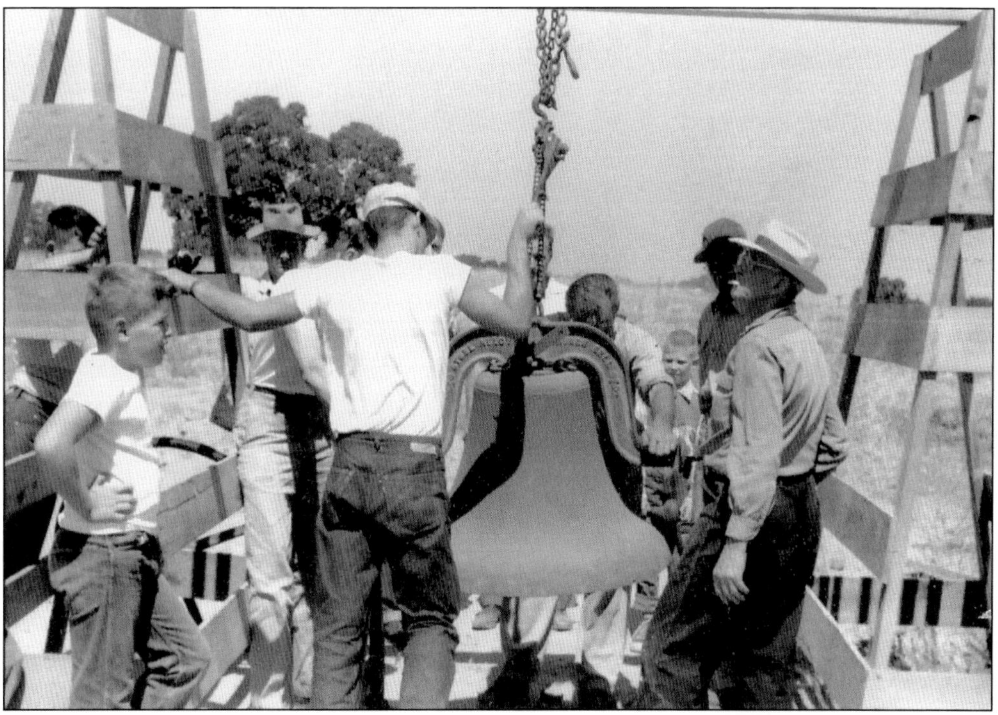

In 1954, the Presbyterian church moved the old bell that had been on the Methodist church to the new site. It still sits atop the sanctuary. (Courtesy Fair Oaks Presbyterian Church.)

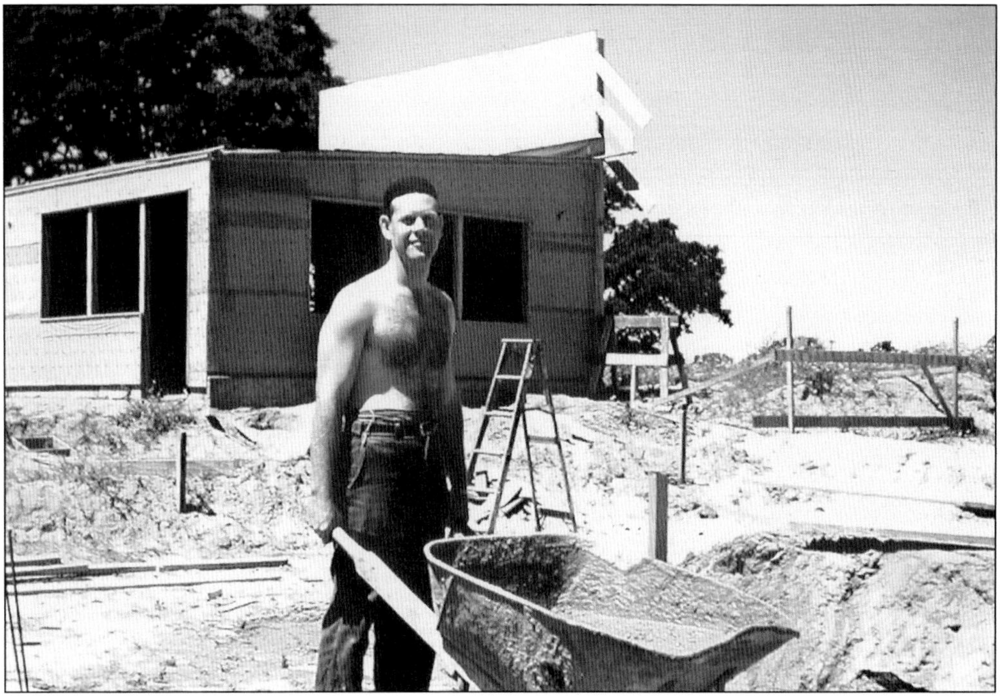

Jim Broadley, grandson of original pioneer Joseph Broadley, who helped to build the Federated Church of Fair Oaks, is seen here in July 1954 working on the construction of the new Presbyterian church. He had helped to tear down the old one his grandfather had built. Below, in January 1954, construction of the new sanctuary building began. (Courtesy Fair Oaks Presbyterian Church.)

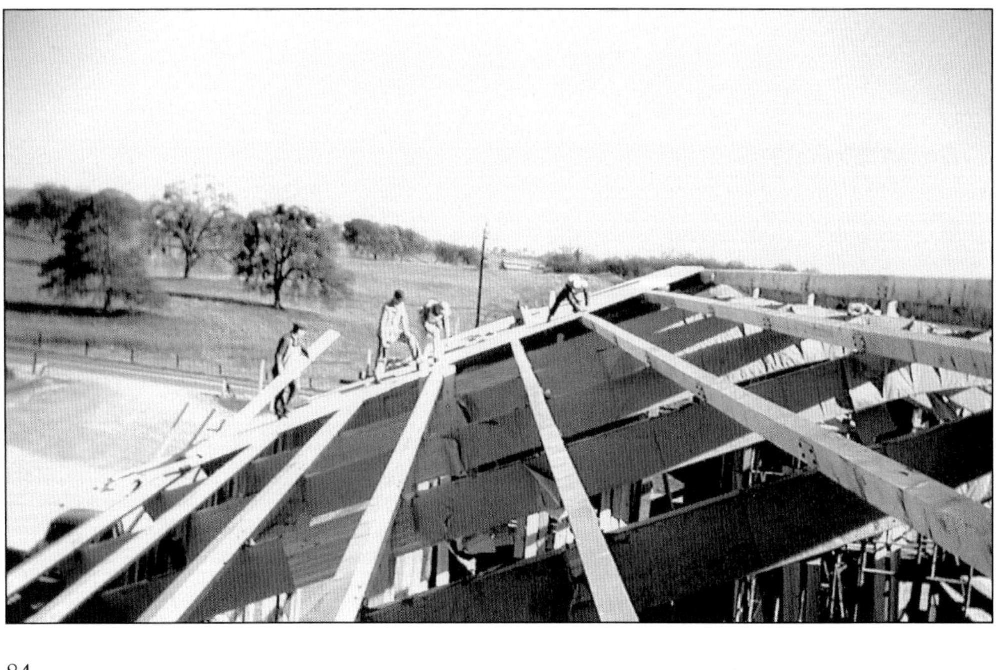

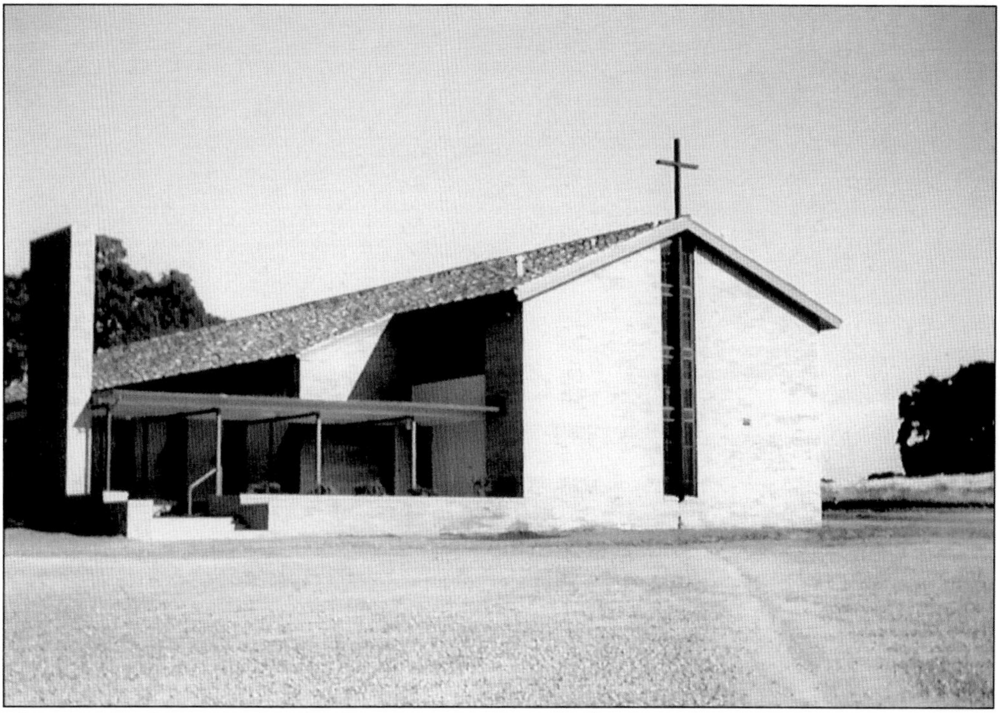

The new Presbyterian church, shown in August 1958, has continued to serve the Fair Oaks faithful for 50 years. (Courtesy Fair Oaks Presbyterian Church.)

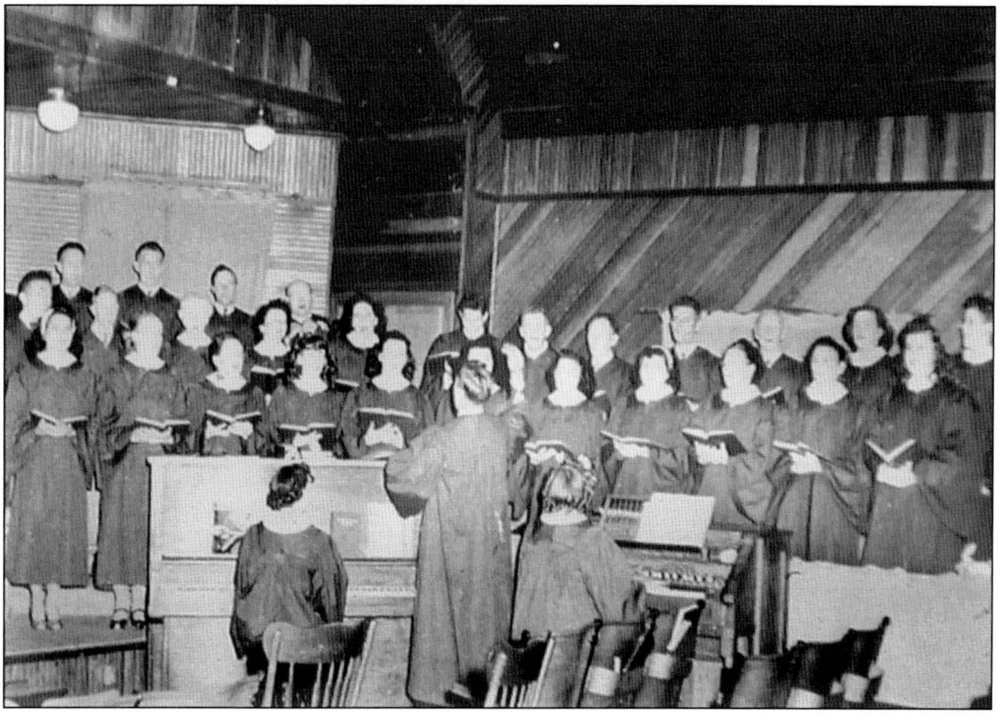

Church choirs, such as the Federated Church choir in 1946, have blessed the community with their songs. (Courtesy Fair Oaks Presbyterian Church.)

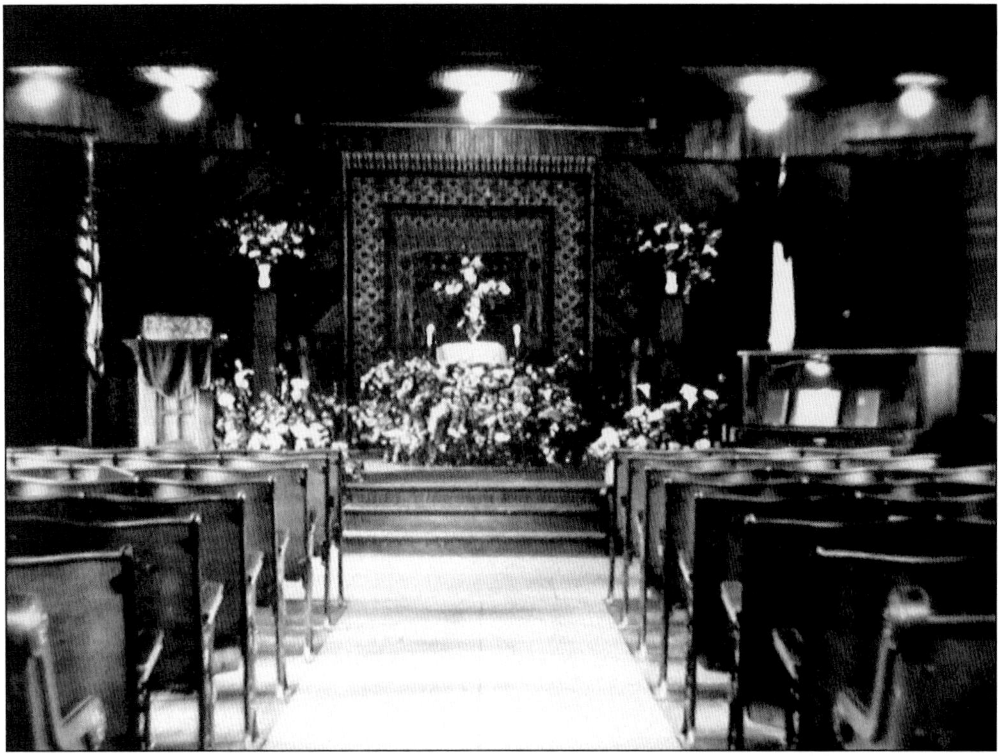

These interior views of the Federated Church of Fair Oaks (above, *c.* 1940) and St. Mel's Catholic Church on Bridge Street (below, *c.* 1950) show the beautiful altars where pastors were able to share their comforting message with Fair Oaks' devout churchgoers and where many of Fair Oaks' residents were married. (Above courtesy Fair Oaks Presbyterian Church; below courtesy St. Mel's Catholic Church.)

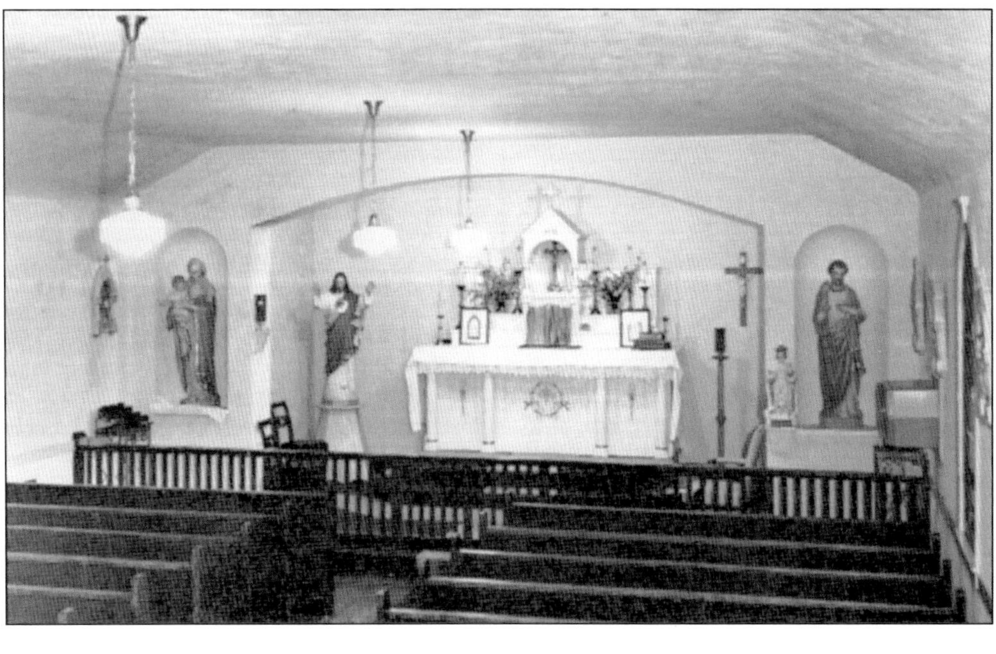

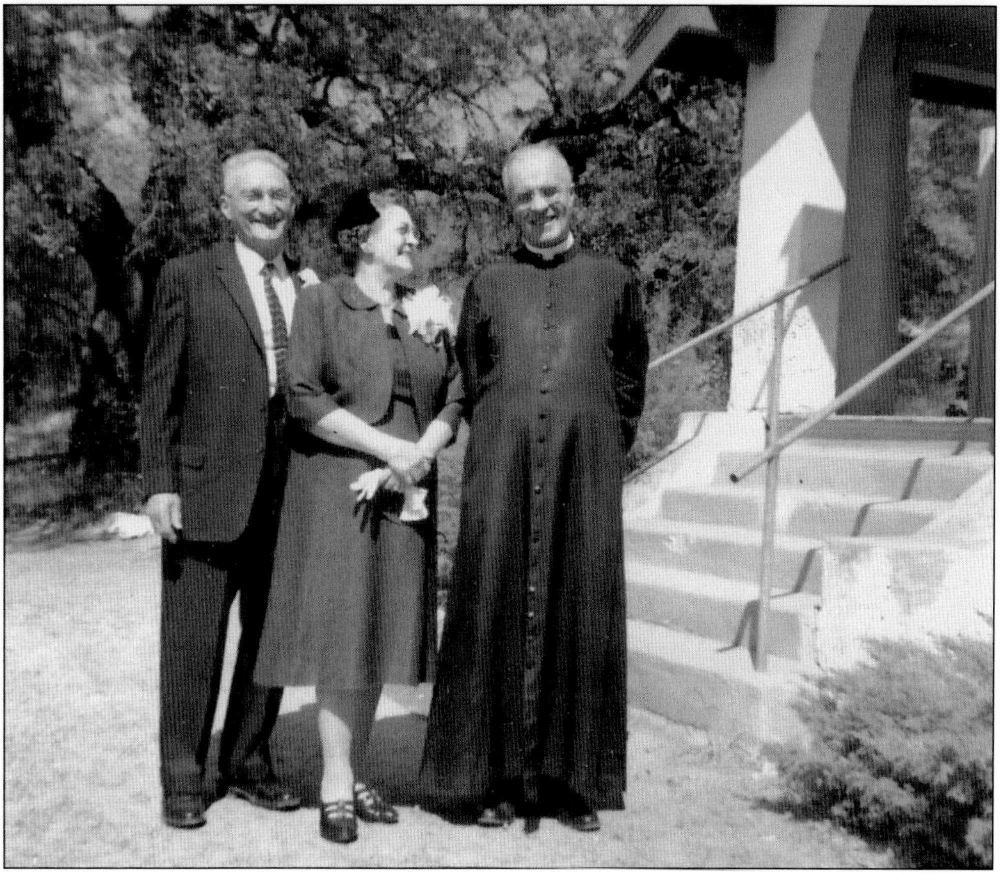

Fr. William Horgan posed with parishioners in front of St. Mel's Catholic Church on Bridge Street in the late 1950s, just before the congregation moved to a new site on Pennsylvania Avenue. (Courtesy St. Mel's Catholic Church.)

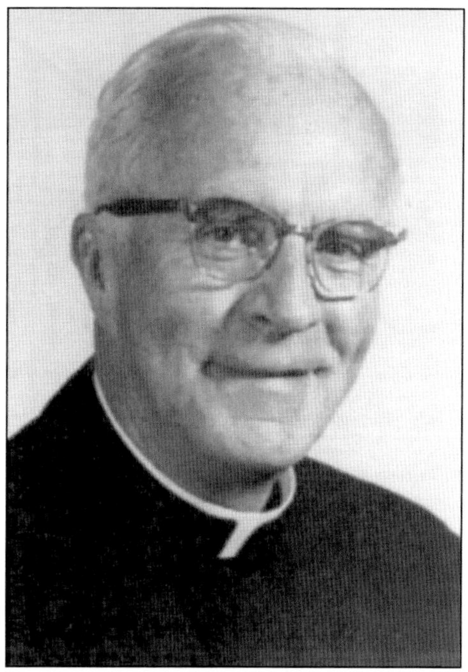

Father Horgan, known as the "building pastor" for moving the church from Bridge Street to Pennsylvania Avenue in the 1960s, served St. Mel's for nearly 20 years from 1956 to 1974. (Courtesy St. Mel's Catholic Church.)

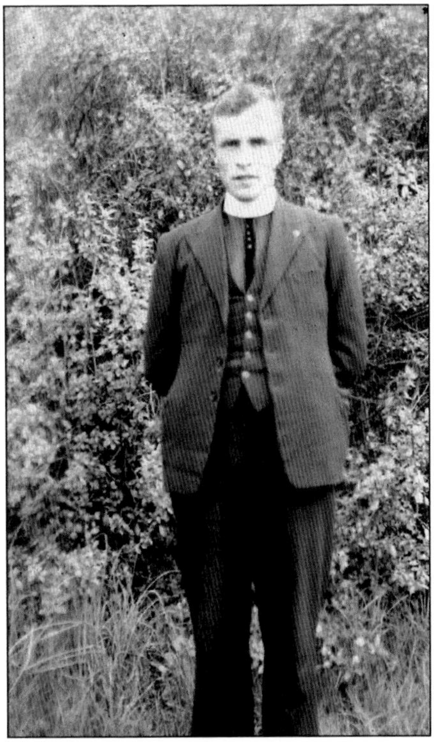

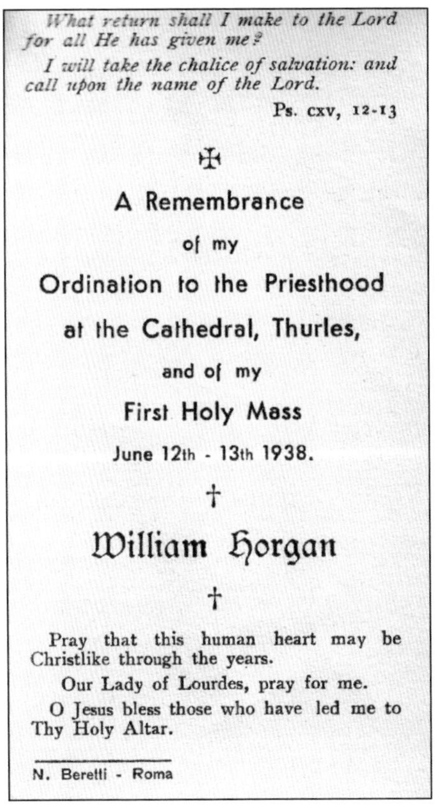

What return shall I make to the Lord for all He has given me?

I will take the chalice of salvation: and call upon the name of the Lord.

Ps. cxv, 12-13

✠

A Remembrance

of my

Ordination to the Priesthood

at the Cathedral, Thurles,

and of my

First Holy Mass

June 12th - 13th 1938.

†

William Horgan

†

Pray that this human heart may be Christlike through the years.

Our Lady of Lourdes, pray for me.

O Jesus bless those who have led me to Thy Holy Altar.

N. Beretti - Roma

On June 12, 1938, Fr. William Horgan was ordained in Ireland. Below is the invitation to his ordination ceremony, June 12–13, 1938. On October 9, 1938, Father Horgan arrived in America. After serving in various positions in Woodland, Grass Valley, Placerville, and Galt, he came to Fair Oaks on April 16, 1956, serving for nearly 20 years until his retirement in 1974. In 1985, Father Horgan finally returned to Ireland. (Courtesy St. Mel's Catholic Church.)

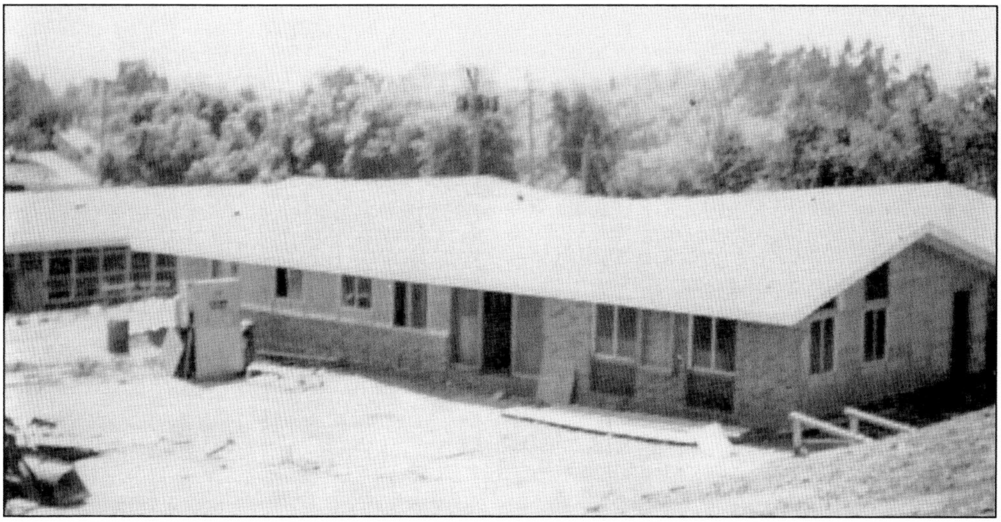

The new convent for the St. Mel's Catholic Church is seen here on Pennsylvania Avenue in 1959. (Courtesy St. Mel's Catholic Church.)

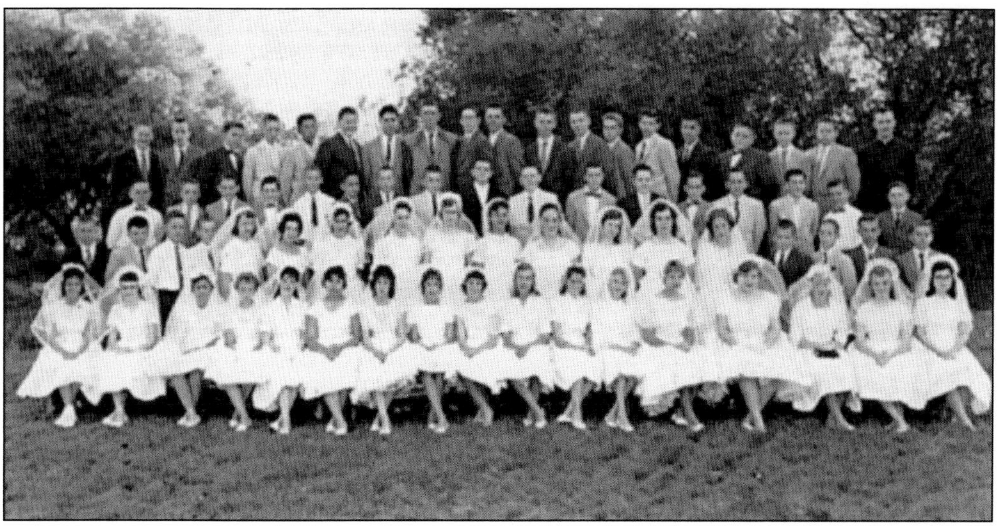

The St. Mel's Catholic Church confirmation class of the Confraternity of Christian Doctrine posed for this May 1960 photograph. (Courtesy St. Mel's Catholic Church.)

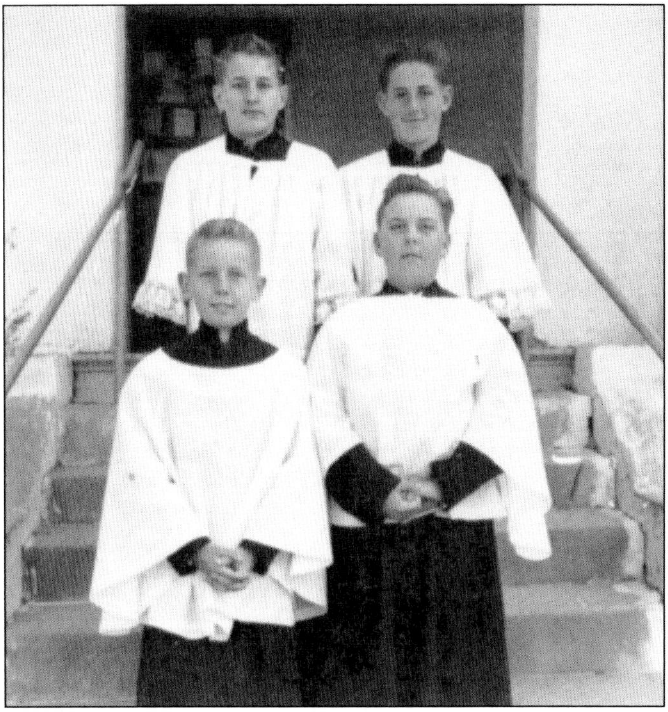

In the early 1950s, some altar boys for Fr. Patrick J. Cronin (pastor from 1948 to 1956) posed on the steps of the Bridge Street church. (Courtesy St. Mel's Catholic Church.)

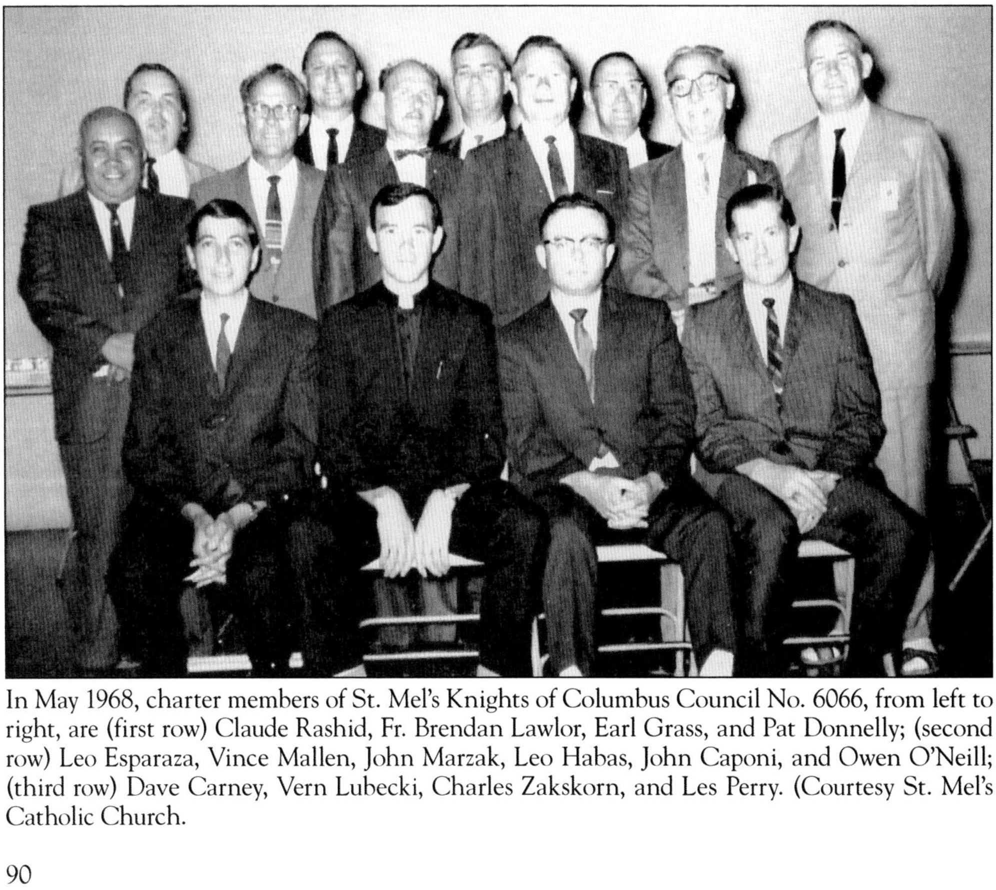

In May 1968, charter members of St. Mel's Knights of Columbus Council No. 6066, from left to right, are (first row) Claude Rashid, Fr. Brendan Lawlor, Earl Grass, and Pat Donnelly; (second row) Leo Esparaza, Vince Mallen, John Marzak, Leo Habas, John Caponi, and Owen O'Neill; (third row) Dave Carney, Vern Lubecki, Charles Zakskorn, and Les Perry. (Courtesy St. Mel's Catholic Church.

Eight

CLUB LIFE

It is noticeable that wherever there is a woman's clubhouse there is public spirit, yes, and social life and enterprise and flourishing public schools and libraries and other things that go to improve a community. The woman's clubhouse stands for progress wherever it is to be found.
—*The Club Woman*, 1902

Human beings are social creatures and clubs have emerged in a multiplicity of forms to serve social needs. Political clubs, woman's clubs, improvement clubs, and a score of others help to unite, in some manner, people of various backgrounds in some sort of common purpose. The history of clubs in Fair Oaks is as rich as the history of any of its leading institutions or organizations and mirrors the club life that sprang up across the country throughout the late-19th and early 20th centuries.

In 1902, The Woman's Thursday Club of Fair Oaks organized for the purpose of "social intercourse and intellectual betterment of its members." The first clubhouse, built in 1913, served to accommodate the club's activities for over 40 years until they moved in 1955 to their present location on Fair Oaks Boulevard. The Woman's Thursday Club enthusiastically participated in a variety of activities to benefit the community, such as donations to child welfare services, mental health services, and schools. The club helped to plant trees, sponsor scholarships, and even helped to entertain and provide for troops in cooperation with the USO during World War II. Indeed, the list of actions for the betterment of all of Fair Oaks society and the surrounding Sacramento community is an impressive and overwhelming tribute to the care, support, and devotion of the club's members.

Not to be outdone by the women, on November 23, 1912, Harold Dewey, Charles Heidt, Florence Ricketts, and Charles Peck were elected officers for the newly established San Juan Social and Improvement Club. According to the club's constitution, the group formed for "the promotion of social functions and good times." For three and half years, the club sponsored picnics, masquerade parties, and trips to the river. Club members represented the most prominent names and well-known citizens of Fair Oaks' remarkable history: Adams, Dewey, Dickson, Green, Gregory, Hinsey, O'Donnell, and Ricketts to name a few. As the United States prepared to join the fight to "end all wars" in World War I, the club recorded its last official meeting on May 13, 1916. When the club held a reunion in the summer of 1948, the *San Juan Record* recorded that over 100 of the most "highly exclusive; only genuine old-timers, and the sons and daughters of old-timers, were invited."

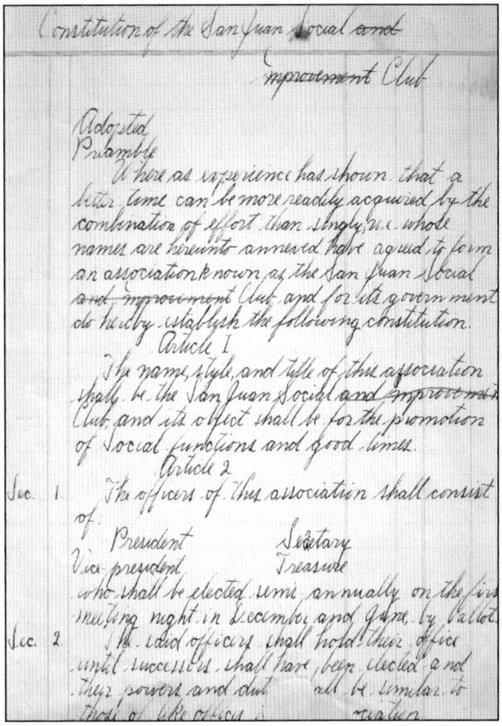

Constitution of the San Juan Social and
Improvement Club

Adopted
Preamble
Whereas experience has shown that a better time can be more readily acquired by the combination of effort than singly, we whose names are hereunto annexed have agreed to form an association known as the San Juan Social and Improvement Club and for its government do hereby establish the following constitution.

Article I
The name, style, and title of this association shall be the San Juan Social and Improvement Club, and its object shall be for the promotion of Social functions and good times.

Article 2
Sec. 1 The officers of this association shall consist of:
President Secretary
Vice-president Treasurer
who shall be elected semi annually on the first meeting night in December and June, by ballot.
Sec. 2 The said officers shall hold their office until successors shall have been elected and their powers and dut[illegible] all be similar to those of like offices [illegible] nature

On November 23, 1912, members of the San Juan Social and Improvement Club in Fair Oaks met for the first time and drafted a constitution. The constitution preamble read: "Whereas experience has shown that a better time can be more readily acquired by the combination of effort than singly, we whose names are hereunto annexed have agreed to form an association known as the San Juan Social and Improvement Club, and for its government do hereby establish the following constitution." (Courtesy Eileen Dewey Thomas.)

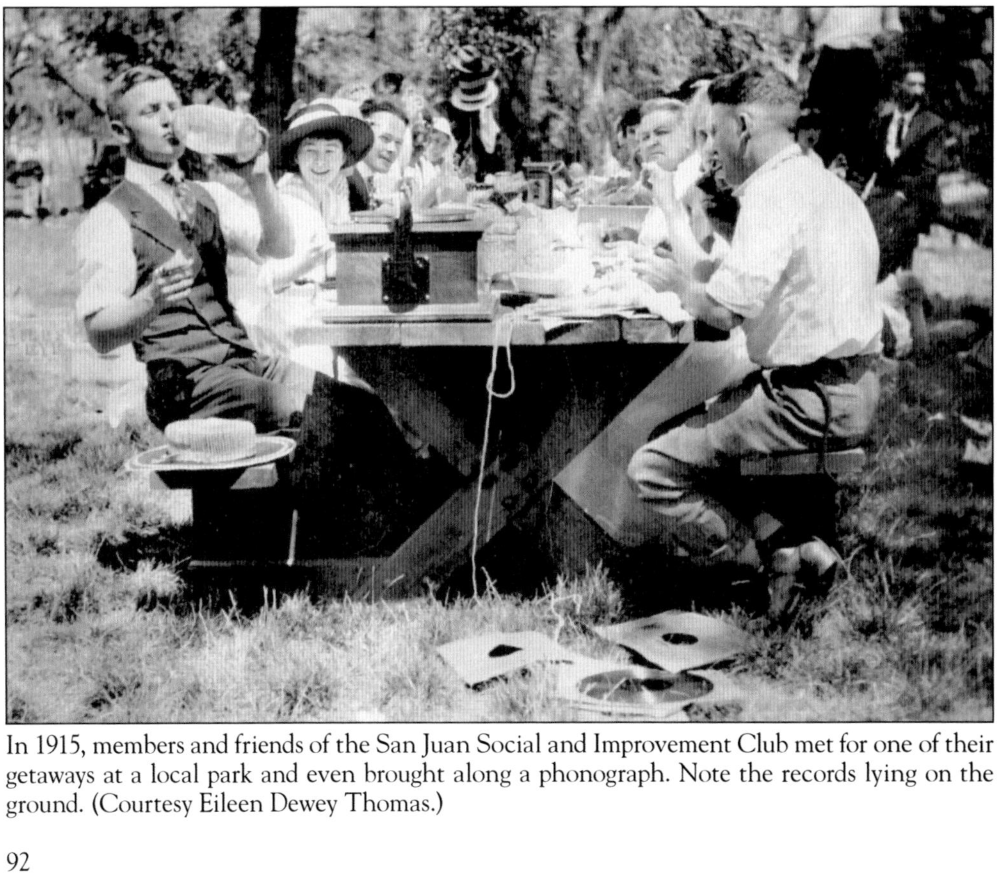

In 1915, members and friends of the San Juan Social and Improvement Club met for one of their getaways at a local park and even brought along a phonograph. Note the records lying on the ground. (Courtesy Eileen Dewey Thomas.)

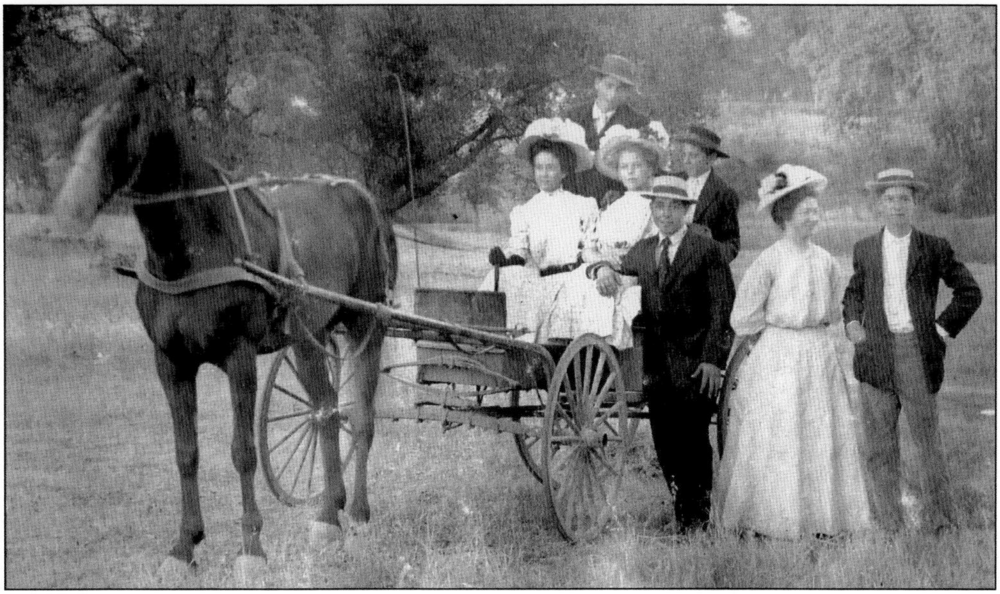

Around 1914, members of the San Juan Social and Improvement Club are dressed up as they head out for another event. Below, members of the San Juan Social and Improvement Club relax during a picnic. (Courtesy Eileen Dewey Thomas.)

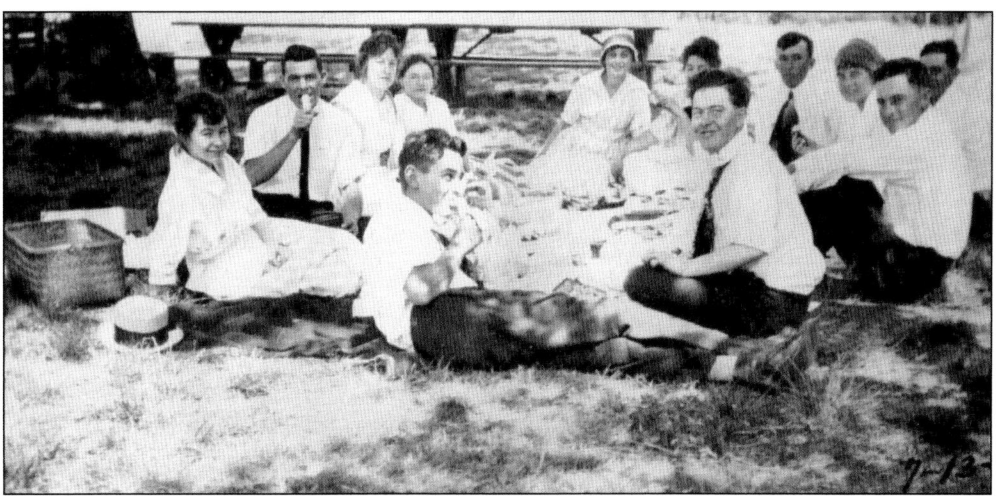

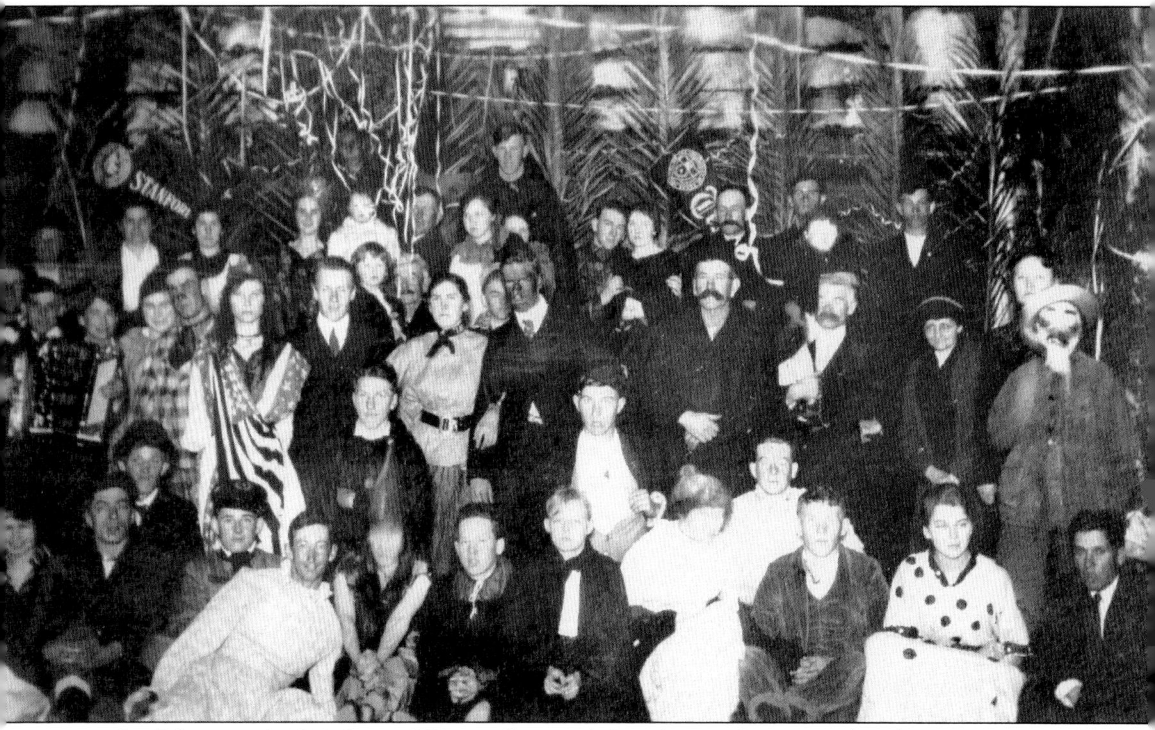

On February 19, 1913, James O'Donnell moved that the San Juan Social and Improvement Club host a masquerade party. The masquerade, held on March 29, 1913, included not only members from the San Juan club, but also other community members and surrounding area organizations, such as a social club from Carmichael. Among the many faces, Alta Dewey is seen in the first row, third from the right. (Courtesy Eileen Dewey Thomas.)

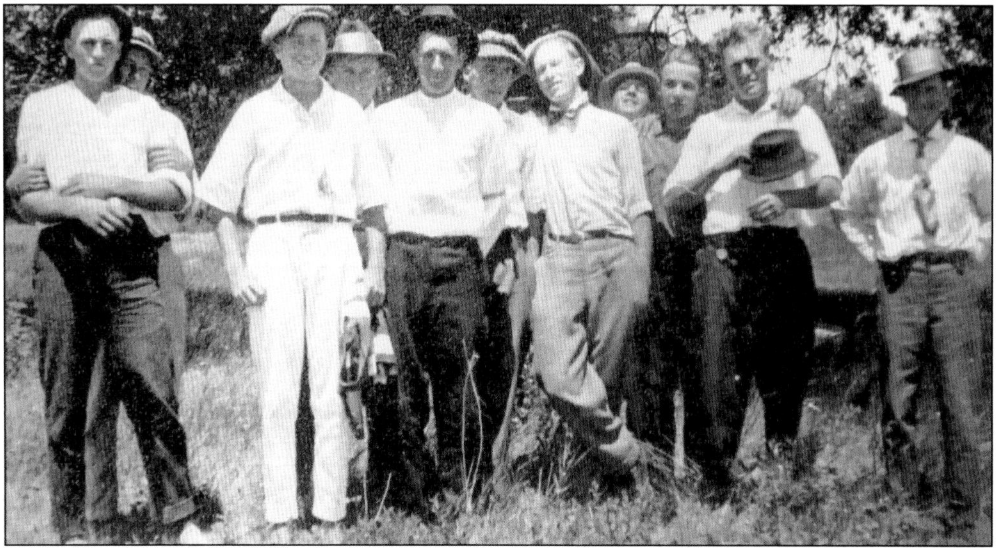

Gentlemen from the San Juan Social and Improvement Club took time out from one of their events to pose for a group picture, *c.* 1914. (Courtesy Eileen Dewey Thomas.)

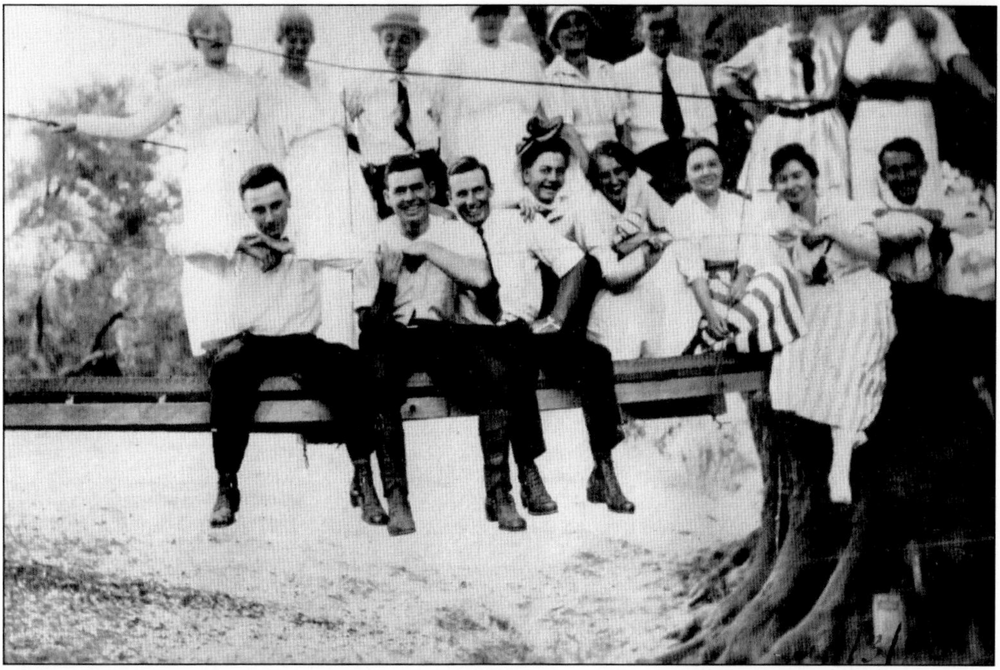

Members of the San Juan Social and Improvement Club met for one of the last times on September 13, 1916, and posed for this photograph on a bridge. (Courtesy Eileen Dewey Thomas.)

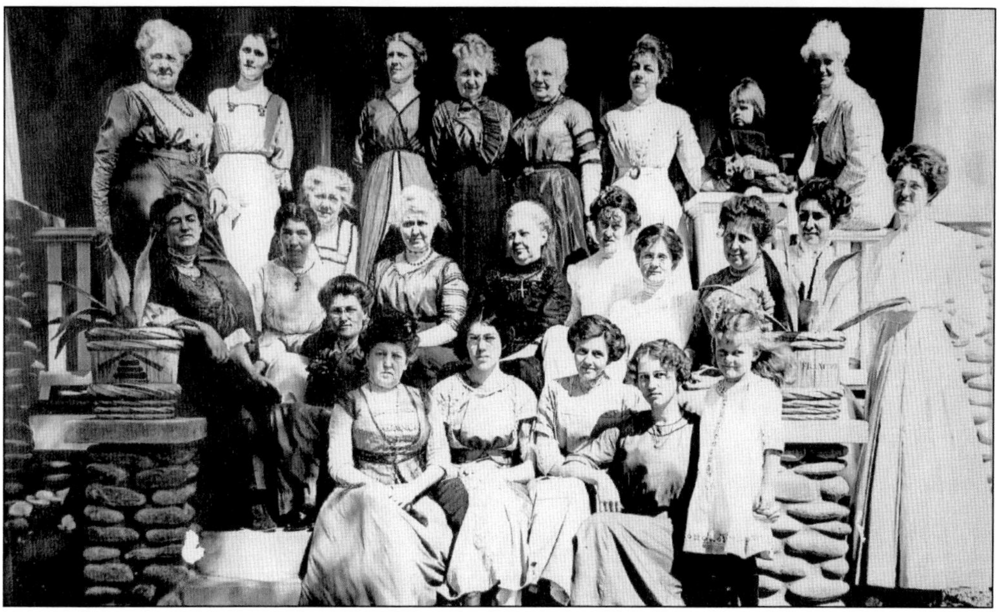

Pictured here in 1912, The Woman's Thursday Club of Fair Oaks, from left to right, are (first row) Bertha Sprague, Mrs. J. H. Buffum, Hortense Gore Slocum, Mrs. Haven Sargent, Gladys Wrangham, and Lorraine Wilson (Dupen); (second row) Madam Buffum, Mrs. Wrangham, Cherry Sargent, Agnes Hodge, Mrs. Caulfield, Mrs. C. E. Wilson, Mrs. C. W. Ruggles, Mrs. Beach, Mrs. Harvey, Mrs. W. Ralph Gore, Mrs. Watson, Mrs. Woods, Mrs. Jas White, Mrs. Harry Studarus, Ida Hodgo, Roberta Ruggles, and Clara Burkar Buffum. (Courtesy The Woman's Thursday Club of Fair Oaks.)

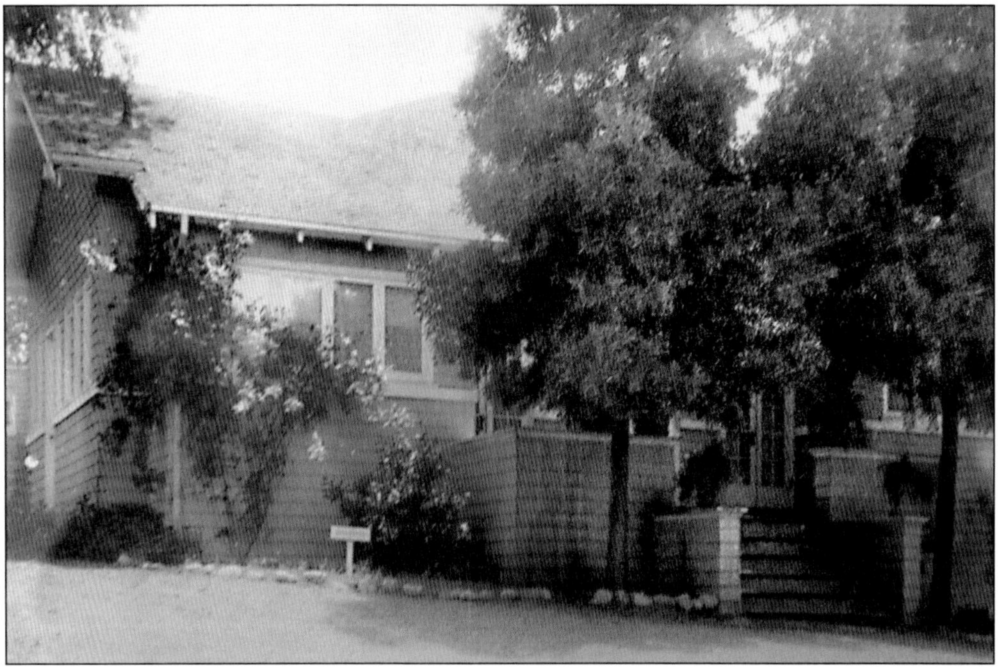

When The Woman's Thursday Club of Fair Oaks first organized, they met in the homes of their many members. The first clubhouse (above, 1930s), on the corner of Fair Oaks and Sunrise Boulevards, was built in 1913 and served to accommodate the club's activities for over 40 years. The club moved in 1955 to their present location (below) on Fair Oaks Boulevard just before Watkins. (Courtesy The Woman's Thursday Club of Fair Oaks.)

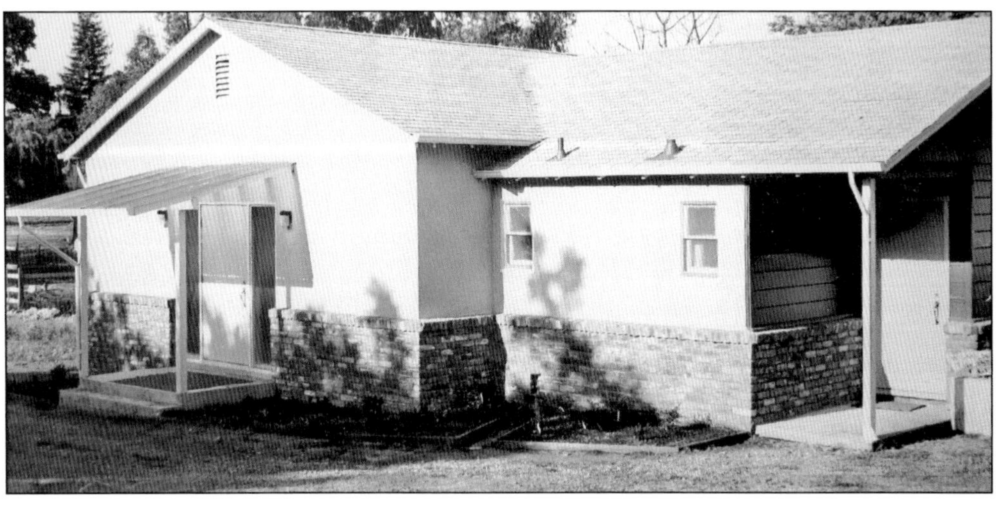

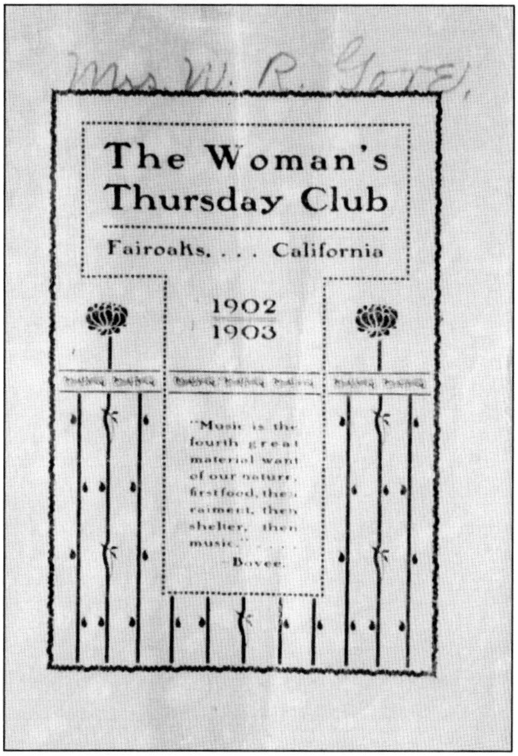

In 1902, The Woman's Thursday Club of Fair Oaks produced their first brochure and program guide, complete with their newly drafted constitution. The brochure was owned by Mrs. W. Ralph Gore, whose husband ran a small grocery store with Charles H. Slocum. Throughout the club's history, they sponsored a variety of programs, such as the ones seen inside Mrs. Gore's brochure. (Courtesy The Woman's Thursday Club of Fair Oaks.)

PROGRAM

O music, sphere descended maid,
Friend of pleasure, wisdom's aid!
—*Collins.*

NOVEMBER 13, 1902.

Guest Evening.

There is a good time coming.
—*Scott.*

Music—Vocal Solos..............Mrs. William T. Murcell

DECEMBER 5, 1902.

George Friedrich Handel.

Music is the child of prayer, the companion of religion. —*Chateaubriand.*

Music—Vocal Selection from Messiah............ . ... Mrs. William T. Murcell

Reading—Sketch of Handel's Life.................. ....Mrs. LaFayette Cozzens

Music—Piano Solo, Dead March in Saul.......... ....Mrs. Anna B. Crafts

DECEMBER 19, 1902.

John Sebastian Bach.

By music minds an equal temper know,
Nor swell too high, nor sink too low.
—*Pope.*

Music—Selection from Bach............Miss Daisy Chase
Reading—Life of Bach...........Mrs. Charles Caulfield
Music—Selection from Bach...........Miss Daisy Chase

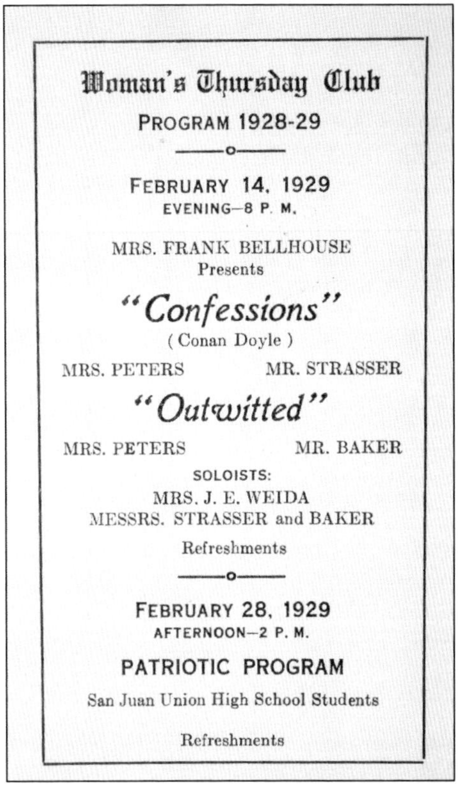
Woman's Thursday Club

PROGRAM 1928-29

FEBRUARY 14, 1929

EVENING—8 P. M.

MRS. FRANK BELLHOUSE
Presents

"Confessions"

(Conan Doyle)

MRS. PETERS MR. STRASSER

"Outwitted"

MRS. PETERS MR. BAKER

SOLOISTS:

MRS. J. E. WEIDA
MESSRS. STRASSER and BAKER

Refreshments

FEBRUARY 28, 1929

AFTERNOON—2 P. M.

PATRIOTIC PROGRAM

San Juan Union High School Students

Refreshments

This 1928–1929 program guide for The Woman's Thursday Club of Fair Oaks mirrors many of the club's brochures produced throughout its history and included such programs as a recital and a play. (Courtesy The Woman's Thursday Club of Fair Oaks.)

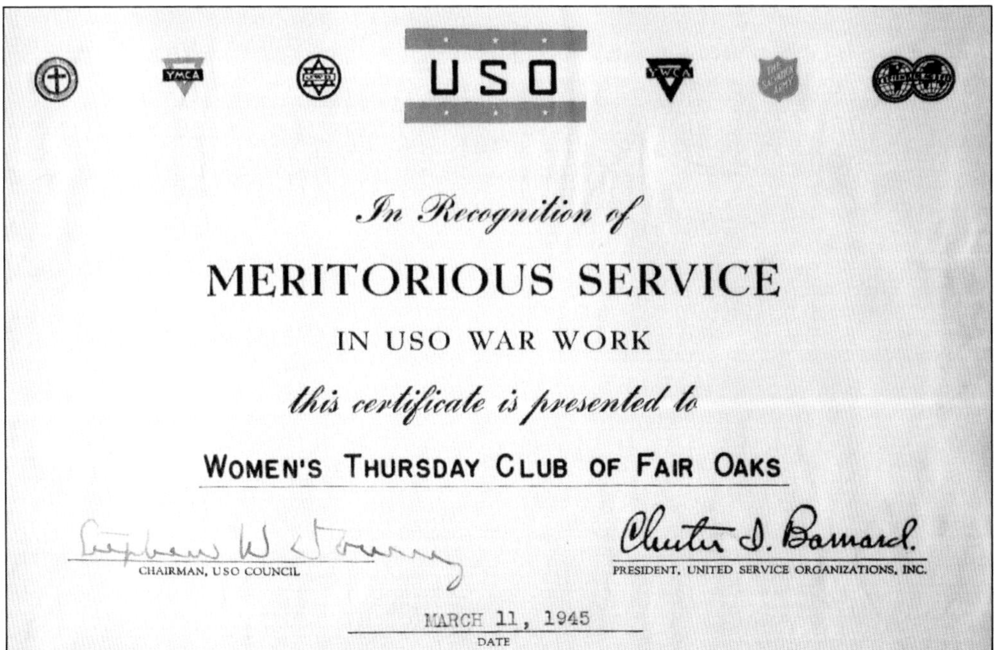
YMCA USO YWCA

In Recognition of

MERITORIOUS SERVICE

IN USO WAR WORK

this certificate is presented to

WOMEN'S THURSDAY CLUB OF FAIR OAKS

CHAIRMAN, USO COUNCIL

Chester I. Barnard
PRESIDENT, UNITED SERVICE ORGANIZATIONS, INC.

MARCH 11, 1945
DATE

In March 1945, The Woman's Thursday Club of Fair Oaks received a certificate from the Sacramento Council on United Service Organizations for the club's "meritorious service in USO war work" during World War II. (Courtesy The Woman's Thursday Club of Fair Oaks.)

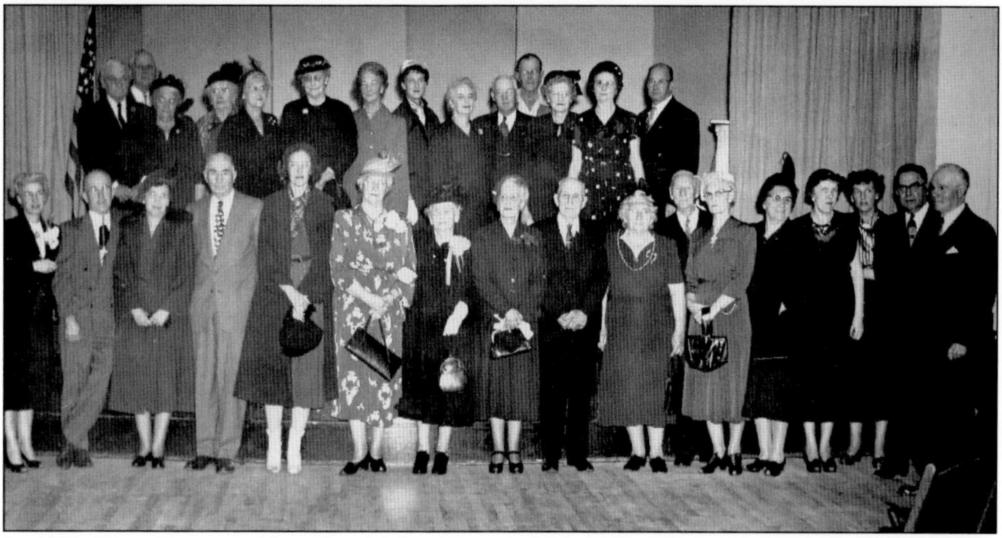

In 1952, The Woman's Thursday Club of Fair Oaks hosted a Pioneer Tea Party honoring the early pioneers and settlers of Fair Oaks. Pictured here, from left to right, are (first row) Iva Rice Langness, Arthur Broadley, Hazel Slocum Broadley, Arch McDonald, Elinor Bramhall, Mrs. K. N. Bramhall, Catherine Van Maren, Mae Van Maren Stock, John Holst, Lillian Shannon, Charles Woodmansee, Mabel Cunningham Collins, Ella Vaughan, Esther Kirschman, Vivian Archer, Judge Joseph Diestel, and Charles Deterding; (second row) William Gregory, DeWitt Rice, Mesdames Mae McDonald, E. W. Glafcke, Eva Gregory, Agnes Cunningham, Margaret Beach, Barbara Beach, Ethel Osgood Kerns, Bert Kerns, A. M. Fowler, Geneva Watson Smith, Abby Green, and Sim Green. (Courtesy The Woman's Thursday Club of Fair Oaks.)

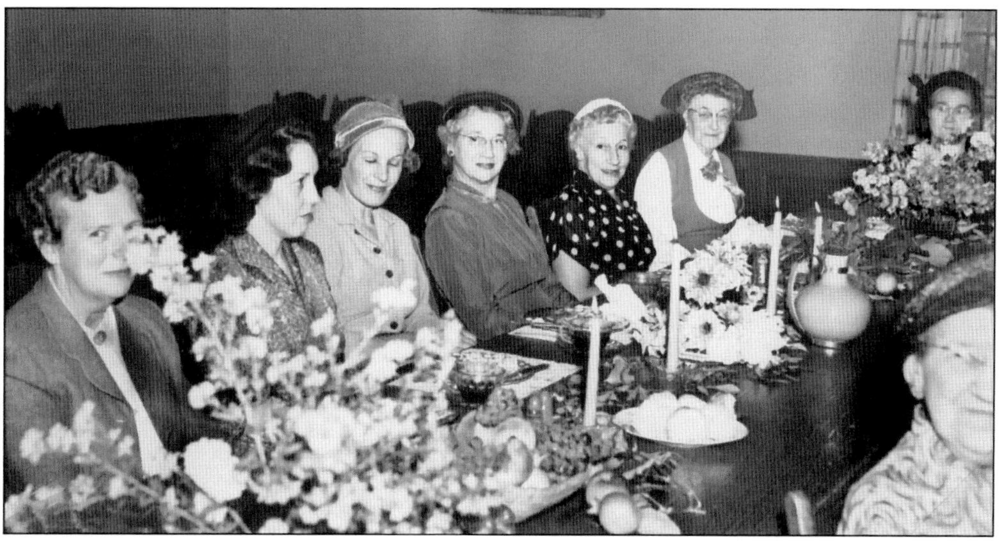

In October 1953, The Woman's Thursday Club of Fair Oaks hosted one of their many luncheons. According to the annual scrapbook, pictured, from left to right, are Mrs. Ralph Graham, Mrs. Frazier, Mrs. John Fryer, Mrs. Shoemaker, Annette Brown, Grace Hammond, Mrs. Brown, and Alice Miller. (Courtesy The Woman's Thursday Club of Fair Oaks.)

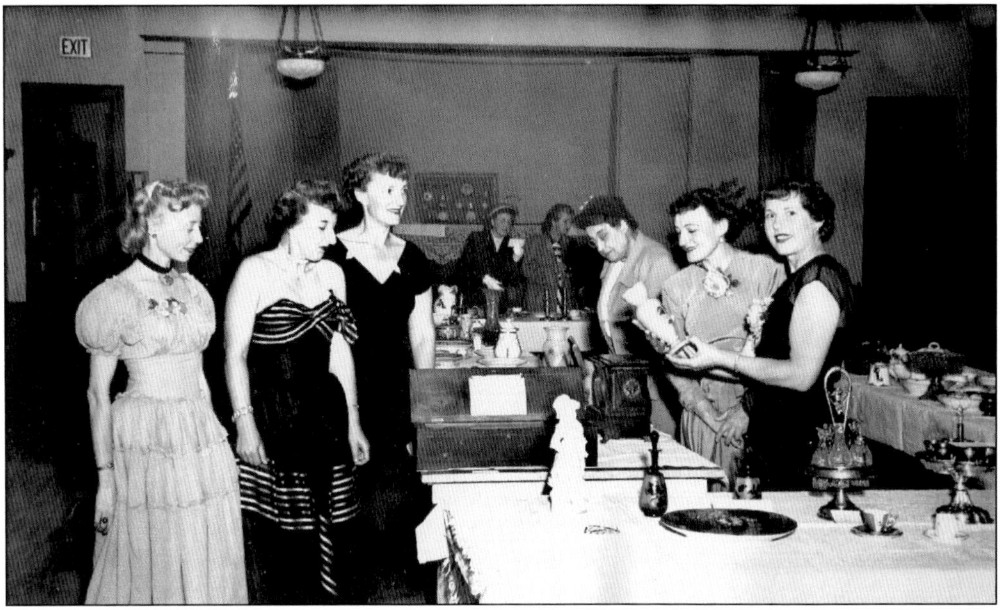

Among the many activities sponsored by The Woman's Thursday Club of Fair Oaks were antique shows (above, mid-1950s) and the Good Earth Garden Club (below, 1951). (Courtesy The Woman's Thursday Club of Fair Oaks.)

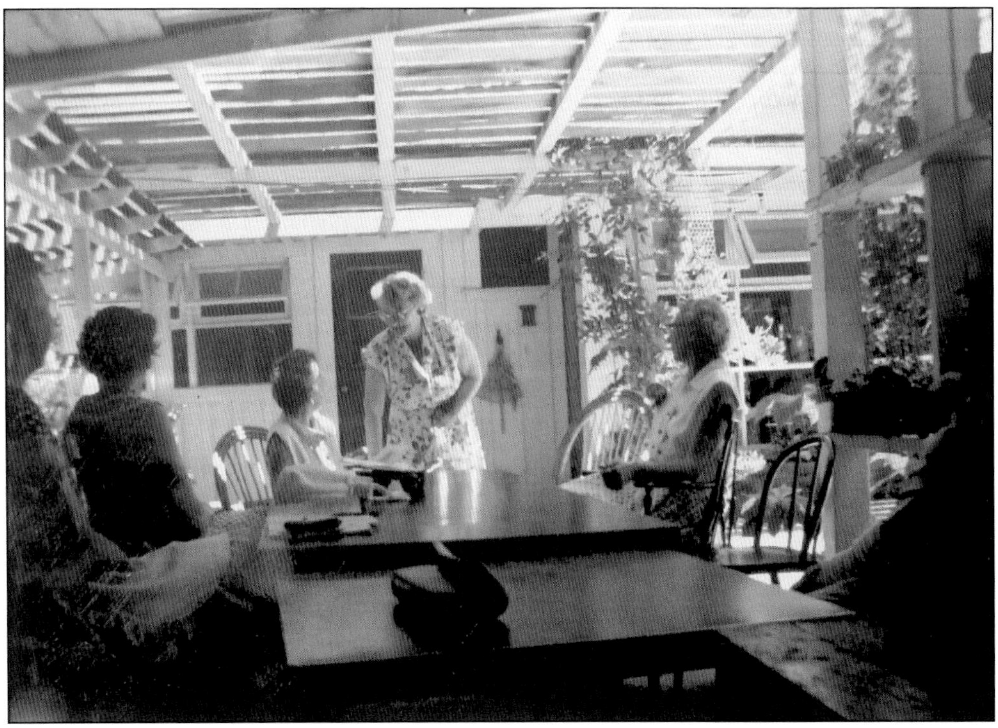

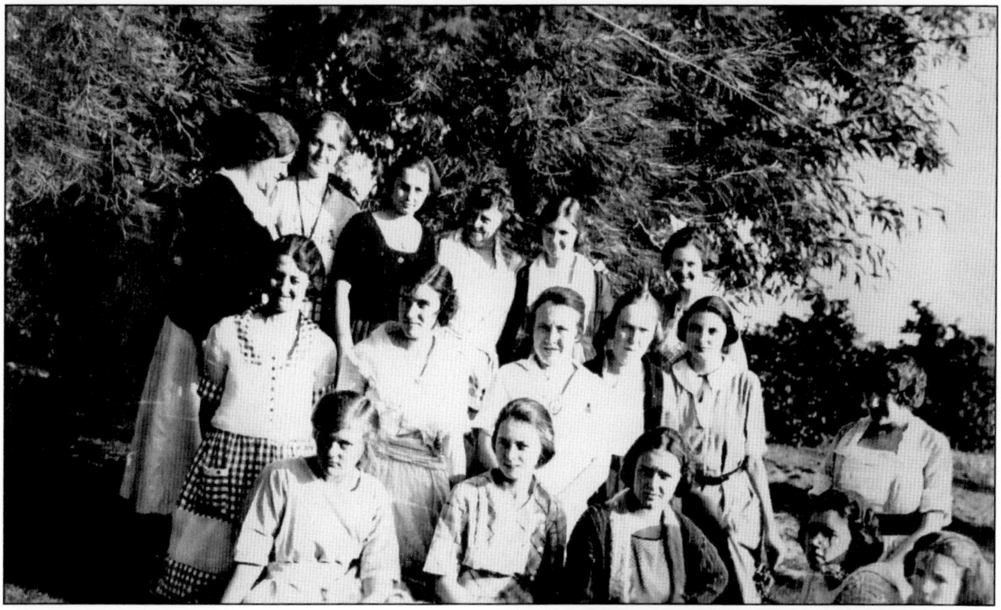

Among the prolific activities of The Woman's Thursday Club of Fair Oaks, the club also sponsored a Girl's Club. Both photographs show members of the Girl's Club as they enjoy one of their outings in the mid-1940s. (Courtesy The Woman's Thursday Club of Fair Oaks.)

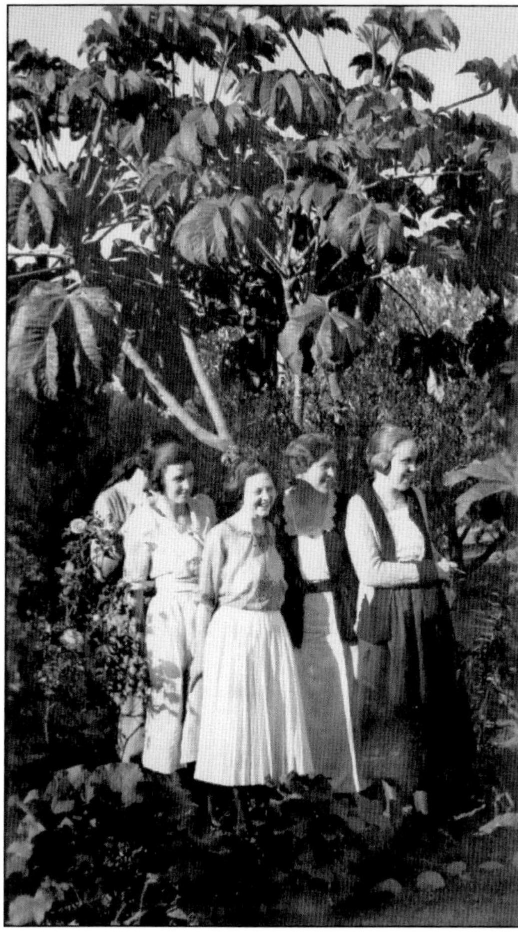

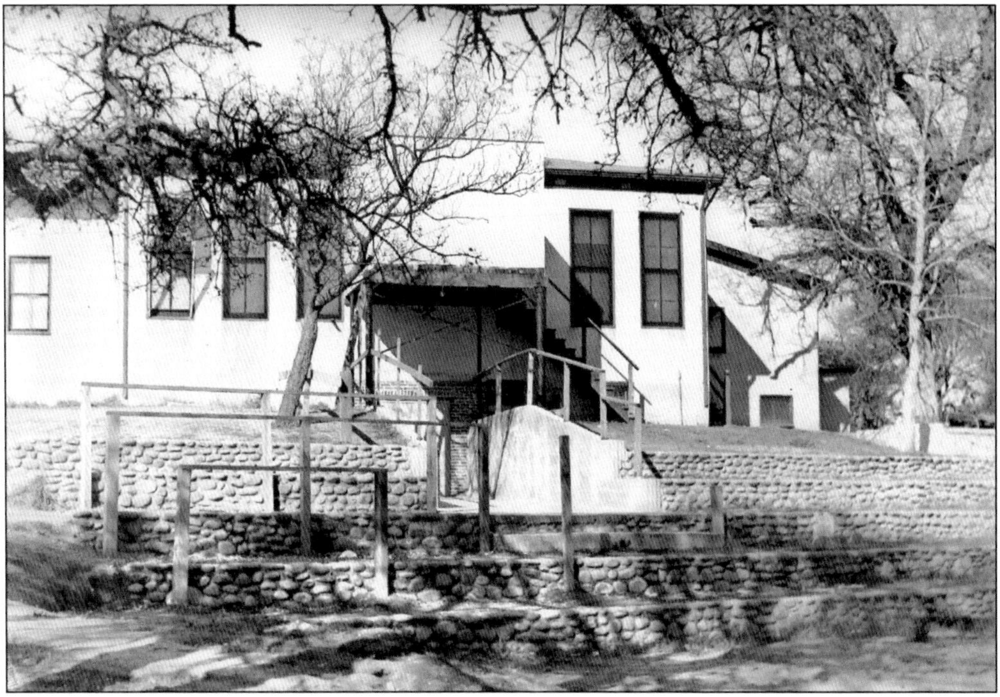

In 1947, the Fair Oaks Recreation and Park District, which formed in 1945, took over the Park Plaza and the Community Clubhouse. The clubhouse above, in March 1947, was immediately put to use to host many different activities, such as the Fair Oakie Art Faire in 1971, below. (Courtesy Fair Oaks Recreation and Park District.)

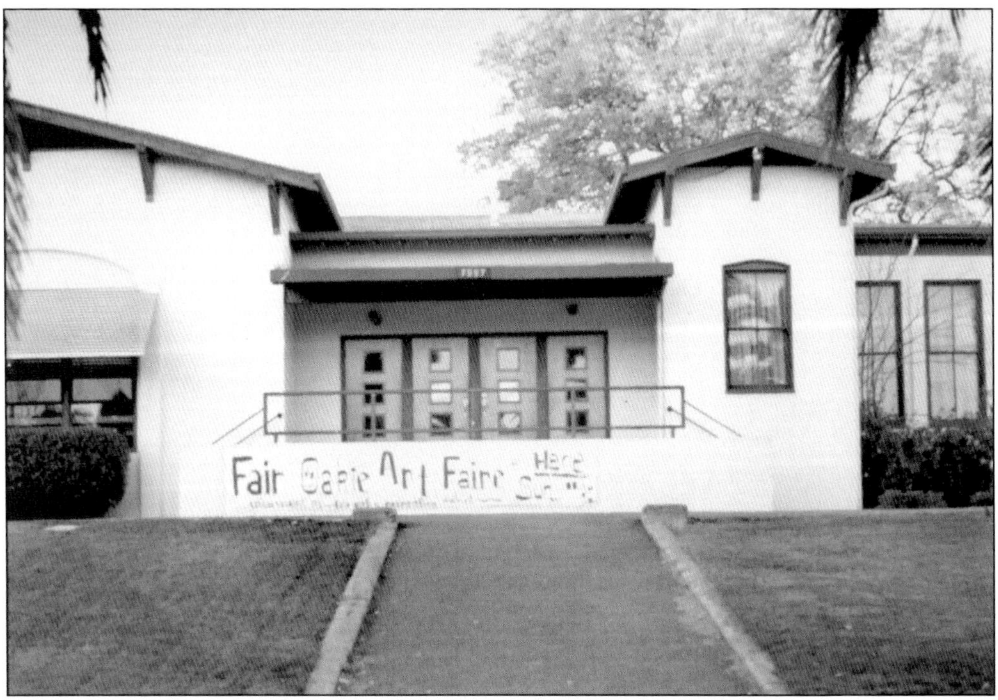

Nine

The Sporting Life

In order to form a just estimation of the character of any particular people, it is absolutely necessary to investigate Sport and Pastimes most generally prevalent among them.
—Joseph Strutt, *Sports and Pastimes of the People of England*, 1838

Generations of scholars and historians have neglected the study of sports and recreation, perhaps, because of other important topics to research, intellectual snobbery, career concerns, or a conviction that a detailed analysis of sports and recreation fails to increase new historical knowledge or explain important questions. Sports and recreation history, however, has proven a veritable field for scholars interested in urban and local dynamics. Scholars are uncovering the role of a town or city as both a site and a process in the evolution of sports and recreation. Likewise researchers are discovering the important role sports and recreation plays as an agent in the further development of local culture, as well as an agent in the dissemination of urban and democratic ideals. Indeed, the study of sports and recreation provides researchers of urban and local history with details that highlight the coevolution and interdependence of one on the other.

Whether filled with dreams of striking out the mighty Casey or calling a home run shot in the World Series like the Great Bambino, Fair Oaks fields and parks, like the many makeshift parks scattered over the American historical landscape, have been filled with the dreams, hopes, and excitement of sports and recreation. Families and friends, looking for a break from the busy hum of work, have found a variety of leisure activities to ease the daily stresses of life. Tennis, football, basketball, baseball, picnics in the park, strolls along the river, ice cream socials, and dances featuring a local band, have been just some of the many ways that the citizens of Fair Oaks have been able to play, relax, and, most importantly, have fun.

Formed in 1945, the Fair Oaks Recreation and Park District provides recreation and park facilities and programs for the citizens of Fair Oaks. Indeed, Fair Oaks residents have a long history of dedication to parks and recreation. It soon began to acquire a number of park properties and recreation facilities beginning with the Fair Oaks Plaza in 1947. Today the Fair Oaks Recreation and Park District owns 123 acres of parkland, including nine developed parks. For over 50 years, the Fair Oaks Recreation and Park District has provided the community of Fair Oaks with a wide range of recreation programming, including special events, day camps, teen programs and trips, adult sports leagues, senior activities, youth programs, leisure enrichment classes, and year-round recreation programs.

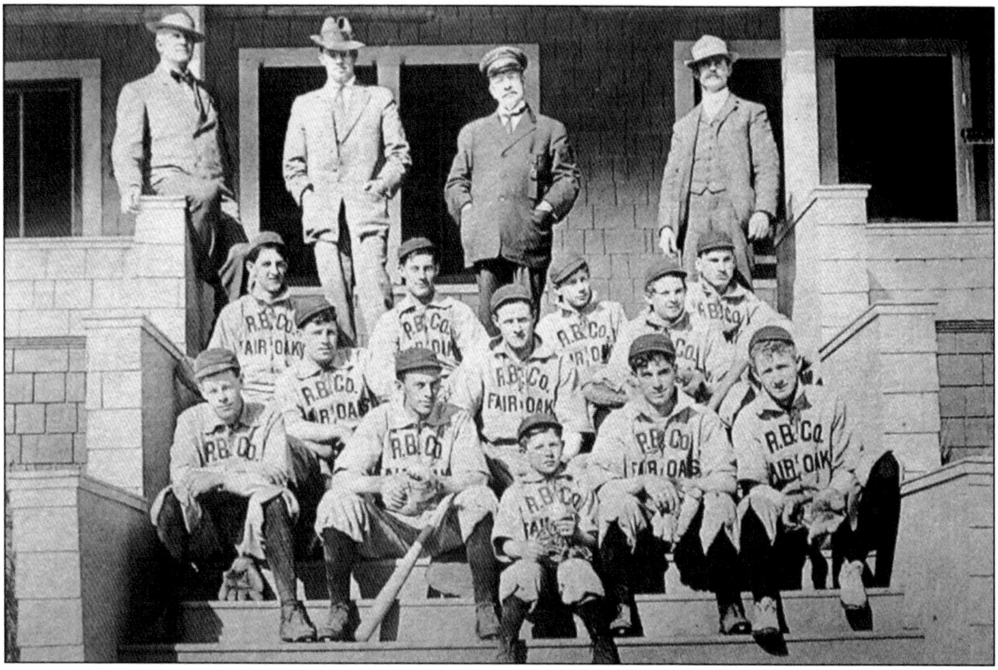

Organized in 1909 by Dr. J. H. Buffum and George Robinson, the Robinson-Buffum Company distributed water in Fair Oaks until the Fair Oaks Water District was formed in 1917. Around 1910, the company sponsored a baseball team. (Courtesy Fair Oaks Presbyterian Church.)

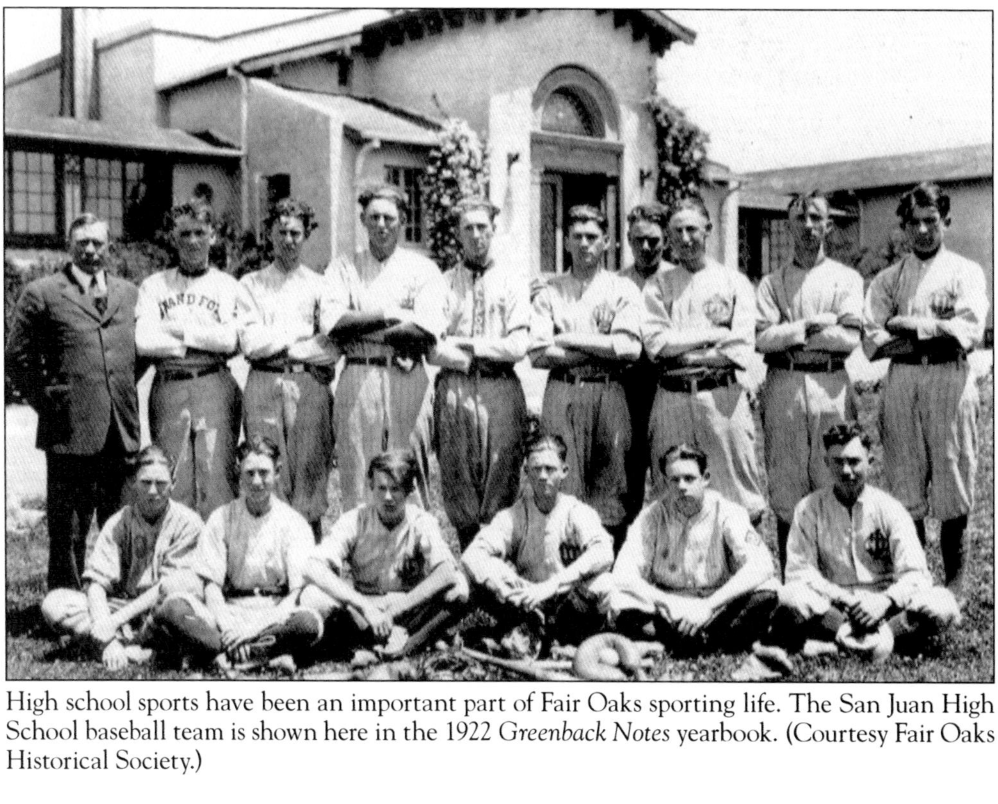

High school sports have been an important part of Fair Oaks sporting life. The San Juan High School baseball team is shown here in the 1922 *Greenback Notes* yearbook. (Courtesy Fair Oaks Historical Society.)

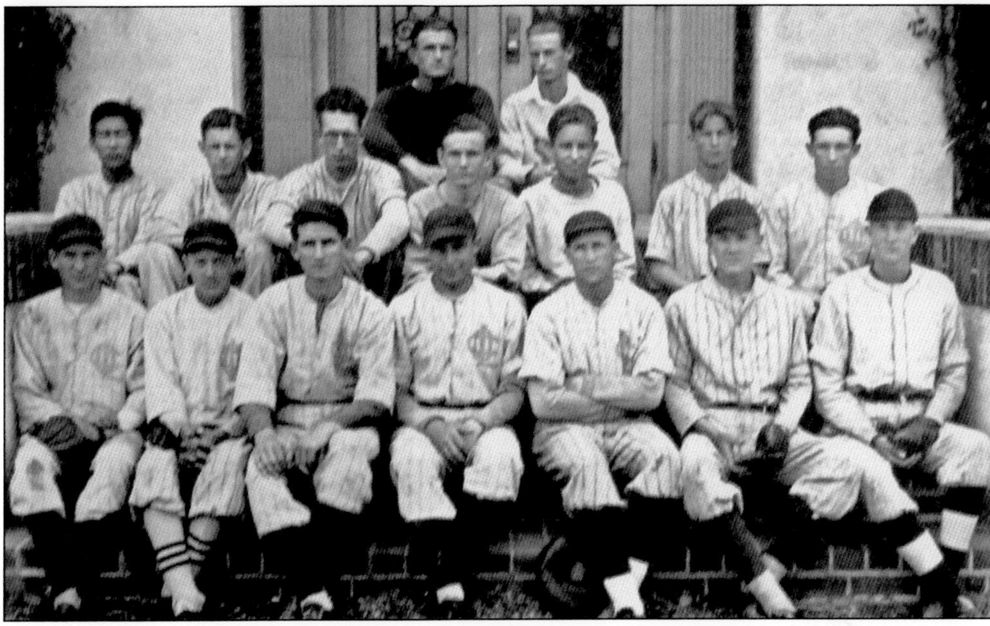

At the height of the Great Depression, these San Juan High School baseball players found a respite from the economic disaster. They are shown here in the 1933 *Greenback Notes* yearbook. (Courtesy Fair Oaks Historical Society.)

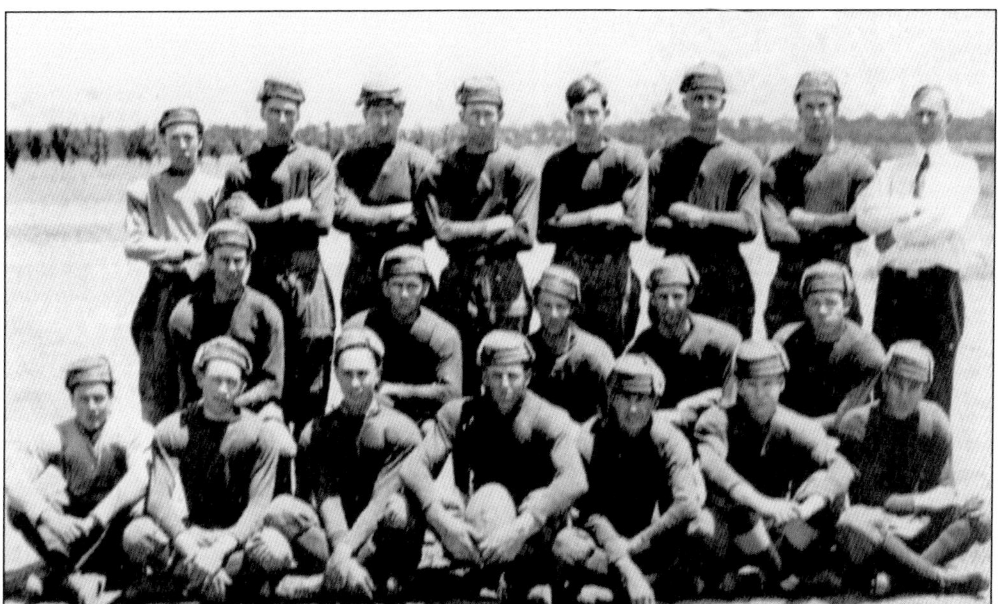

Heroes of the high school gridiron, the 1922 San Juan High School football team posed for their yearbook picture. (Courtesy Fair Oaks Historical Society.)

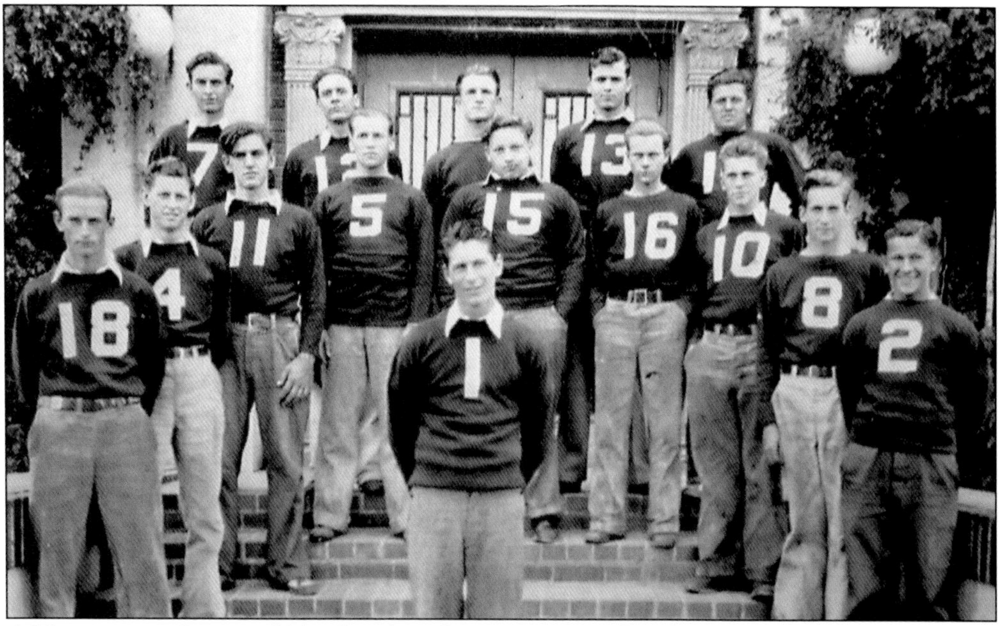

Athletic camaraderie could be found in the San Juan High School Boys' Block. The athletes expressed their dedication to "the good old school spirit which is so evident on the athletic field and which will make for good, clean sportsmanship—the aim and ideal of the Boys' Block S. J." in the 1933 yearbook. (Courtesy Fair Oaks Historical Society.)

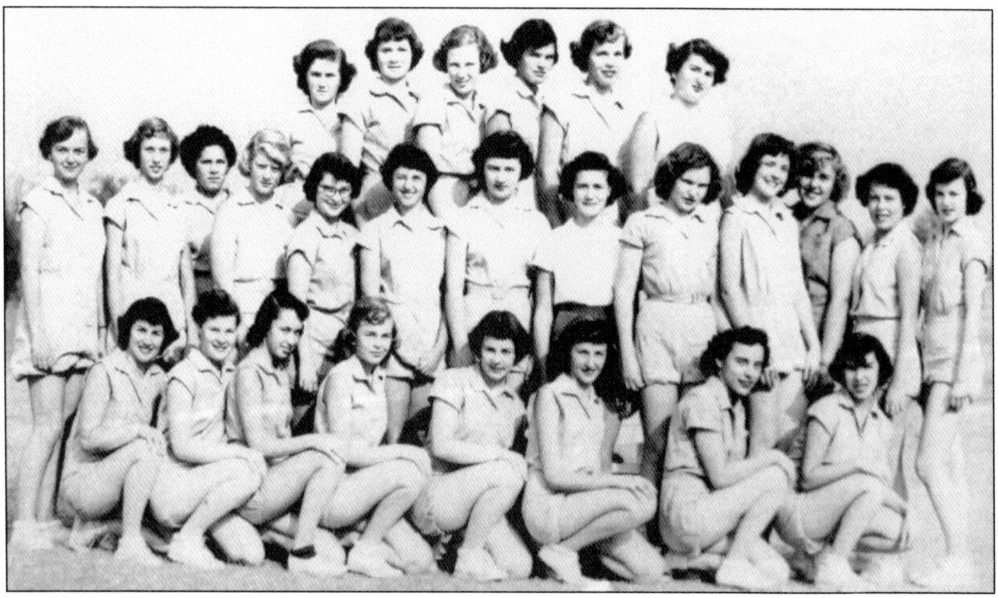

Not to be outdone by the boys, the San Juan High School Sophomore Girls' Athletic Association posed for this picture in the 1952 yearbook. Pictured, from left to right, are (first row) G. Gooch, R. Harris, N. Rose, J. Allen, R. Call, R. Shankle, J. Boucher, and H. Heredia; (second row) E. Putman, J. Pippitt, B. Farnham, B. Agee, E. Royce, L. Tremp, S. Rice, M. Pittman, S. Pritchard, G. Aragon, B. Kelly, E. Oliva, and S. Huston; (third row) N. Volkert, J. Graham, J. Quincey, B. Husu, D. DeGough, and M. Ford. (Courtesy Fair Oaks Historical Society.)

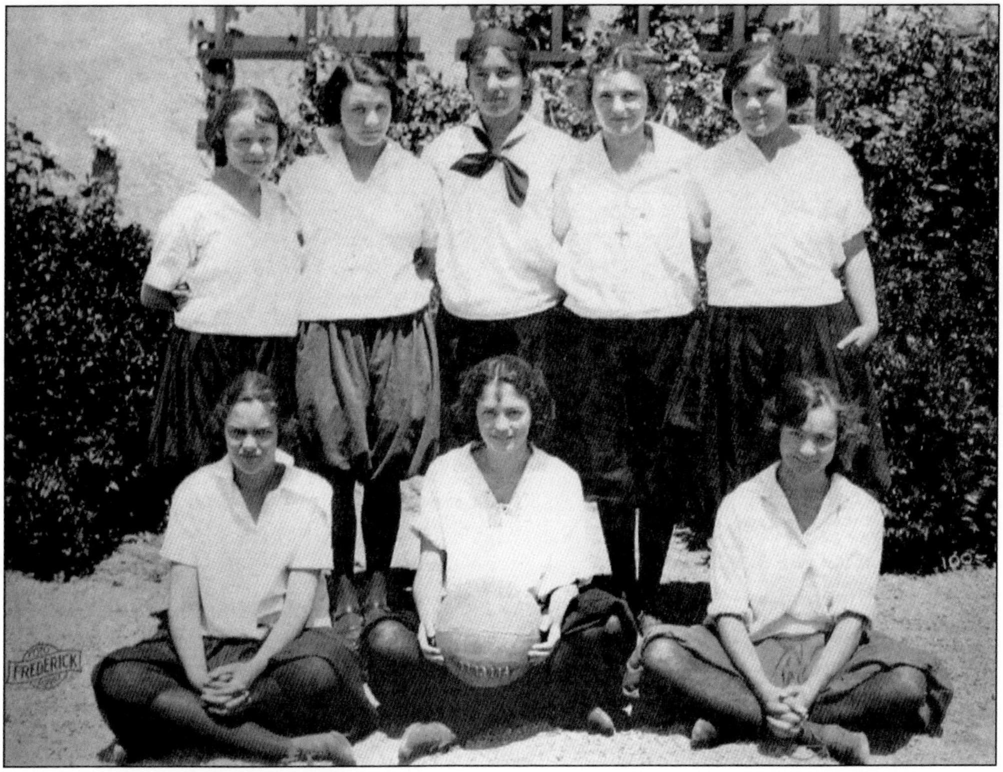

Young women athletes played for the 1922 San Juan High School Girls' basketball team. (Courtesy Fair Oaks Historical Society.)

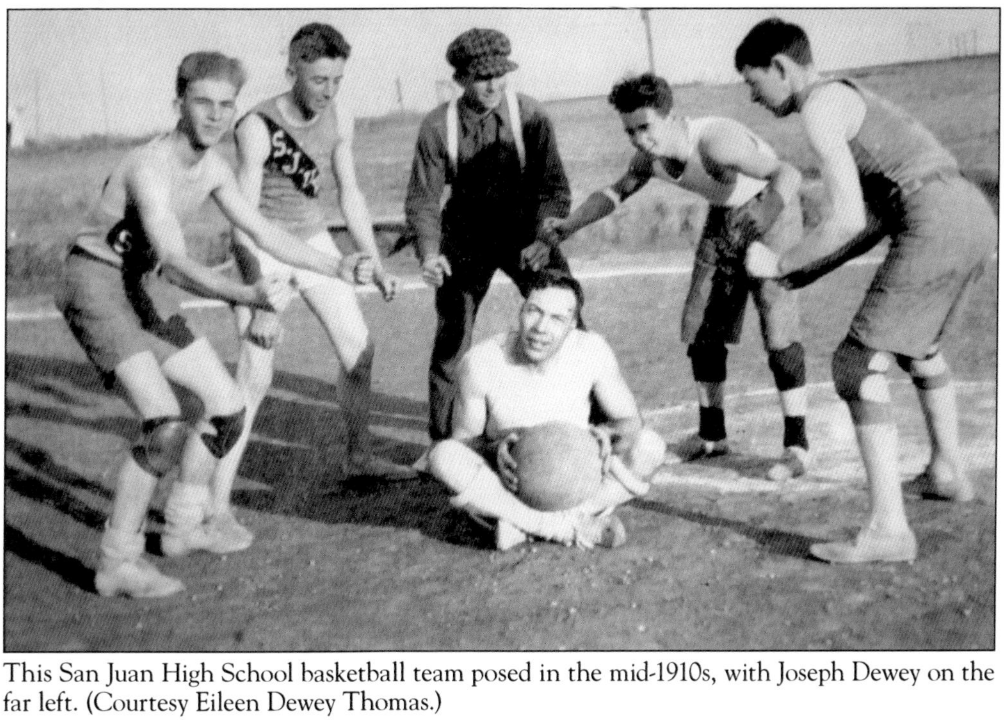

This San Juan High School basketball team posed in the mid-1910s, with Joseph Dewey on the far left. (Courtesy Eileen Dewey Thomas.)

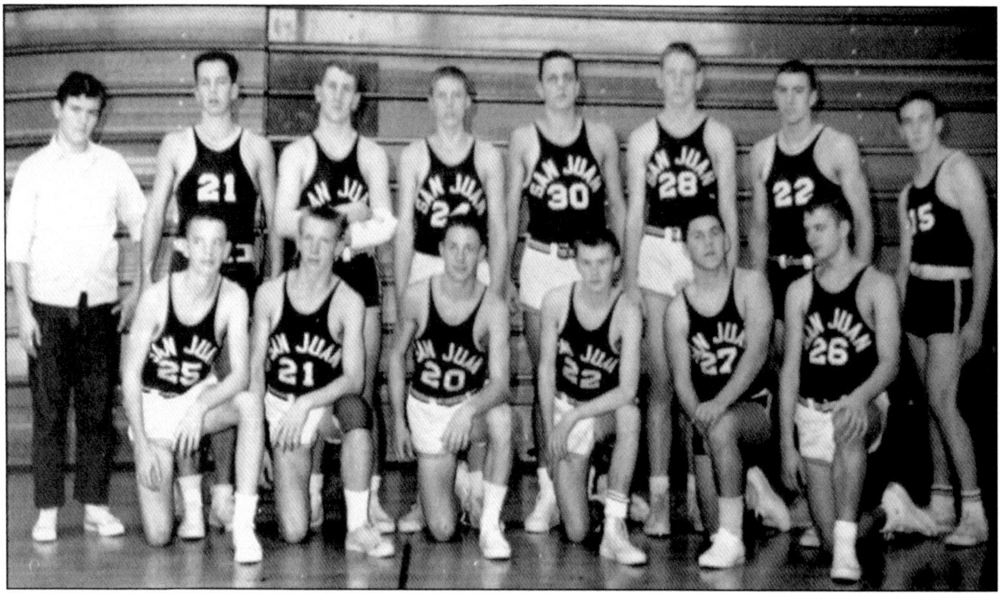

Pictured in the 1962 yearbook, the JV basketball team, from left to right, are (first row) C. Madill, D. Bryant, P. Borgos, R. Moorhead, B. Cummins, and T. Carty; (second row) M. Tabler (manager), M. Talbot, M. Richardson, J. Wheeler, D. Ashby, D. Giblin, B. Stoeckmann, and D. Dailey. (Courtesy Fair Oaks Historical Society.)

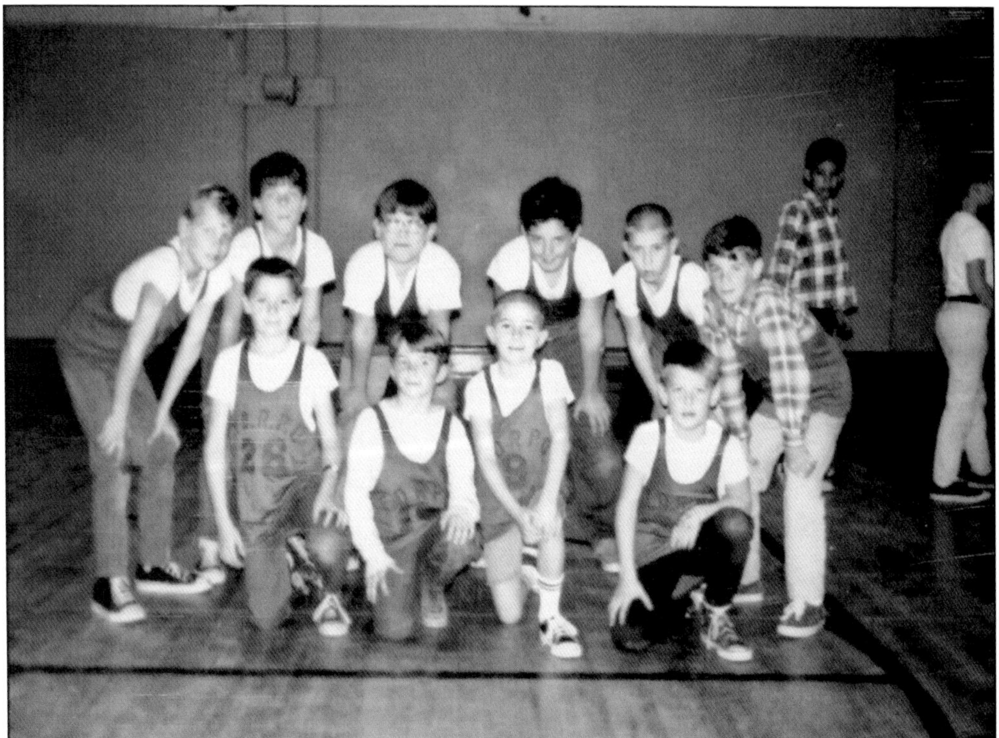

In this 1969 photograph, the Earl LeGette School basketball team is shown on the court. (Courtesy Fair Oaks Recreation and Park District.)

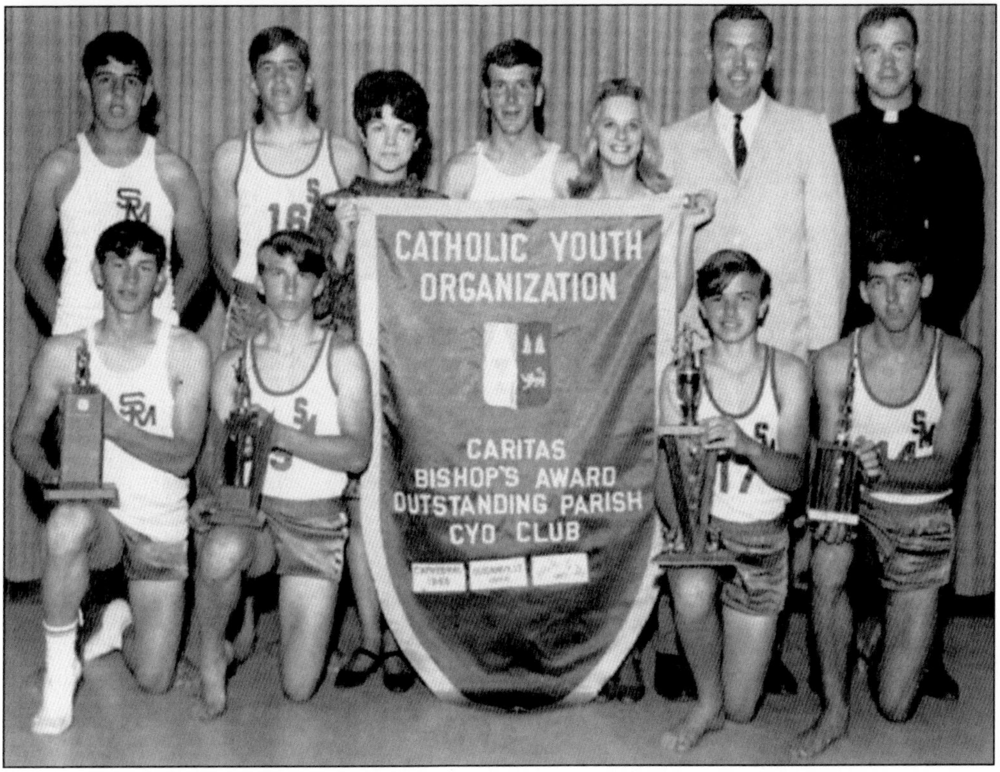

At the CYO awards ceremony in 1968, St. Mel's award-winning basketball team took time to pose without their shoes. Pictured here, from left to right, are (first row) Chuck Friedrich, Mickey Riley, Tom Mullen, and Mike Morrison; (second row) Joe Gordon, Glen Woodruff, Sandy Harrington (advisor), Rick Martin, Cathy Morrison, Bill Harrington (advisor), and Fr. Brendan Lawlor. (Courtesy St. Mel's Catholic Church.)

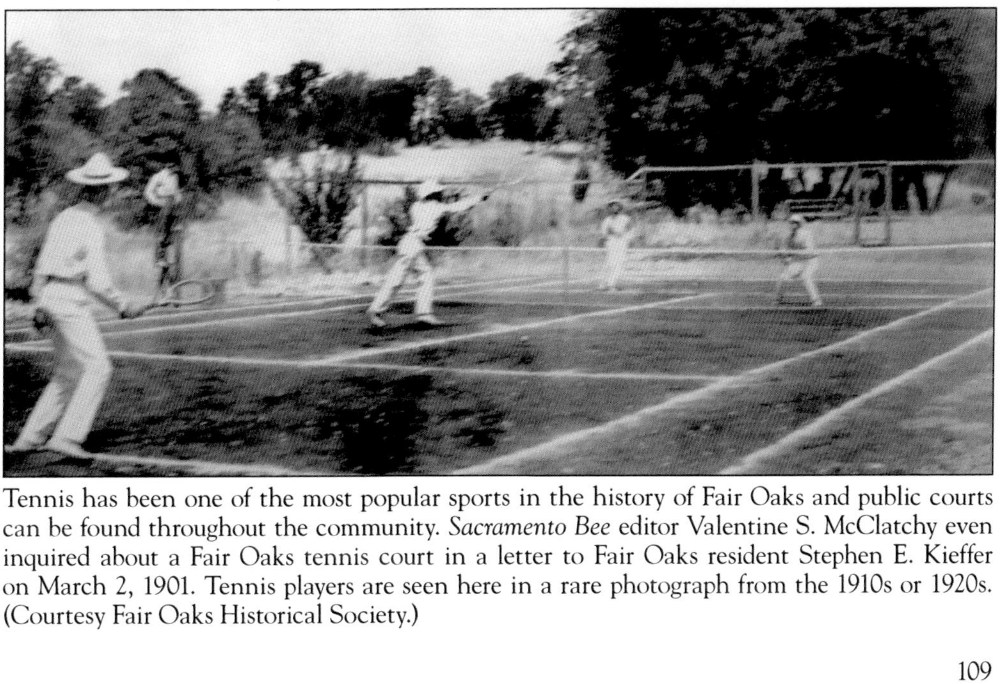

Tennis has been one of the most popular sports in the history of Fair Oaks and public courts can be found throughout the community. *Sacramento Bee* editor Valentine S. McClatchy even inquired about a Fair Oaks tennis court in a letter to Fair Oaks resident Stephen E. Kieffer on March 2, 1901. Tennis players are seen here in a rare photograph from the 1910s or 1920s. (Courtesy Fair Oaks Historical Society.)

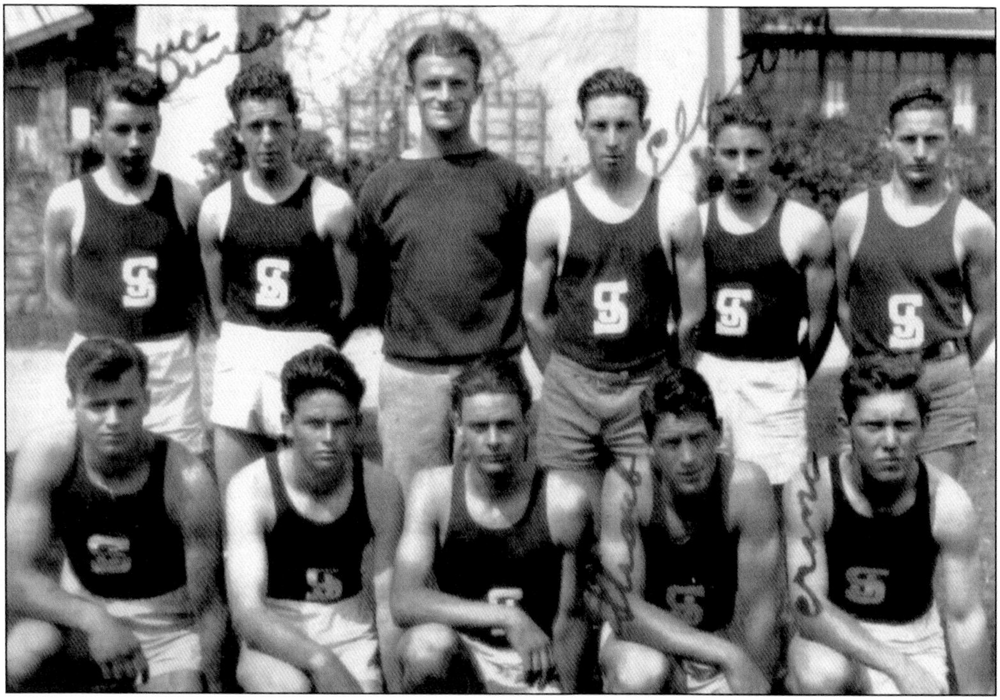

Members of the 1933 San Juan High School track and field team identified in this photograph include Clarence Hall (middle, first row), Bruce Duncan (far left, second row), and Elbert McGee (third from right, second row). (Courtesy Fair Oaks Historical Society.)

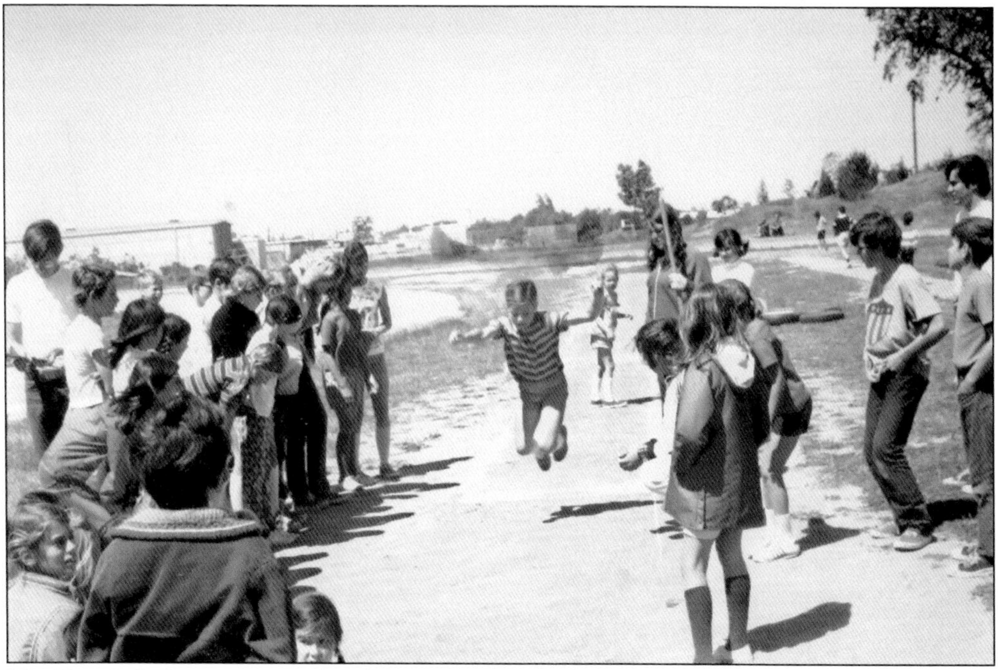

The Fair Oaks Recreation and Park District sponsored a variety of athletic contests, including this track meet in April 1972 for the Jr. Olympics. (Courtesy Fair Oaks Recreation and Park District.)

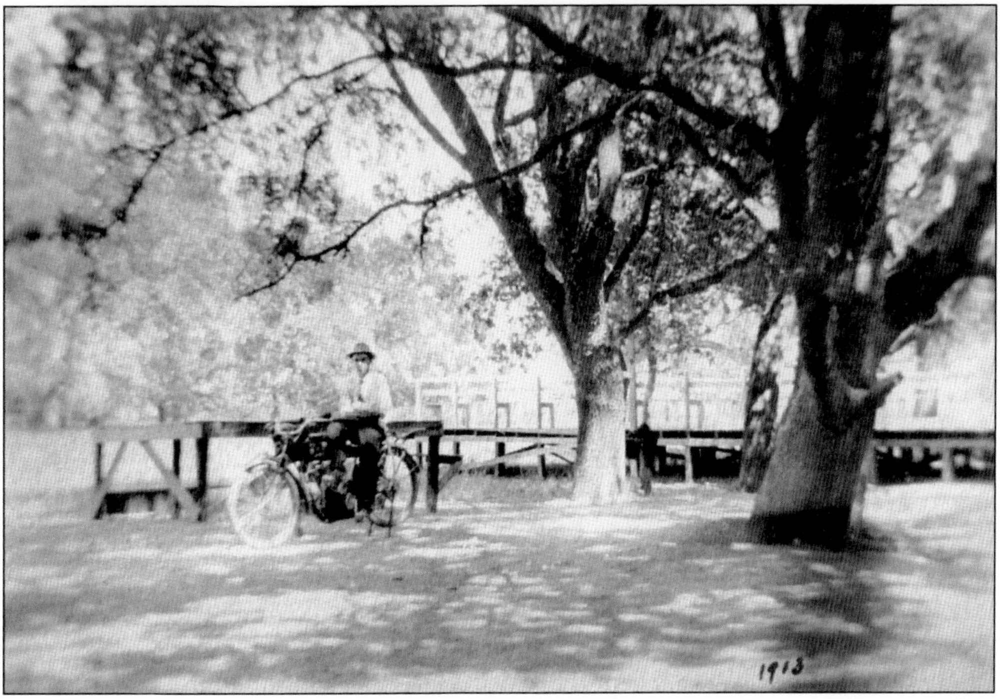

Residents enjoyed taking leisurely bicycle rides under the lush scenery of Fair Oaks, much like this Dewey family member did in 1913 (above). The Fair Oaks Recreation and Park District sponsored "Bicycle Drags" throughout the years, such as the one below in 1970. (Above courtesy Eileen Dewey Thomas; below courtesy Fair Oaks Recreation and Park District.)

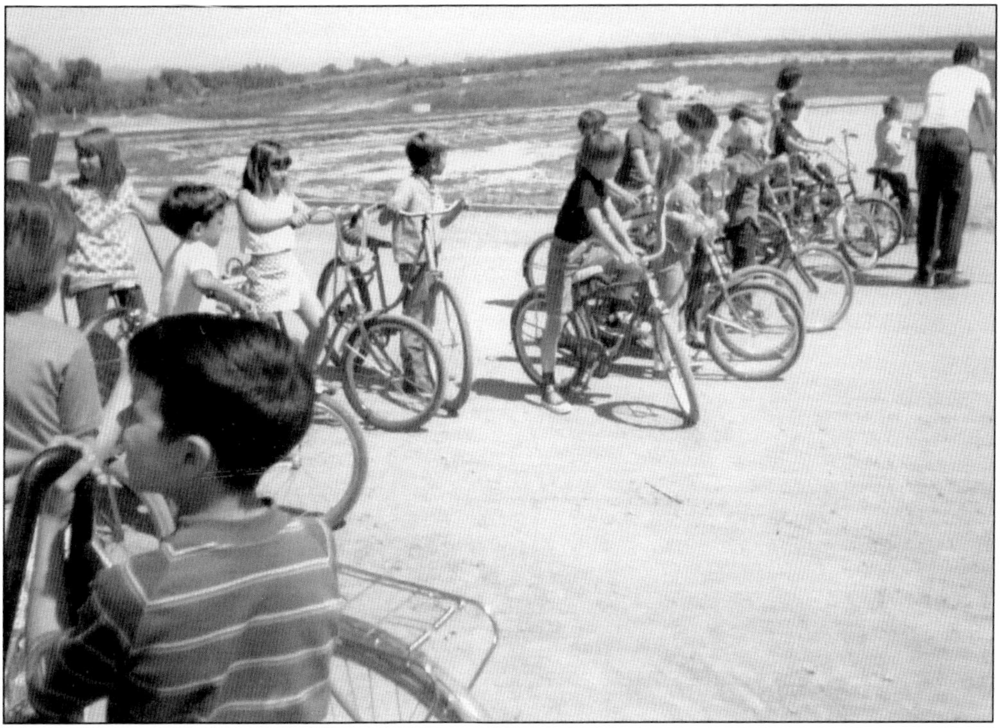

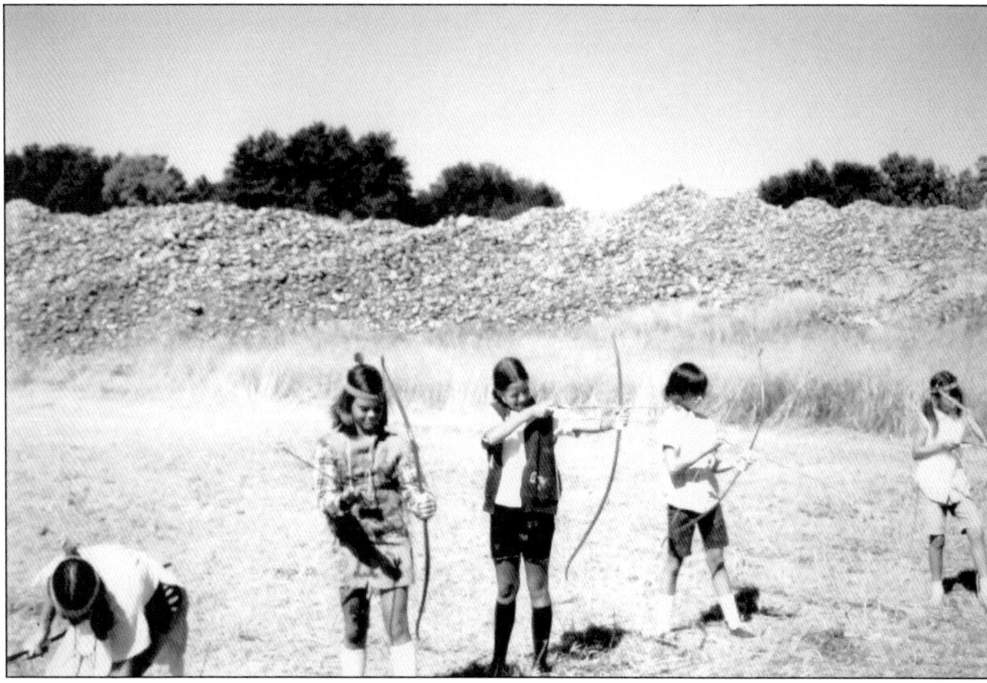

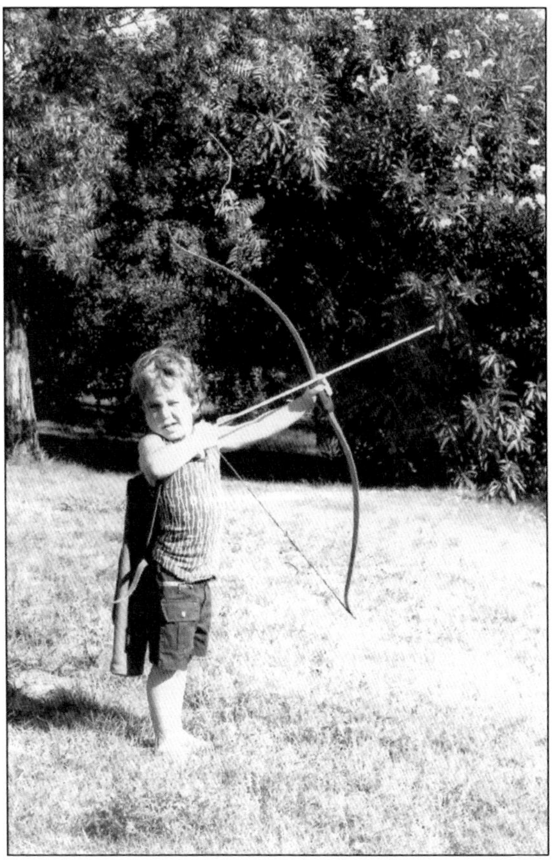

In 1969, the Fair Oaks Recreation and Park District sponsored an archery event at Sailor Bar (at the bottom of Illinois Avenue). Archery was also popular with many, evidenced by Karl Francis Speth as he played in front of his home on Magnolia Avenue in 1975. (Above courtesy of Fair Oaks Recreation and Park District; below courtesy Janice Speth.)

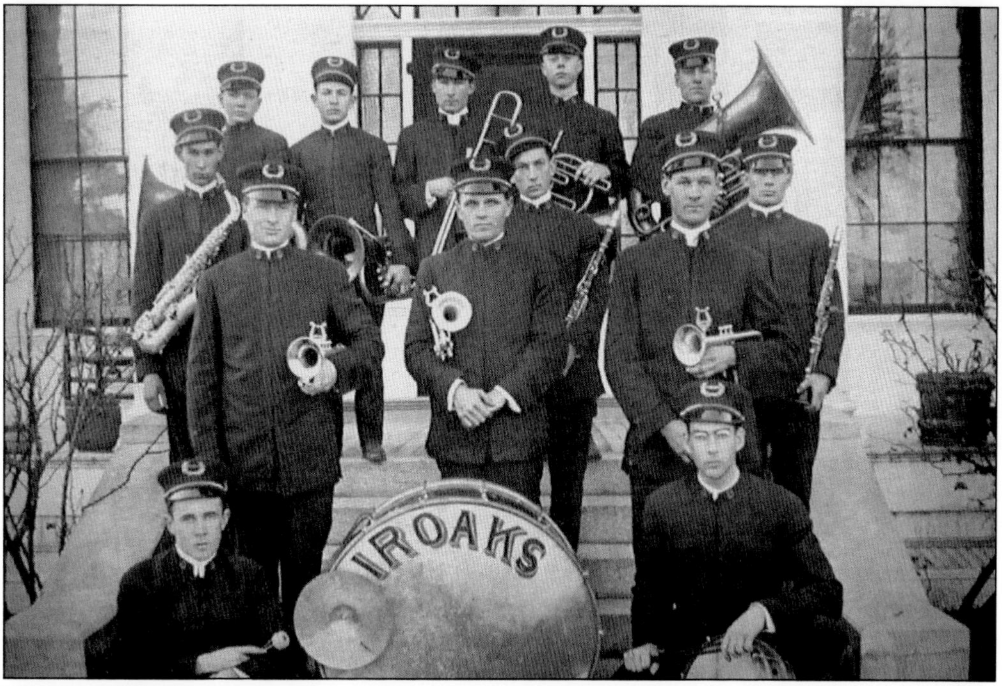

The Fair Oaks Band, started by Will Gregory and Dr. Buffum in 1914, played for picnics, American River Grange, Orangevale Grange, Folsom Fourth of July, and other local events. Unfortunately, by 1917, World War I put an end to the band. The band, seen around 1915 in dark uniforms above and white ones below, featured, from left to right, the following: (first row) William Gregory Sr. and Frank Odem; (second row) Ira Dickson, Elmer Green, Fred Bishop, Bill Gregory, Howard Buffum, Gus Schoen, and Wylie Dickson; (third row) Bob Fisk, Bill Raymond, Frank Bishop, Pete Holst, Art Broadley, Walt Hinsey, and Ted Crosby. (Above courtesy Fair Oaks Presbyterian Church; below courtesy Linda Morris.)

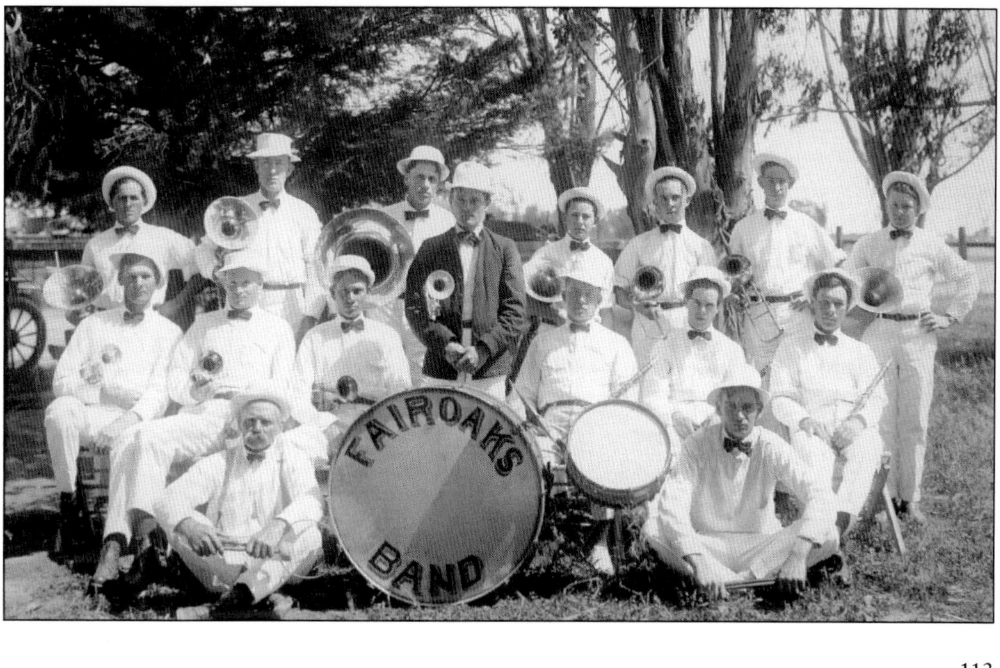

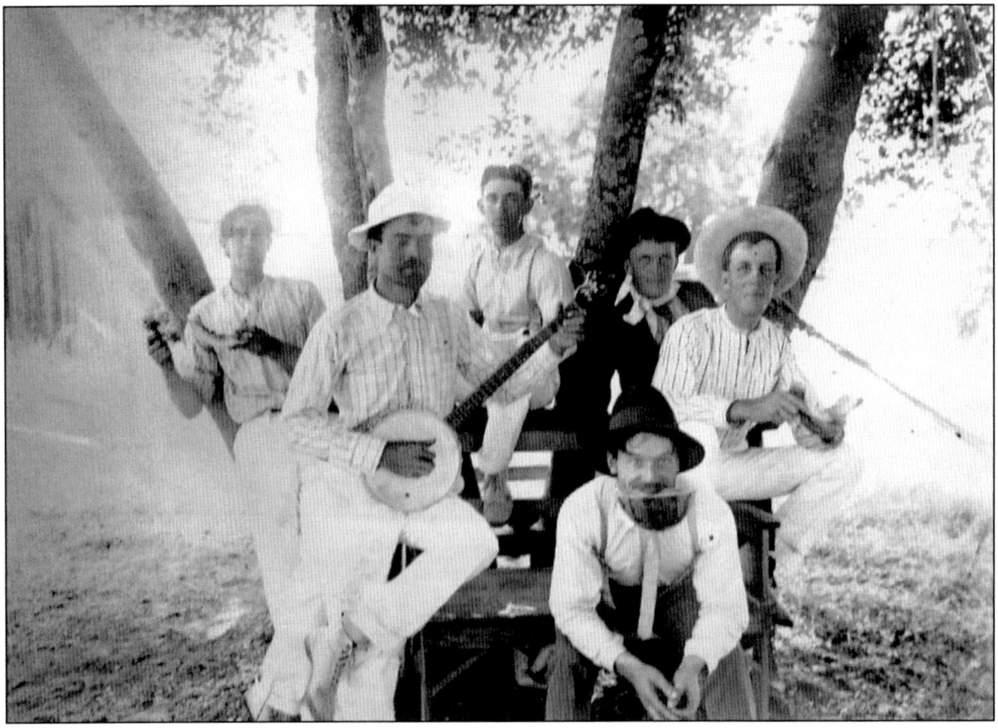

In the 1910s, this "banjo band" that played at an ice cream social and pancake dinner included Paul Midler, Dr. Eugene Buffum (with banjo), Thomas Ward, Donald Beaton, and ? Strickland. Below, in 1972, an orchestra gathered to play during the Fair Oaks Fiesta. (Above courtesy Fair Oaks Historical Society; below courtesy Fair Oaks Recreation and Park District.)

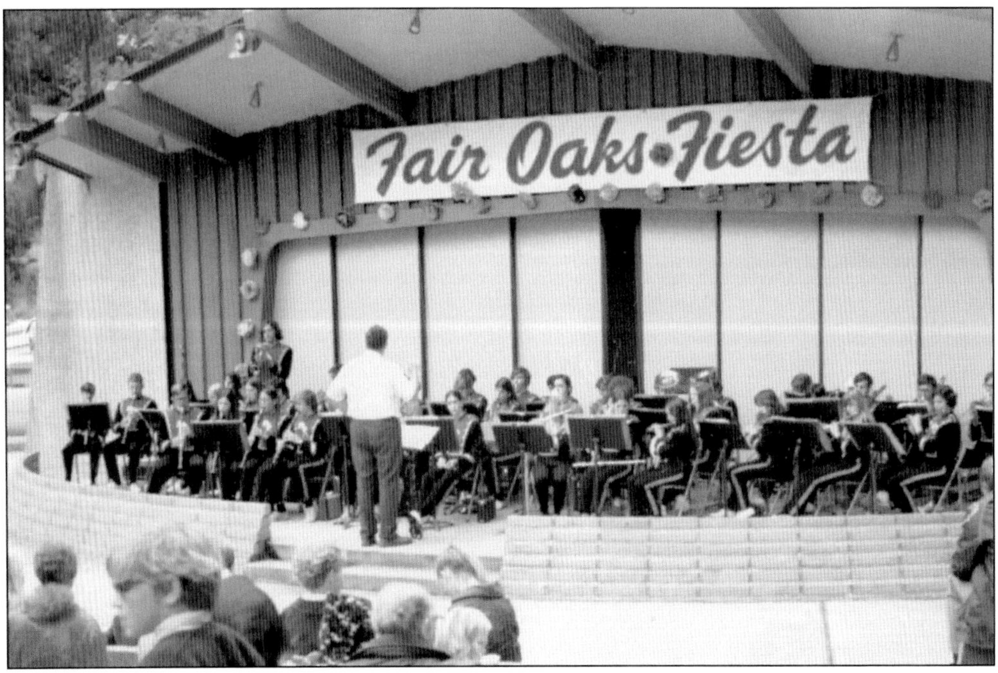

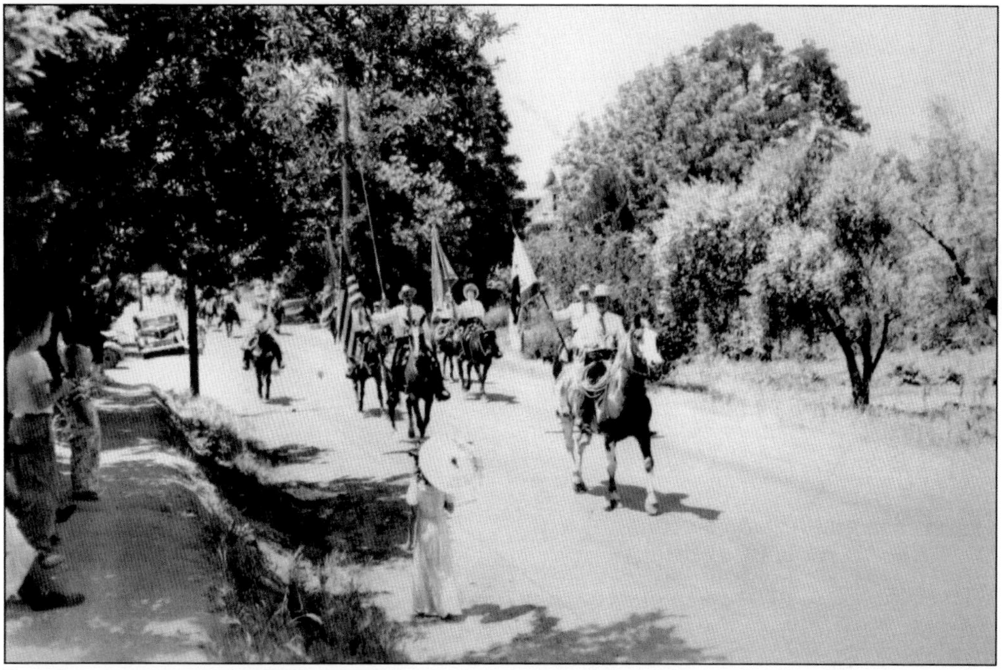

Parades were a marvelous way to celebrate the sporting life. In the mid-1950s, Sheriff Dan Cox leads horses down the street during the first parade in Fair Oaks. In the late 1950s or early 1960s, children marched down Fair Oaks Boulevard through Old Town (below). (Above courtesy Fair Oaks Historical Society; below courtesy Fair Oaks Chamber of Commerce.)

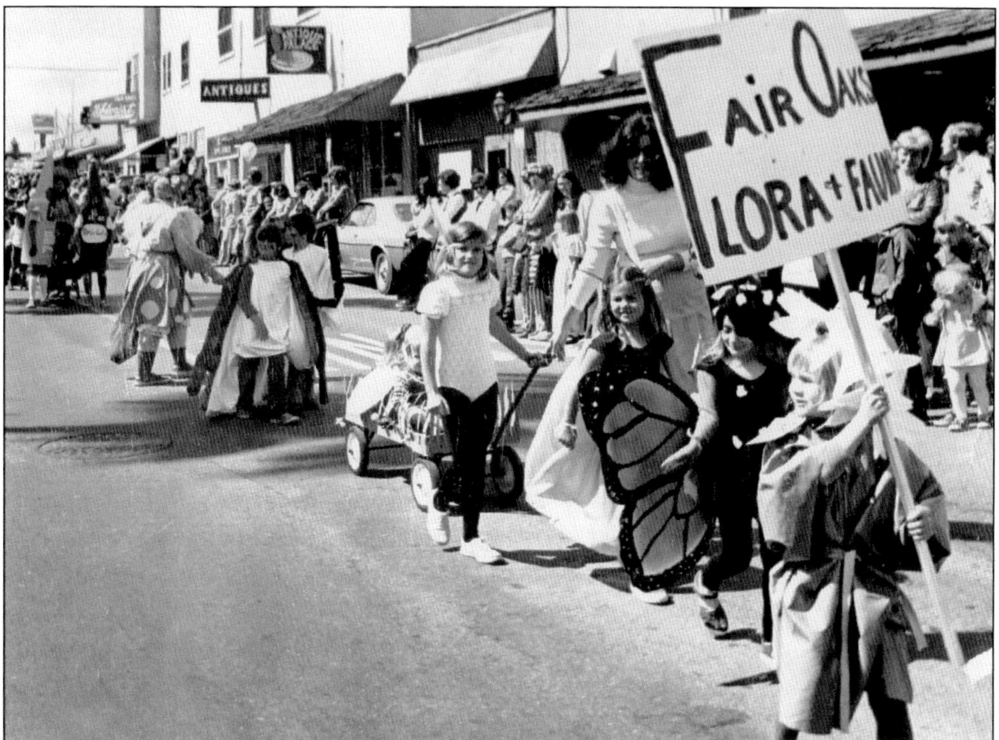

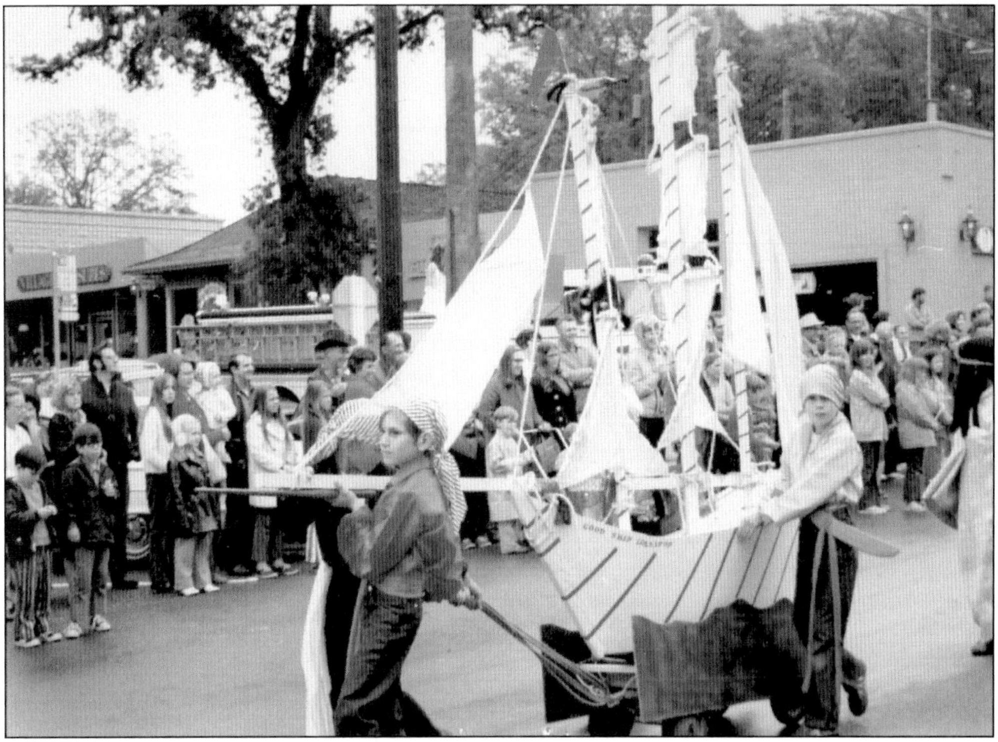

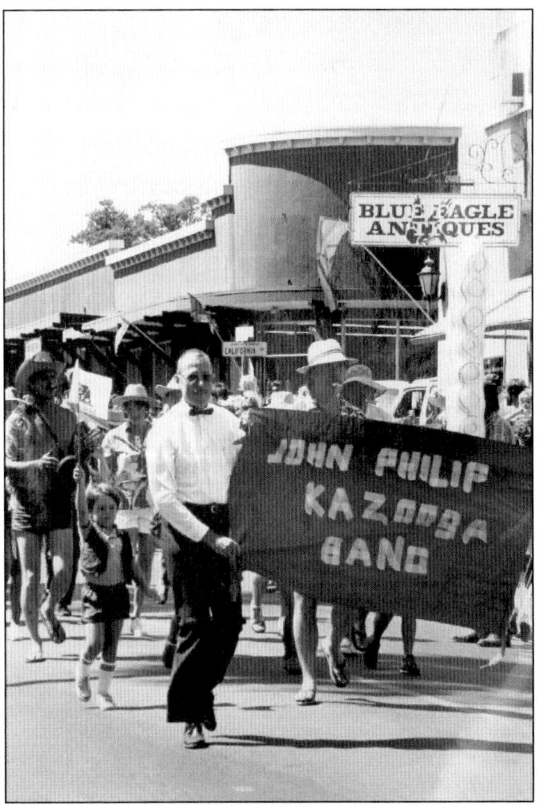

Since the 1950s, the Fair Oaks Fiesta has been an entertaining tradition in Fair Oaks. During that time, many enjoyable parade participants, including this boat full of pirates (above, 1972) and a kuzooga band (left, early 1980s), have strolled down Fair Oaks Boulevard in Old Town to show off their floats, signs, organizations, and the like. (Above courtesy Fair Oaks Recreation and Park District; below courtesy Hugh Gorman.)

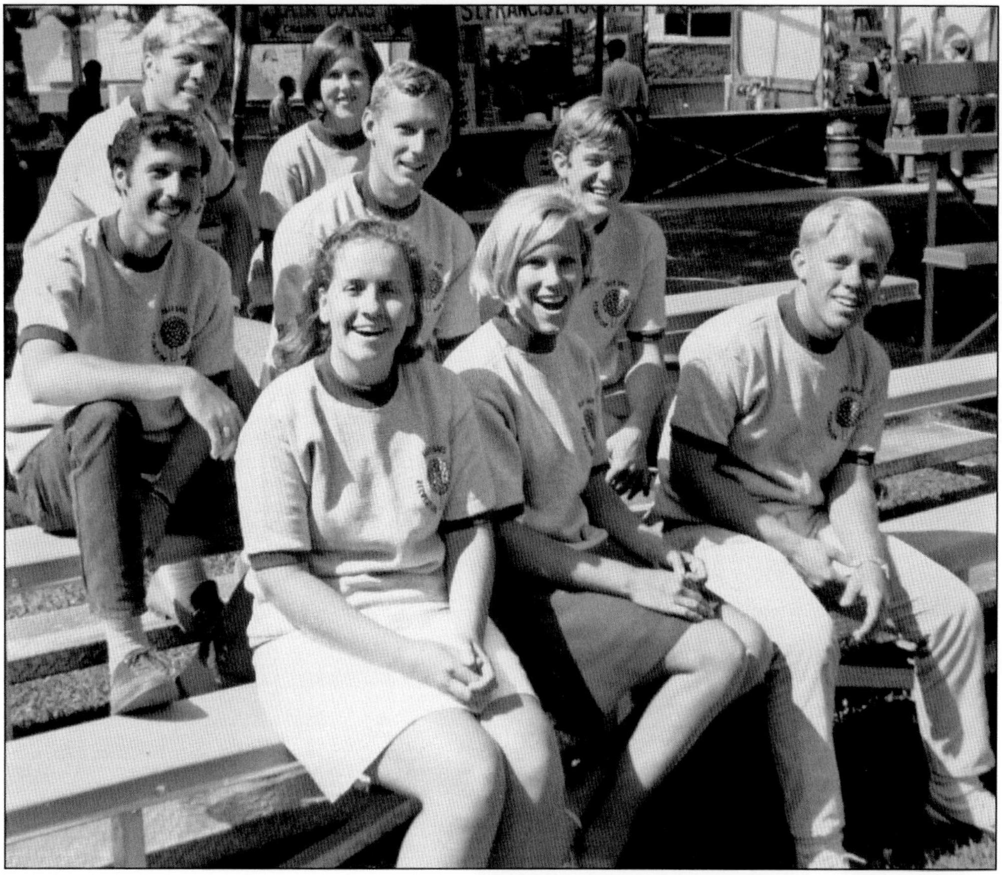

For the Fair Oaks Recreation and Park District to succeed in its many programs, they have relied on the support of volunteers and staff, such as the Recreation and Day Staff. Pictured here in 1969, from left to right, are (first row) Pamela Jenkins, Cindy Bridges, and Steve Cassell; (second row) Wayne Lowery, Rick Janecke, and Tom Peterson; (third row) Steve Somers and Nancy Geandrot. (Courtesy Fair Oaks Recreation and Park District.)

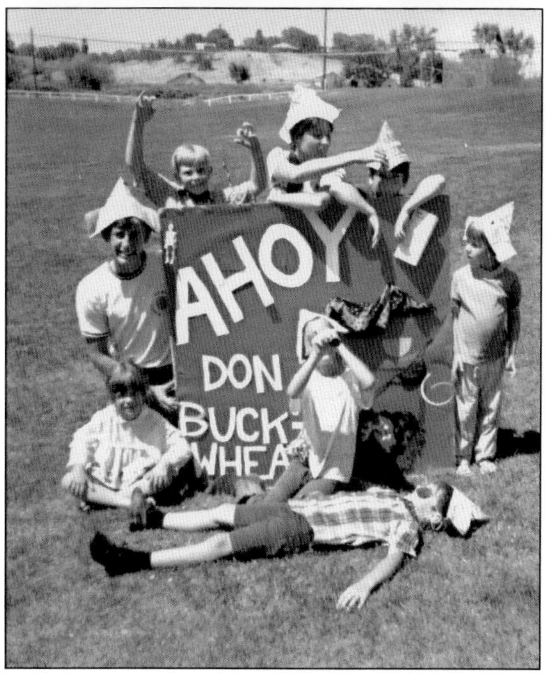

Another one of the Fair Oaks Recreation and Park District's many events was the "Pirate Ships and Underwater Wonders Week" in 1970. (Courtesy Fair Oaks Recreation and Park District.)

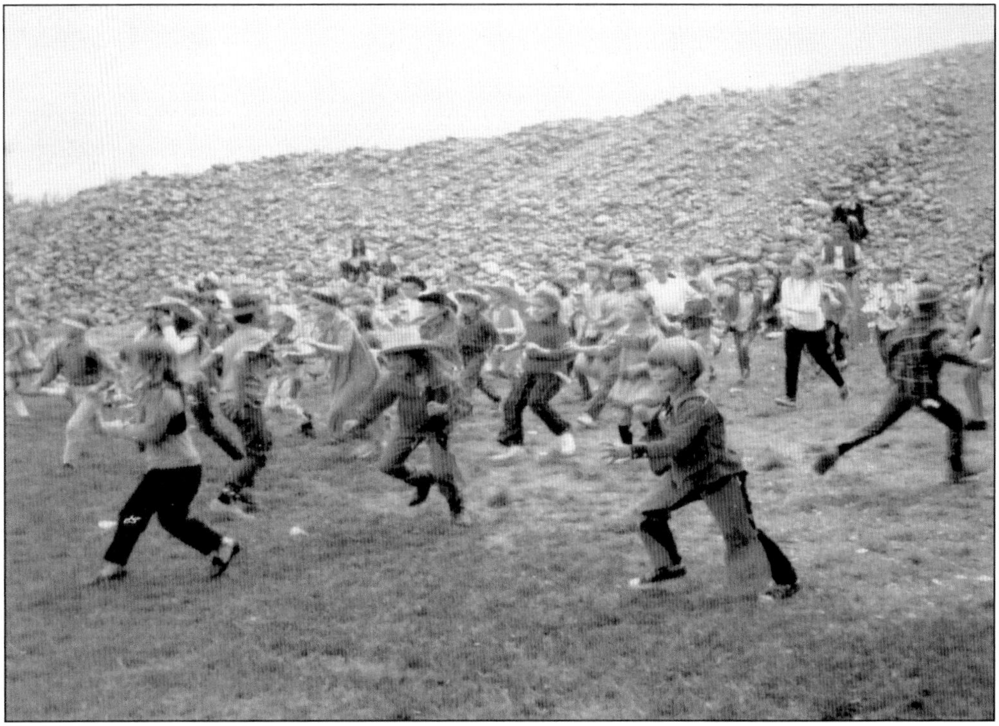

In 1969, the Fair Oaks Recreation and Park District put together a "Western Roundup" at Sailor Bar Park (above), while 1972 brought a pet show to Fair Oaks (below). (Courtesy Fair Oaks Recreation and Park District.)

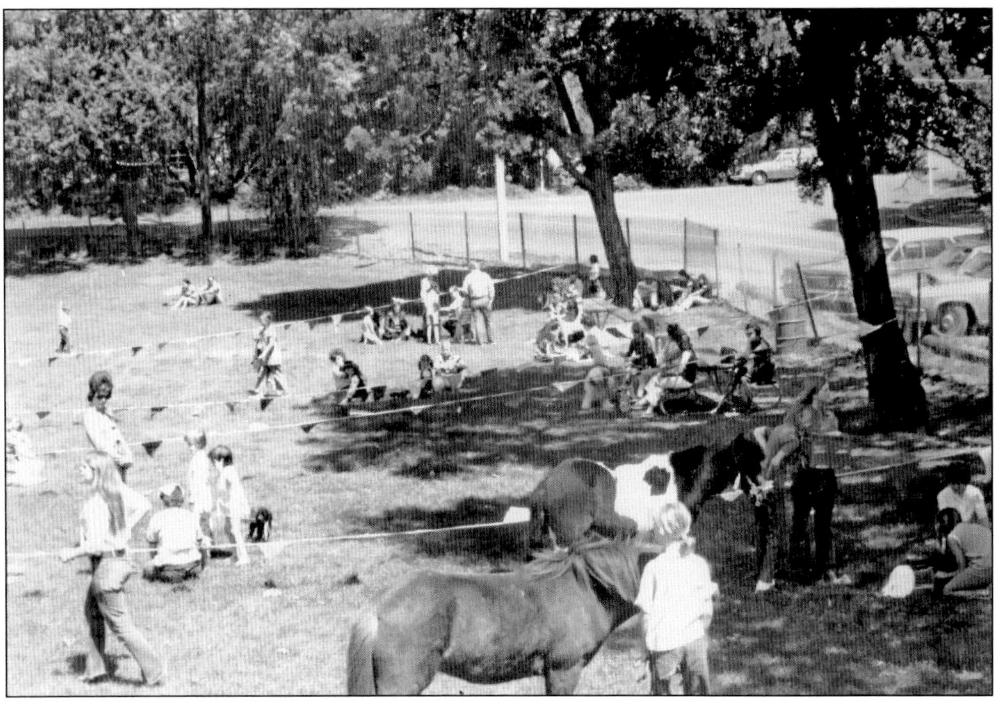

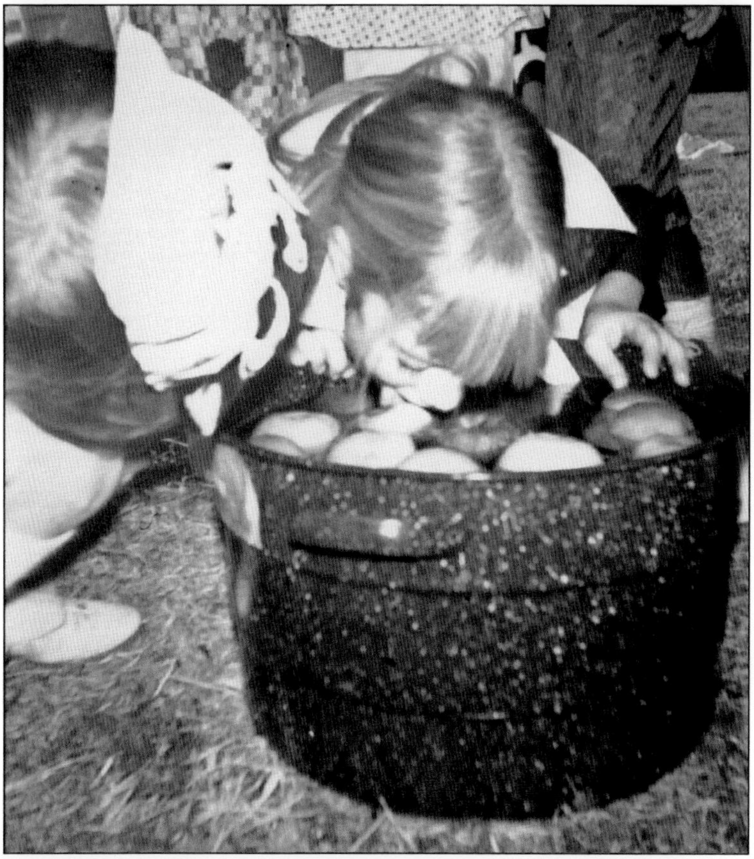

The Fair Oaks Recreation and Park District sponsored many holiday programs, such as a 1971 Halloween event, which included apple bobbing (above) and dressing up in costumes for trick-or-treat. (Courtesy Fair Oaks Recreation and Park District.)

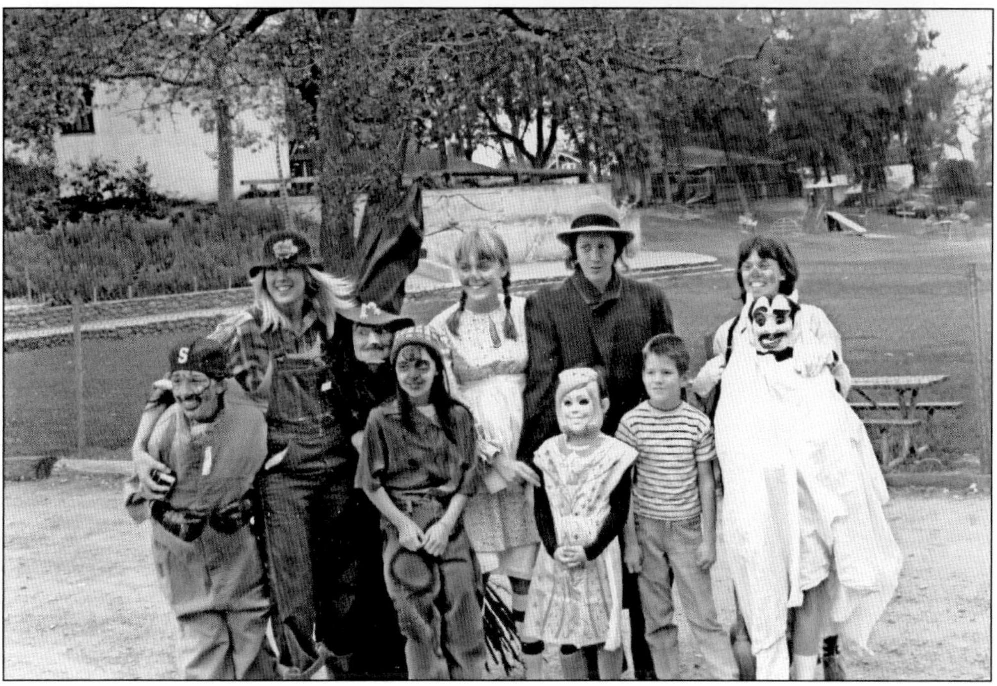

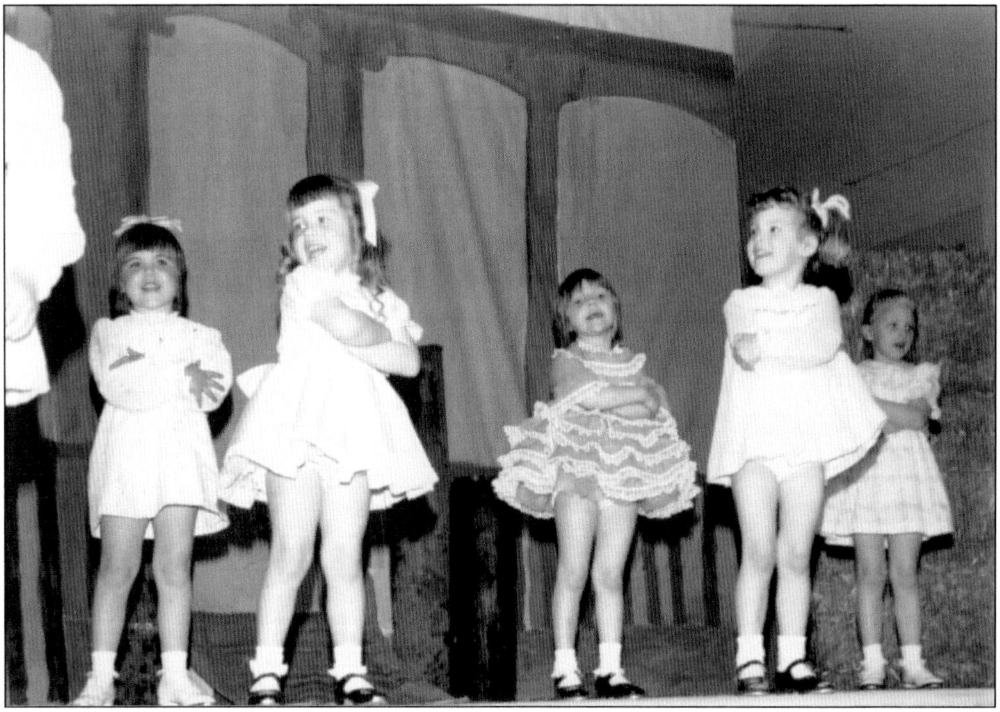

In March 1973, some of Fair Oaks' aspiring ballerinas performed at the Fair Oaks Recreation and Park District's tap and ballet recital. (Courtesy Fair Oaks Recreation and Park District.)

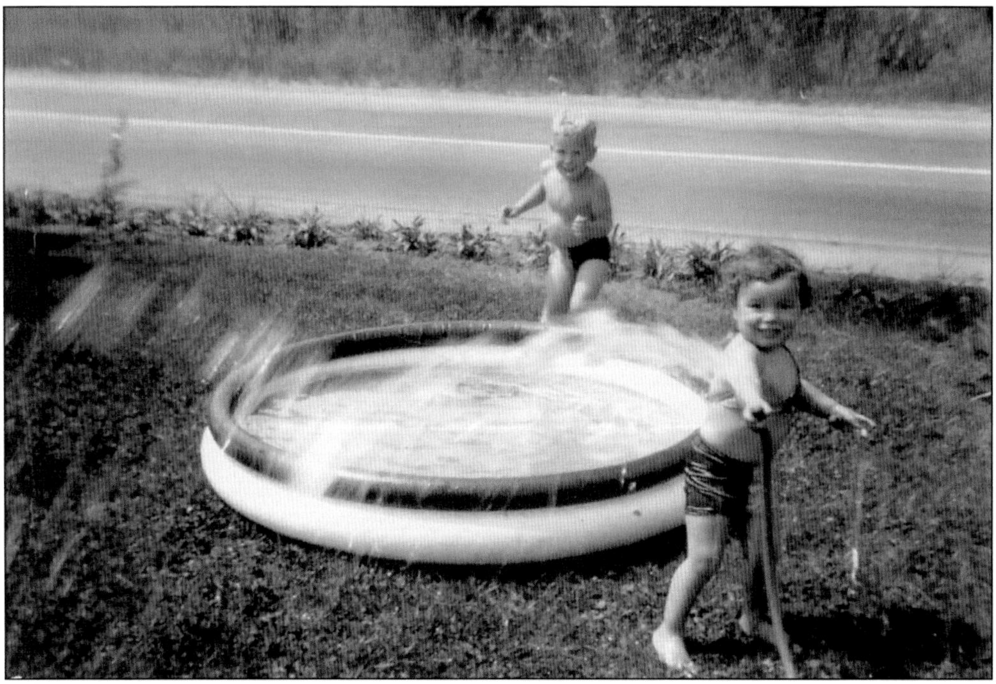

Although Fair Oaks Boulevard is a major street with heavy traffic today, it once was rather small and tranquil. In 1950, Ritchie and Sherry Lynn Wood play around a small pool outside their home on Fair Oaks Boulevard. (Courtesy Sherry Lynn Wood.)

Ten

THE RIVER

Sometimes, if you stand on the bottom rail of a bridge and lean over to watch the river slipping slowly away beneath you, you will suddenly know everything there is to be known.

—*Pooh's Little Instruction Book*, inspired by A. A. Milne

The American River is known for its remarkable beauty and as the location of one of Fair Oaks' most enduring and beloved structures and symbols—the Old Fair Oaks Bridge. The river runs from the Sierra Nevada Mountains through Sacramento and flows into the Sacramento River on its way to the San Francisco Bay. Throughout the years the river and its surrounding areas has been popular for its lush canyons, fishing, and whitewater rafting. Also, along the southern boundaries of Fair Oaks many thousands of acres of rich farm land were dredged up by such companies as the El Dorado Dredging Company, Natomas Dredging Company, Ashburton Mining Company, and the California Dredging Company in search of gold along the American River. The dredging mainly ceased by World War II, but made a lasting mark on the landscape as evidenced by the still visible dredger trailings along the bluffs of the river.

The river passes through an urbanized area, but its beauty is still captured by the American River Parkway that runs from Folsom Lake to the river's confluence with the Sacramento River. The bluff at Fair Oaks is the last piece of scenic bluff accessible to the public along the American River Parkway and allows all who visit to stroll quietly and enjoy the beauty that once helped promote a colony, provide enjoyment and relaxation, and become a symbol of a proud and treasured history. Indeed, while the rushing waters of the American River may drown out the hum of traffic and screams of development, the Fair Oaks Bluff, as well as the Old Fair Oaks Bridge, is also responsible for further development, promotion, and economic expansion of Sacramento's boisterous concrete urban and suburban jungles.

The Fair Oaks Bluff at the American River has been called "The Crown Jewel of the American River Parkway" and offers perhaps the most spectacular vista in all of Sacramento County. Since the 1800s, this historic and scenic spot has been enjoyed by residents and visitors of the Sacramento Valley. Its vegetation includes California prairie and a dense blue and interior live oak forest where wildlife and wildflowers abound. The area is currently inhabited by deer, wild turkeys, raccoons, hawks, and opossums. Recently, to protect this cherished part of Fair Oaks and Sacramento County's history, a local contingent formed as the "Citizens to Save the Bluffs" and purchased the area so that visitors could continue to wander among the native trees and wildflowers and enjoy the breathtaking views of the river like the many generations before did. Swimming, fishing, and picnicking were as popular with the pioneers and early settlers of Fair Oaks as they are today.

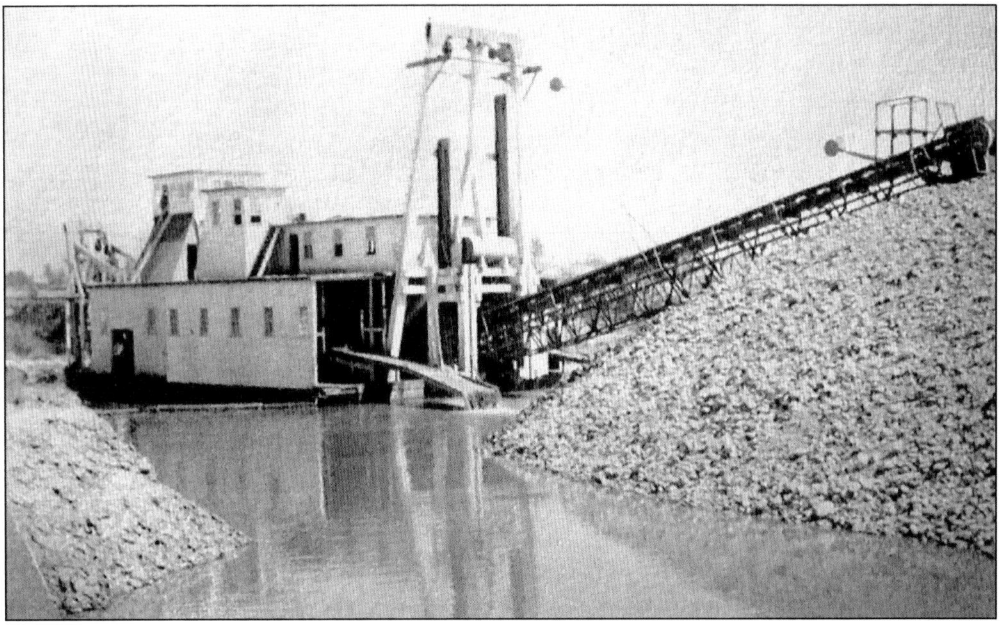

The American River experienced the heaviest amount of dredging in California's history. A walk along the American River Parkway still leaves visitors with visible evidence of dredger trailings. Massive gold dredgers, like the one above during the 1940s, could be seen up and down the river, particularly at Sailor Bar or Sacramento Bar. (Courtesy Fair Oaks Recreation and Park District.)

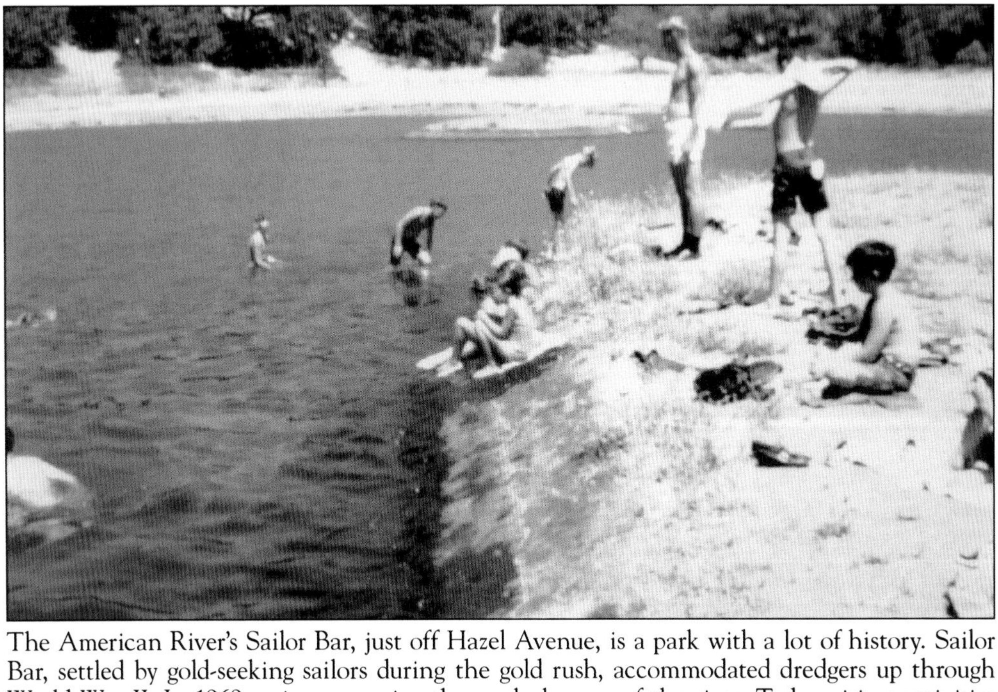

The American River's Sailor Bar, just off Hazel Avenue, is a park with a lot of history. Sailor Bar, settled by gold-seeking sailors during the gold rush, accommodated dredgers up through World War II. In 1969, swimmers enjoy the cool pleasure of the river. Today visitor activities such as swimming, rafting, fishing, horseback riding, and nature gazing, are enjoyed by many. (Courtesy Fair Oaks Recreation and Park District.)

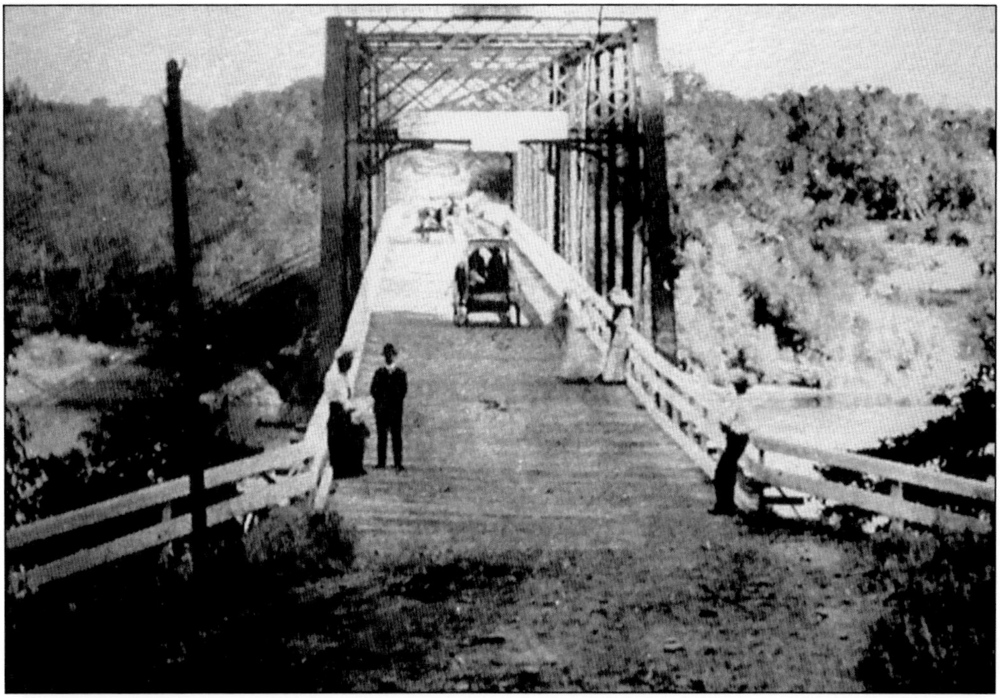

The original bridge over the American River at Fair Oaks, seen above around 1902, was built by the Pacific Improvement Company, who won the bid for the Fair Oaks Bridge at a cost of $24,800—with another $1,500 added for a trestle approach. Construction of the bridge began in January 1901 and spanned out for travel by early March that same year. The bridge served the community and helped for the faster transport of fruit from 1901 to 1906, when it washed out during a flood (below). (Courtesy Fair Oaks Presbyterian Church.)

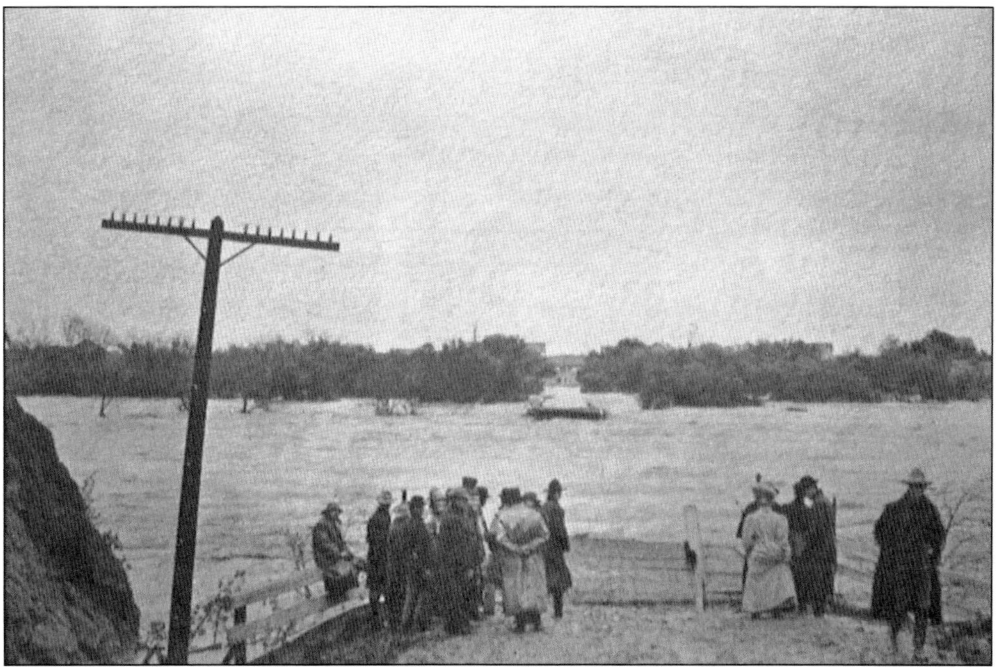

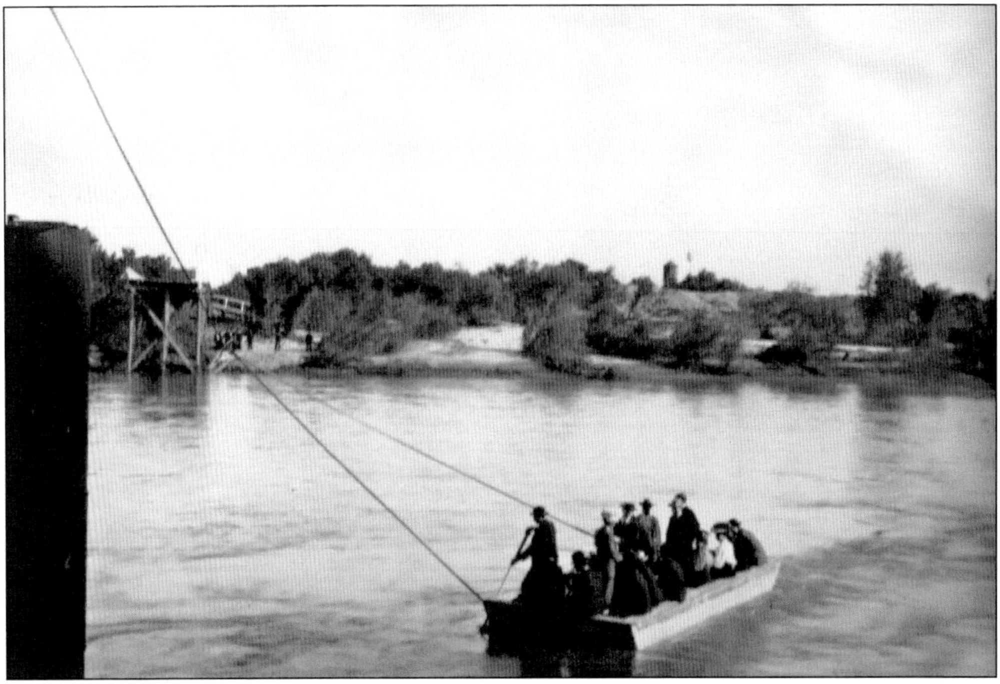

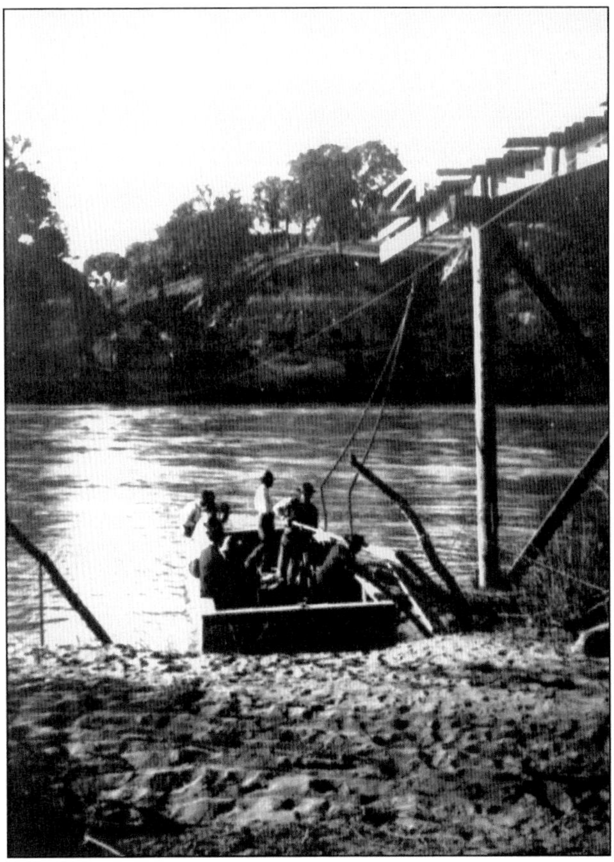

To get across the river after the bridge was washed out, a ferry service was established to help. The images seen here not only show the ferries crossing the river, but also the destruction to the original bridge. (Courtesy Fair Oaks Historical Society.)

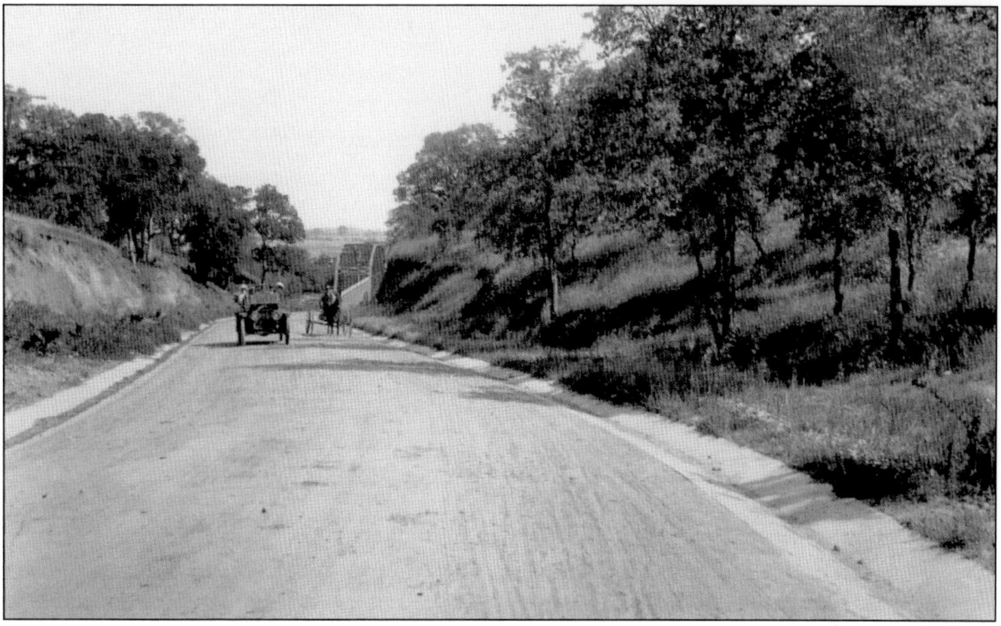

The road to access the Fair Oaks Bridge, Bridge Street, was built after the completion of the 1901 bridge and is shown above around 1915. The actual structure that is the current Old Fair Oaks Bridge (below, 1970s) is an excellent example of bridge construction and technology advancement in the mid-to-late 19th century. The Fair Oaks Bridge, a Pennsylvania Petit through Pratt truss that extends nearly 700 feet across a wide bend in the American River, is one of the more extraordinary truss bridges in California. The Western Bridge and Construction Company of Omaha completed the double truss bridge in 1907. It still survives and services the community today. (Above courtesy Fair Oaks Historical Society; below courtesy Fair Oaks Presbyterian Church.)

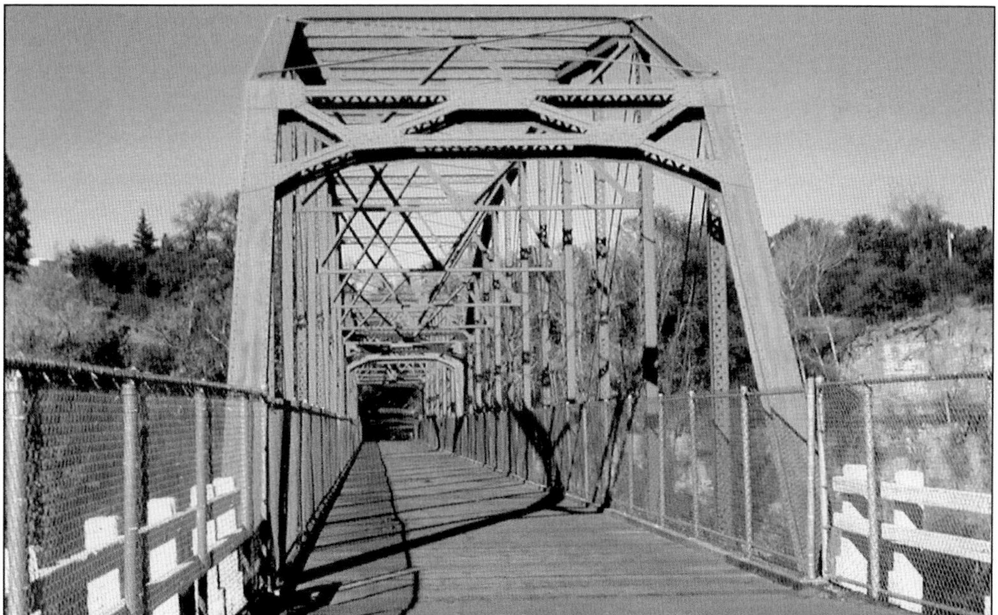

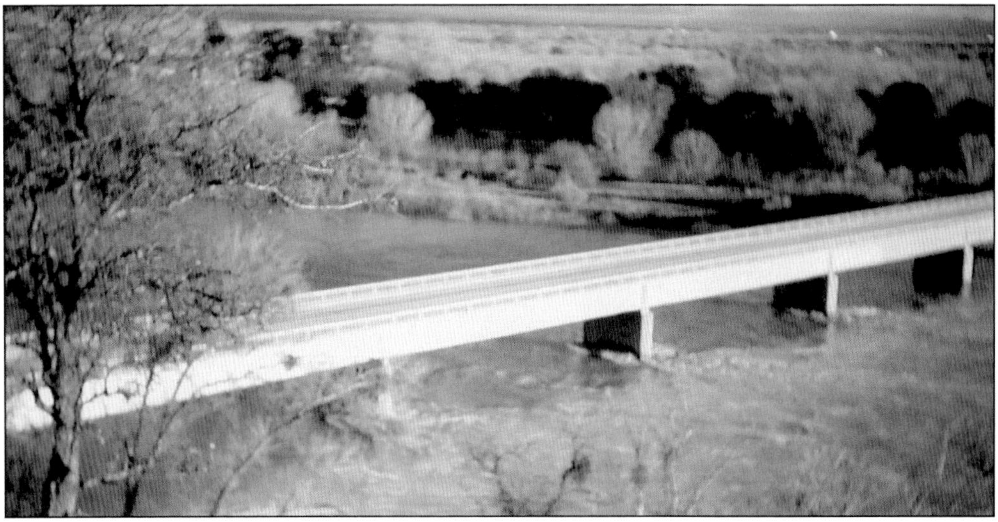

The Sunrise Avenue Bridge, pictured here in December 1955 as a simple two lane road, helped relieve the workload of the Old Fair Oaks Bridge, after nearly 50 years as the only major crossing over the lower American River in the area. (Courtesy Fair Oaks Presbyterian Church.)

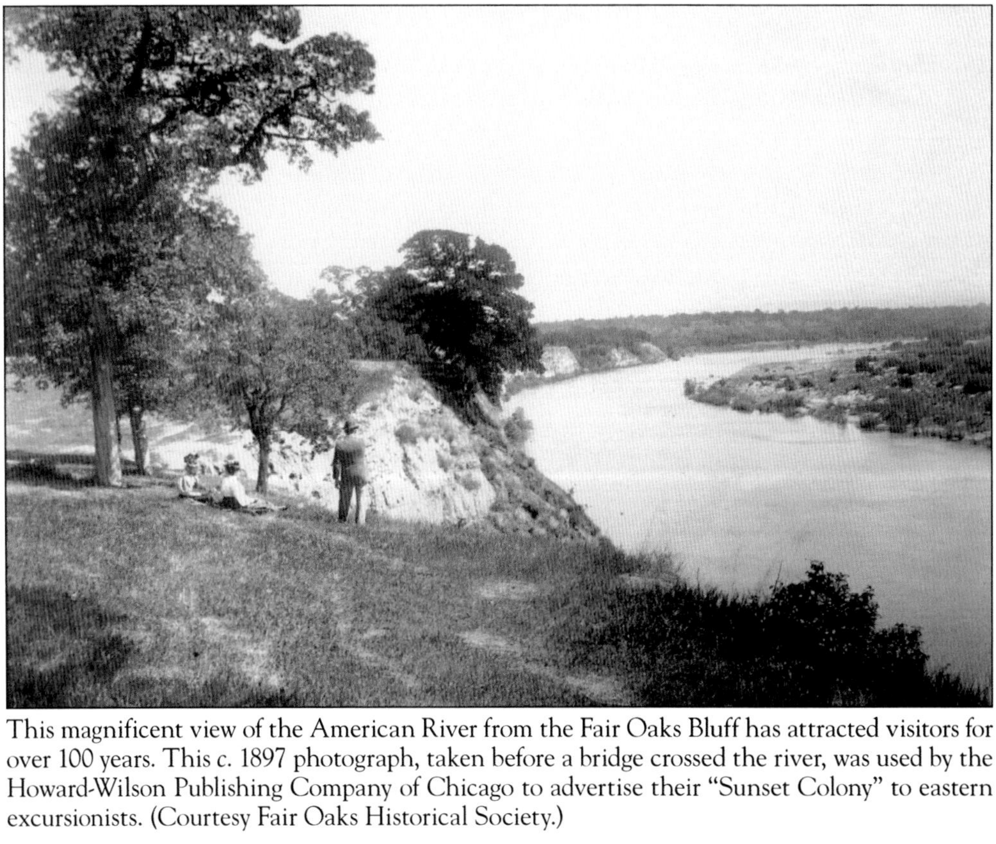

This magnificent view of the American River from the Fair Oaks Bluff has attracted visitors for over 100 years. This *c.* 1897 photograph, taken before a bridge crossed the river, was used by the Howard-Wilson Publishing Company of Chicago to advertise their "Sunset Colony" to eastern excursionists. (Courtesy Fair Oaks Historical Society.)

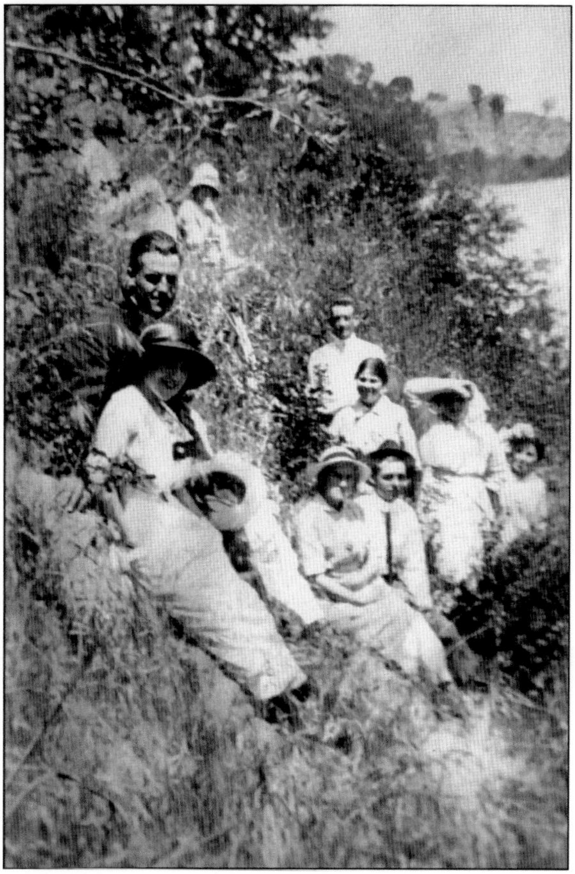

Like many families throughout the years, the Dewey family (Harry Dewey, left, and Alta Dewey, third from the right, middle) also visited and enjoyed the view of the Fair Oaks Bluff. Around 1915, the family also enjoyed playing in the American River. (Courtesy Eileen Dewey Thomas.)

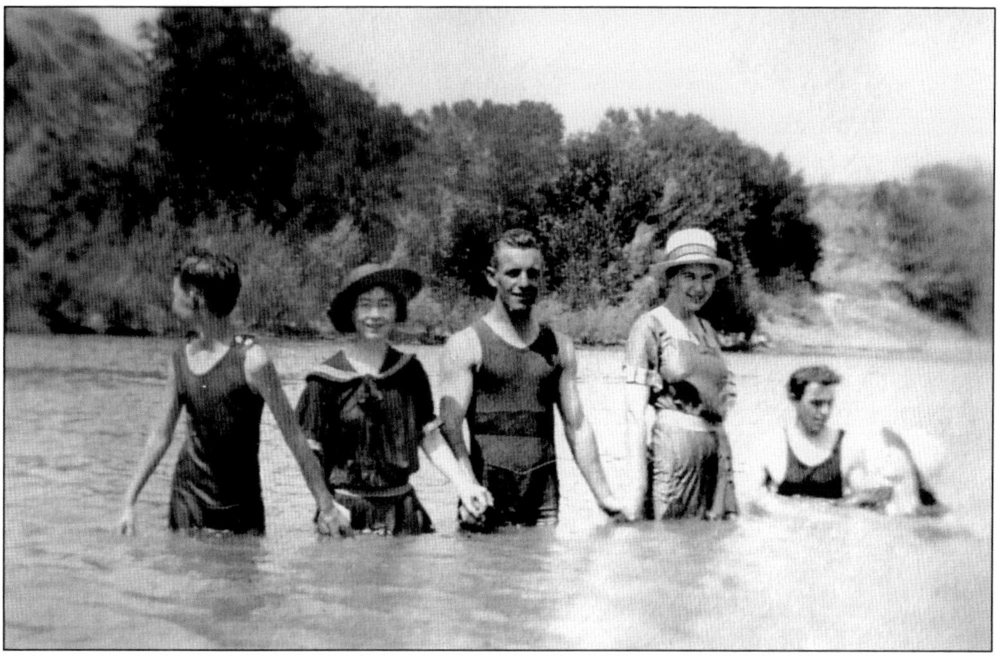

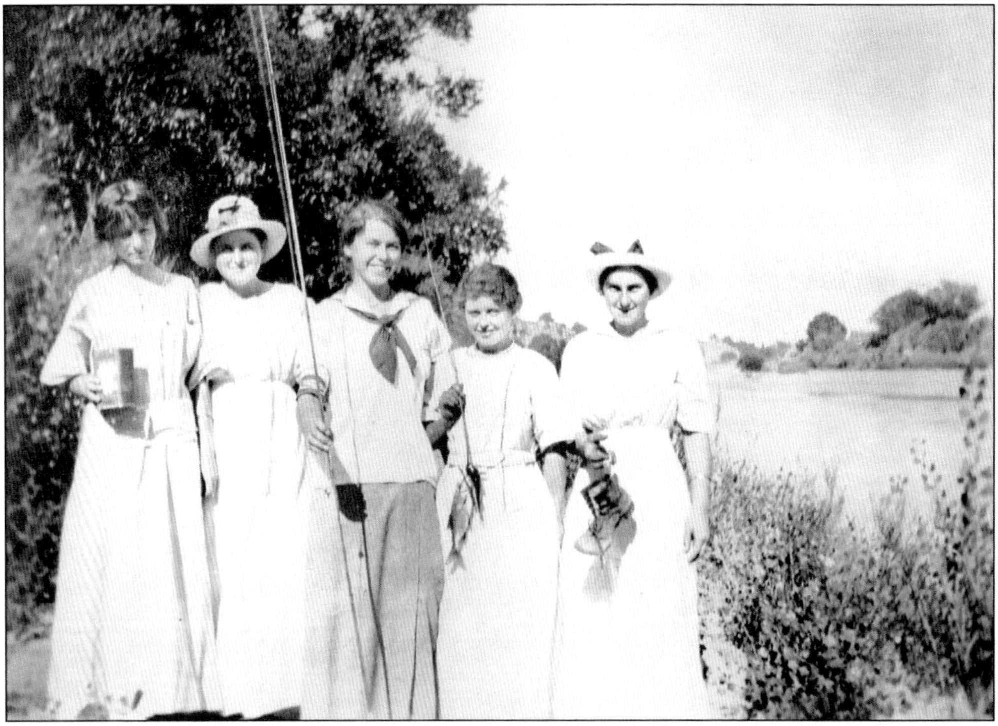

Fishing was just as popular at the American River in the early 1900s as it is today. Alta Dewey (center) and some of the Dewey family women (around 1915) show off their prized catch—a fish for Alta, and the others left holding a tin can and a boot! (Courtesy Eileen Dewey Thomas.)

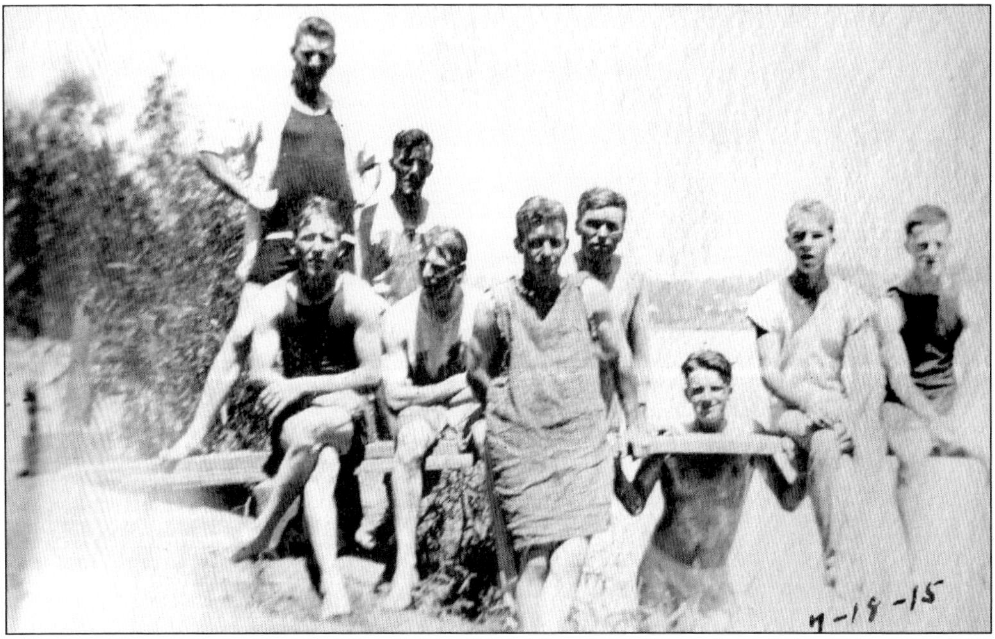

On July 18, 1915, the Dewey boys and their friends set up a diving board along the Fair Oaks Bluff and enjoyed, like so many before and after them, playing around in the cool river air and getting wet to beat the hot summer days. (Courtesy Eileen Dewey Thomas.)